SNP: THE TURBULENT YEARS

1960 – 1990

A history of the Scottish National Party

Gordon Wilson

Scots Independent (Newspapers) Ltd

Published by
Scots Independent (Newspapers) Ltd
51 Cowane Street
Stirling FK8 1JW
Scotland
www.scotsindependent.org

ISBN: 978-0-9512820-7-6

Printed by Trendell Simpson
Tel: (01382) 825629

CONTENTS

But this was the dark before the dawn – even though the nationalist movement, then and now, has had great familiarity with 'false dawns'. It did have the advantage from 1955 onwards of having internal peace and a settled strategy. It was also fortunate in its remaining leaders.

Chief amongst these was its President, Dr Robert McIntyre. Robert McIntyre had been involved in the national movement for some considerable time. In 1945, prior to the end of the war, he had been elected as MP for Motherwell, and although he lost the seat in the ensuing General Election a few weeks later, he still carried the prestige that came from being the first nationalist to be elected under the SNP banner. Robert was a consultant chest physician, specialising in tuberculosis. He was a cautious man and not someone to be budged over new fashions in politics – or by new people. Philosophically, he wished Scottish society to operate on a decentralised basis. As a former Party Secretary who believed in organisation and discipline, he had helped to keep the Party together. In later years, he became Provost of Stirling and gave hope to SNP members that success could be achieved in local government.

Another leader was Arthur Donaldson, National Chairman, (1960-1969), a steadfast nationalist who never evaded controversy. Latterly, he had occupied the post of Convener of Publications and been responsible for writing new policy leaflets, one of which with 300,000 copies printed, was distributed free to the branches. He had been a journalist with D C Thomson, Dundee before migrating to the States in the 1920s. His patriotism brought him back to Scotland where he became a chicken farmer in Ayrshire and Editor of the SNP newspaper, the Scots Independent.

When he attacked the government for their actions in conscripting young Scottish women to work in the war matériel factories in the South of England, he touched a raw nerve and was arrested and held without trial under war-time regulations in Barlinnie prison before being sprung by the efforts of James Maxton, one of the Independent Labour Party MPs in Glasgow. Subsequently, he moved to Forfar where he became a Councillor and Editor of the Forfar Dispatch.

Arthur Donaldson was easily the best public speaker the SNP has had. Good at small meetings and also capable of motivating the Party at large Conferences, he could expound a masterly case for self-government.

David Rollo was a consultant electrical engineer and as National Treasurer, quite frequently made up the pay of the Office Secretary out of his own limited pocket. He helped keep the office going and attempted to raise funds. His special interest was broadcasting in Scotland. His son has described him as a character out of James Thurber. Always smiling, with what seemed to be a twinkle in his eyes, he had a capacity, as they say now, to 'think out of the box'.

Chapter 1
Roots of Revival

'The Ayes to the right 311. The Noes to the left 310. The Ayes have it. The Ayes have it'
It was 28 March 1979 in the House of Commons. The Speaker had just announced the result of a vote of confidence against the Labour Government of 1974/1979. A Government had been defeated, the first time in living memory, and on a vote triggered by its failure to deliver a devolved Scottish Assembly! Prime Minister James Callaghan rose to the Despatch Box and cleared the way for a General Election. Five weeks later, the Scottish National Party, responsible for the pressure for the Assembly, crashed losing nine of its eleven MPs. It was in despair. But twenty years earlier, the election of two MPs would have been a dream. And ten years later, the Party had made a partial recovery and returned to prominence. This is the story of these turbulent years.

The early history of the Scottish National Party is fully reported in 'Independent and Free, Scottish Politics and the Origins of the Scottish National Party, 1918-1945' by Richard J. Finlay. In the period covered, the SNP started from weakness. Frequently fissile, the SNP had been fragmented in the forties when its powerful National Secretary and effective leader, Dr. John MacCormick, defected in 1942 (taking with him half of the Party's conference delegates[1]) to found the all-party devolution body, The Scottish Convention (later the Covenant Association). This was compounded by the suspension of almost one third of the Branches in 1955 after members had left to form the short-lived Nationalist Party of Scotland.[2] By 1956, the nationalist movement was badly fragmented. The left wing Scottish National Congress had several branches but as it was devoted to Ghandi-style passive civil disobedience – without having the manpower to be effectively disobedient - it issued pamphlets through The Scottish Secretariat, a publishing company owned by the venerable industrialist and socialist millionaire, Roland E. Muirhead.

The Scottish Patriots, under their flamboyant leader, Wendy Wood were active, but had few members. She spoke at the Mound in Edinburgh and, although undoubtedly charismatic and talented, there was always a touch of the eccentric that made it difficult for her, despite all the publicity, to do more than titillate the public.

After the various disruptions, the SNP had come down to a hard core of 23 branches, most of which had difficulty in reaching the minimum constitutional figure of 20 members, with total membership, at its lowest, of between 200 to 500 – the figures vary. The Party was seemingly moribund.

DEDICATION AND THANKS

This personal history of the Scottish National Party over the turbulent decades of the sixties, seventies and eighties is dedicated to the many thousands of members, some still alive, but many now dead, who contributed to making the SNP what it is today – a power in the land.

My thanks go particularly to my wife Edith and daughters, Margaret and Katie who patiently – and sometimes not so patiently – allowed me to be so absorbed in the world of politics at their expense.

Additionally, I wish to thank my contributors for their willingness to push the boat from the shore and offer their different perspectives of events. Angus Lyon and Andrew Scott have also devoted much time to editing the text and correcting my enthusiasm! Any errors are mine.

I also wish to acknowledge the assistance of Dr Maria Castrillo of the National Library of Scotland for her cataloguing of the profuse SNP records in the collection and to thank the SNP for allowing me access to them.

The last of the major quartet was James Halliday, National Chairman (1956-60), who became Chairman at the age of 27, an impossible task when newly qualified and with a young family. Jimmy was a history teacher who later moved to Dundee to become a lecturer in history at the Northern College of Education. Always realistic and frequently acerbic, James Halliday added bite to the leadership. In later years, he became Convener of the Party's Election Committee which was responsible for vetting potential parliamentary candidates.

These four, along with Vice-chairman Sandy Milne, had been candidates in the 1959 election, and it is then that some observers place the flickers of life in the Scottish National Party. I was not involved much in the 1959 election. The Edinburgh Branch did not contest elections. Because of my involvement as Director of Programmes with Radio Free Scotland (RFS) from 1960 onwards, I interviewed the SNP leaders and came to the conclusion that, in them, rested the future of the cause of independence. With RFS, I came through to Glasgow to broadcast at the Bridgeton By-election and learned my first lesson in Glasgow politics. As part of the campaign, there was a special election edition of the Scots Independent, a monthly publication affiliated to the SNP, and armed with these, I was sent round the Bridgeton pubs. To put it mildly, this was not safe territory. It was a very rough area and the pubs were all male 'howffs' of the 'spit and sawdust' variety. Hardly surprisingly, and with none of the acceptance enjoyed by vendors of the War Cry produced by the Salvation Army, I found sales slow to the point of non-existence.

At last success – a buyer. I took the price of 2d and handed him a copy. It fell to the ground. I leant down, picked it up and handed it over. This time, he took it but observed:

'Look, son, I could have kicked you in the face.'

I was grateful he had restricted his advice to a verbal warning only. Bridgeton was the real turning point for the SNP. Two new members had joined the National Executive - Ian Macdonald and Alan Niven. Ian was the candidate and Alan, the election agent. They were backed up by a regular team, Unity Miller from Glasgow, David Rollo, George Leask, three members from Hamilton and twelve others on a casual basis, who worked steadily for months through a long summer and autumn, distributing leaflets and canvassing. This was the first time that the SNP had fought a by-election campaign systematically and effectively, yet to put matters into perspective, at its conclusion, only 10% of the constituency had been canvassed. At the beginning, nobody expected much. This was the first by-election fought by the Party since Dundee East in 1951. Glasgow SNP was also notorious for chaos and feuding. As Ian Macdonald observed[3]:

'It was ridiculous to put a farmer up in Bridgeton, but there was no one else.'

Ridiculous or not, he proved to be an excellent candidate whose public presence, affable manner and sincerity brought in support. More importantly, the excellent staff work of Alan Niven gave longer term encouragement to SNP members as they realised that hard work, good organisation and confident electioneering could pay dividends. So when the election result was declared on 11 November 1961, the SNP had gained 18.7% of the vote, very close to the Scottish Unionists' share of 20.7%.

Glasgow Bridgeton By-election Result (November 1961)

Labour	57.5%
Scottish Unionists	20.7%
SNP	18.7%
ILP	3.1%

For Ian Macdonald, it was an epiphany.[4]

> 'I joined the SNP in 1952 at University. Keen but inactive until Uni. and National Service were over. Then in late '56 or early '57 while working on a farm in Killearn, I started the Balfron Branch. Got my own farm at Newmilns May '57 and started the Irvine Valley Branch. Shortly after, I was elected to the Nat. Exec. and the Organisation Committee – anyone who was semi-active was on the Nat. Exec. ... I had started a number of Branches in '57, but I don't remember any other new ones until I was Nat. Org. We did contest 5 seats in the Election of 1959 it may be we were on the way up. However I have no doubt that had I not become N.O., we would have taken an awful lot longer to get anywhere.
> At Bridgeton, I realised there was a huge demand for a Scottish Parliament, but people wouldn't vote for a Party contesting a handful of seats. I was still single, and thought no real progress would be made if I continued farming and I was confident that I could build on organisation. The agreement with the Nat. Exec. was that I would get half of the increased income to the Party.'

It would be difficult to over-state the contribution made by Ian Macdonald. As his words show, he was an expansionist in branch formation well before he became National Organiser. To form two branches in the dog-days of 1957 was remarkable. So, too, were his decisions to fight a parliamentary by-election in a city seat and to throw up his farm and livelihood to take on the precarious task of National Organiser for peppercorn pay. Ian was never short of optimism or drive. He went round a country, largely free of SNP members, armed with free leaflets and Business Reply Cards (BRCs), holding meetings and spreading the message. Where there was support, he would form a group, give it some leaflets and BRCs and leave it to grow to branch status. If it died, he would come back and repeat the process.

There was no grand scheme. If there were, there was no one else with the energy to implement it. He was a one-man band. He had to cover the ground and, as for after-care, hope that he had recruited people who were self-starters. He also had the advantage of a series of Democratic Party hand-books on organisation which an RFS colleague, Louis Stevenson had sent me from Chicago.

Politically, he was not without support. When it came to public meetings, the Party had many good speakers, especially Arthur Donaldson who could find the time to tour. Also, as the Party developed and grew, new leaders appeared. Pre-eminent amongst them was William (Billy) Wolfe. He was a man of many parts: an accountant in a manufacturing business owned by other members of his family in Bathgate, West Lothian, County Commissioner for Scouting and member of the cultural Saltire Society. Having become disillusioned with the lack of impact made by the Society, and after having canvassed the policies of the main political parties in Scotland, he joined the SNP in 1959 and was to be their candidate in the forthcoming West Lothian By-election.

Ian Macdonald as newly appointed National Organiser came through to help. Unusually for the SNP, there was a core of local members who had been active for many years. They were spread amongst the community. Help also arrived from the Edinburgh University Nationalist Club, led by Donald Stevenson, Allan Macartney, Robin MacCormick and Roy and Anne MacIver.

Radio Free Scotland came from Edinburgh to carry out broadcasts, and subsequently, West Lothian became one of their permanent broadcasting stations.

It was not an easy seat to contest. It had a substantial coal and shale mining industry and had been Labour for generations. But the shale oil industry with around one thousand miners was in trouble owing to Government excise duties that made it artificially uneconomic, and Billy Wolfe skilfully wove this into a central theme of Scottish economic decline and the need for self-government. Stylish and punchy leaflets were designed. Billy employed a slogan, 'Put Scotland First' and used it effectively. The result gave the SNP a great boost. Labour won with 50.9% but the SNP was runner up with 23.3%.

West Lothian By-election Result (June 1962)

Labour	50.9%
SNP	23.3%
Conservative & Unionist	11.4%
Scottish Liberals	10.8%
Communists	3.6%

The effect on SNP morale was dynamic. People now believed that there was a chance of getting a Scottish Parliament if they worked for it. Politically, the SNP had appeared on the electoral horizon, and as the result sank in, it began to attract attention. Not even a comparatively poor result in Glasgow Woodside fought by Alan Niven caused despondency although the Liberal, a well-known Glasgow columnist, had done too well for comfort.

Glasgow Woodside By-election Result (November 1962)

Labour	36.3%
Conservative & Unionist	30.3%
Liberal	21.2%
SNP	11.2%
Others	0.0%

Until now, my connection with the SNP had been through Radio Free Scotland and local involvement in Edinburgh. 1963 was pivotal. I attended the Annual Conference, was invited to speak on a resolution on broadcasting policy and found myself elected to fill one of the 15 places on the National Council and then serve on the National Executive Committee. This startling rise from obscurity was not unknown. Ian Macdonald, then National Organiser had observed that anyone slightly active was earmarked for promotion. Probably of more significance was the election of Dr James Lees, a pathologist in Fife, who would subsequently become a Vice-Chairman. I was also one of the SNP's speakers at the annual Bannockburn Rally, again a new experience. After having reviewed in my speech the reverses of the Scottish economy over the year, I added:

> '...we can no longer stand by in the belief that things will improve tomorrow. The mounting tide of

unemployment, the continued decline of our economy and the projected destruction of our railways force us to realise that unless we take immediate control of our own affairs there will be nothing left of Scotland worth saving.'

In July, I received an invitation from Arthur Donaldson to take over as Assistant to the National Secretary, Malcolm Shaw who was unable to carry out his duties.

James Lees had been chosen as candidate for the Dundee West By-election, expected in the autumn of 1963 and Ian Macdonald had been detached to give preliminary assistance. Hardly had that been arranged when a vacancy appeared in Kinross & West Perth which we had fought in 1959. With 15%, it was one of our better prospects. Our candidate was Arthur Donaldson and expectations were high. The Unionists adopted their new leader, Alec Douglas Home as their candidate.

During the election, Arthur Donaldson was in excellent form. It did not matter. The squeeze was on and we ended up with a 50% drop in the vote to 7.3%, and worse yet, were beaten by a local Liberal. Arthur was very disappointed and at the count, I remember his fortitude and preparations. He had two speeches prepared – one for a reasonable result and the other for defeat. He did not flinch when the result proved as disastrous as feared.

Kinross & West Perth By-election Result (October 1963)

Conservative & Unionist	57.4%
Liberals	19.5%
Labour	15.2%
SNP	7.3%
Others	0.6%

The momentum of Bridgeton and West Lothian had been checked, and several weeks later, the by-election in Dundee West brought a similar vote of 7.4%.

Dundee West By-Election Result (November 1963)

Labour	50.6%
Conservative & Unionist	39.4%
SNP	7.4%
Communist	2.6%

A further by-election in Dumfries beckoned. Even before that election was called, a serious debate had broken out. Billy Wolfe, who had done so well in West Lothian, was seriously worried. He and two experienced representatives from West Lothian conducted a Political Opinion Survey in the Dumfries Constituency dated 13 November 1963 and distributed to the NEC on 16 November:

> 'Our conclusion was that, in the time available, the case is hopeless in this huge constituency. Given three or four months and constant hard work and propaganda (with 30 or 40 regular workers) the situation could be made most favourable for the SNP but we feel that the prospects are not good for a poll in early December especially since the weather is not likely to be favourable for campaigning. The time of year is also against campaigning in country towns and villages.'

He further pointed out that Dumfriesshire was a long way from outside support in the central belt and that a bad vote, following upon the poor result in Kinross & West Perth, would further dent morale.

The survey results were:

Tory	Labour	Liberal	SNP	Don't Know
30	55	10	3	2

Matters came to a head at a special meeting of the NEC in the Dundee election rooms on 16 November when Billy Wolfe sought to find support to recall an earlier decision to fight Dumfriesshire. He failed to find a seconder and had his dissent recorded.

There must have been many who had doubts, but as Robert McIntyre asserted[5]:

> 'He felt it would be worse publicity to back down than to contest in Dumfries.'

In the event, the Party contested with local teacher, John Gair as the candidate and achieved an improved vote of 9.7% - improved that is on the out-turn of the two previous by-elections – but a long way from the results in Bridgeton and West Lothian.

Dumfries By-election Result (December 1963)

Conservative & Unionist	40.8%
Labour	38.6%
Scottish Liberals	10.9%
SNP	9.7%

In two of the elections, we had been outclassed by the Liberals. Billy Wolfe raised this in a memorandum[6]:

'Attitude to the Liberal Party

No one can accuse me or anyone else in West Lothian of being pro-liberal in private or in public but it is more obvious to us now than ever before that the SNP missed a great opportunity last year when it was in a position of strength relative to the Liberal Party. Secret and unofficial 'pacts' are of little value. The SNP is the Party with the real proposals for Scotland but I have no doubt whatsoever that many members and supporters of the Liberal Party are very sincere in their nationalism and that they are held back from us because of lack of knowledge about Scotland or Scotland's resources, and by lack of knowledge of what the SNP outlook and philosophy really is. They are also held back by the sort of things which appear in the current edition of the S.I. On many occasions I have spoken against the Liberal Party for one reason or another but I am quite sure we stand to lose nothing by making an offer to have some kind of official short-term agreement based on the acceptance of such points as:-

The Scottish Liberal Party and the SNP would publicly declare their support of the following action. If there was a Labour/Tory government in London and 36 out of the 71 Scottish seats were held by the SNP or Liberals the SNP and Scottish Liberals members would convene a meeting of all Scottish MPs. They would call on the Government in London to take action to provide Scotland with a Government of her own. If the London Government did not negotiate then the SNP and the Scottish Liberal MPs would convene in Scotland and

form a Government of their own and would draw up a
constitution for Scotland and for a plebiscite or General
Election as soon as possible.'

I had no idea what Billy's earlier proposals had been, but any attempt to
initiate discussions on a pact with the Liberals would have offended long
serving office-bearers - and with good reason. Just a cursory glance at the
history of the Party would demonstrate the dangers. The SNP had been
established as a result of the failure of the Westminster parties to deliver on
home rule. It had then suffered heavily from splits in the thirties, forties and
fifties. Most of these had originated from attempts to co-operate with the
unionist parties. To many it would be revisiting battles that had been won.
To do so, at a period when the SNP was united and making progress, would
seem like folly.

It was a dangerous course. Yet Billy Wolfe did have a serious point. There
was room in 'first past the post' elections for a third party; but none at all for
a fourth. Nor was he being naive. Unlike now, there were prominent
members of the Scottish Liberals who would have been at home in the
emergent Scottish National Party. They could be taken for the picking. Billy
Wolfe was setting a high standard for co-operation. If the Scottish Liberals
rejected the overtures, the SNP would gain. If they accepted, then the
Liberals would have to put self-government to the top of their political
agenda advancing the cause by a mile. However, the potential downside
could be to split the SNP and befog the issue of independence.

The meeting of the NEC in the by-election rooms in Dundee was pre-
occupied with Dumfries and ignored the Liberal issue. Billy Wolfe wrote to
the Scots Independent – a monthly journal associated with but independent
of the Party - to keep the topic alive. Opposition emerged at the National
Council meeting of 7 December 1963. Moved by Billy Wolfe, with the
negative proposed by Party veteran office bearer, T. H. (Tom) Gibson, his
resolution was defeated by a vote of 20 to 11.[7]

Billy Wolfe returned to the attack on 8 February 1964, when he received
the consent of a Special Meeting of National Council to publicise a notice of
motion for discussion at its next regular meeting. At the ensuing meeting of
the Executive on 14 February 1964, Arthur Donaldson, with my support,
sought to sound out the views of the Liberals prior to the Council debate.
William Wolfe who was not present had earlier given his consent. The
proposal was opposed by Alan Niven and defeated by 5 votes to 4.[8] The
Donaldson resolution reappeared as an amendment to the West Lothian
resolution at the Council meeting on 7 March and was amended heavily and
carried.[9] After all the fuss which had illuminated tensions within the Party,
the issue died internally. It had the happy outcome of eventually bringing

some senior Liberal members into the fold. It did not remove the recurrent problem of the Liberals.

Election readiness was the main concern. On 22 November 1963, the Executive reviewed the Kinross & West Perth By-election campaign. Arthur Donaldson as Chairman expressed concern about the readiness of branches to fight elections and was of the view that people should be trained who could go into a constituency to run an election. Worries were expressed by members about the need to organise in selected areas for the oncoming General Election.

The Executive then took a decision which would alter the face of the Party for generations.[10]

'Party Reorganisation

In view of the widespread dissatisfaction with the central organisation, the assistant secretary was instructed to investigate the Party superstructure i.e., the functions of the Executive Committee and National Council, those of the national office-bearers, Standing and Ad Hoc Committees, office efficiency and financial budgeting to decide where these are defective and make recommendations for improving them. Mr Wilson was asked to present his report, if possible, at the next meeting of the committee and members undertook to submit Memoranda within fourteen days.'

It is clear that the Executive had had a nasty shock over the Kinross & West Perth Result. In Billy Wolfe's memorandum[11], he had criticised the emergence of in-fighting in the constituency in the last few days of the campaign, the lack of deployment of man-power and inefficiency over the organisation of resources. The days of amateurism were over. The problem was what to do before the General Election.

Time was my problem. I was dependent on receipt of submissions from more experienced members of the NEC to give me an historical analysis of the problems and their ideas for solutions, all to come in not later than 6 December 1963 in time for a report to go to the NEC scheduled for 20 December. This was an impossible timescale, even for a cursory approach. I received a good response to my request for evidence. The letters and memoranda came in swiftly. Not surprisingly, the submissions from Arthur Donaldson were of greatest use. I have already touched on his expressed criticisms. His further views encouraged me to be more ambitious about the scope of the enquiry, to re-examine the functions of the various bodies and office-bearers, to examine how they worked and to come up with responses. This methodology is covered in a doctoral thesis by Robert Crawford, who served as a Research Officer to the Party: The Scottish National Party, 1960-1974: An Investigation into its Organisation and Power Structure (Glasgow University) and it is not necessary to cover here the descriptive account of the processes.

The more I looked at the project, the greater it expanded. The intellectual challenge was to balance the different functions and powers of each stratum of activity. My obsession was certainly not appreciated by my girl friend (and future wife), Edith Hassall, who had come through to Glasgow only to find that her boyfriend had gone missing – the lesson being never to trust the word of a politician – and was a permanent black mark, especially when she was conscripted to help!

Eventually the Report was compiled. With appendices and organisational charts, it contained 115 paragraphs with facts, analyses and recommendations. The structure lasted for 40 years. It was subject to chopping and changing in minor matters to accord with political pressures and although the symmetry of the original was lost, the basic skeleton remained. As the Party would eventually be prepared for a governmental role, National Council was given a role in policy formation. Care was taken not to diminish the overall authority of National Council. It was the supreme governing body in between conferences. As a delegate body, it had the power to call the office-bearers and the NEC to account. Delegates were now to obtain an overview of executive actions in the reports of the Chairman and the principal office-bearers, sections of which could be contested and go to a vote.

The Executive was to be the centre of decision making. There was to be a Senior Vice-chairman who would stand in for the Chairman in his absence, and two Executive Vice-chairmen, one responsible for Policy and Development (including Publicity) and the other for Organisation (including Finance). These officers would take responsibility for their functions, choose chairmen of sub-committees and report to Conference, National Council and the National Executive.

Of just as great importance was the acknowledgement by Dr Robert McIntyre, the President and a former Chairman, that so far as he was concerned, the Chairman was the main office bearer – and although the terminology was not used in the SNP - the Party Leader. This was a significant clarification. The Report was considered by the NEC on 6 and 31 January 1964[12], with a special meeting of Council scheduled for 8 February 1964. The NEC made some minor changes, the principal one relating to the size and method of election of the NEC. National Council passed the Report with a few minor changes and overruled the NEC on the method of election to the Executive.[13] The Executive Vice-chairmen were in place by June 1964. The first holders were Billy Wolfe (Policy) and Douglas Drysdale (Organisation) The NEC instructed a further report on the areas of branch and constituency organisation from Alan Niven, convener of the Organisation Committee. This was overtaken by the General Election and reconstitution of the Organisation Committee and he was unable to report until November 1964.

True to form in the SNP while all this constructive work was being undertaken, another dog-fight broke out on the issue of contesting the forthcoming Rutherglen By-election. The dispute first emerged at a special meeting of the NEC on 31 January 1964 where my motion to defer a decision was defeated by 4 votes to 2. It was again discussed at a brief additional meeting held before a special meeting of National Council on 8 February 1964. At Council, Arthur Donaldson left the chair and seconded by me, moved a resolution against contesting the election to passionate opposition from local Rutherglen, Cambuslang and Glasgow members. His resolution carried by the margin of 30 votes to 10 although a contest was permitted if Rutherglen Constituency Association could find the funds – which it could not.[14]

The twist in the tail came later. At the next NEC meeting the candidacy for Rutherglen was discussed vehemently and the Chairman and I were defeated by 5 votes to 4. The minute barely disguised a furious row[15]:

'Chairman Vacates Chair

> Having rejected a statement by Mr Niven that it was unethical for the Chairman to have used National Council to overturn an Executive Committee decision, the Chairman left the chair after an interchange with Messrs. Niven and Gray.'

After Arthur Donaldson had left, having intimated his resignation in passing, there was a stunned silence. In the run up to a General Election, the last thing anybody wanted was a resignation of the Party leader – and everyone knew that Mr Donaldson was a man who meant what he said.

Very quickly, I was unanimously asked by the Executive to go after the Chairman to persuade him to withdraw his resignation. I dashed out and managed to catch Arthur and gave him the message of support. He noted our views and undertook to consider his position. It is an understatement to say that the NEC received this news with considerable relief.

Chapter 2
Broadcasting: The Fight for Justice

From the mid fifties, with the growing predominance of television, the political parties moved away from reliance on the traditional methods of campaigning, such as public meetings and leafleting, although in the 1960s, these still had a substantial role to play. The national parties of Scotland and Wales were deprived of access to radio and television. In 1955, the BBC National Broadcasting Council of Wales had proposed setting up a series of Welsh party political broadcasts. The answer from the British Government was swift. Postmaster General, Charles Hill MP used his powers under the BBC's Licence and Agreement with the Government to veto such 'regional broadcasts'. This decision was taken to keep all political broadcasts 'British'. If this fell more harshly on the nationalist parties, so much the better, since it has always been a prime aim of Westminster and Whitehall to keep power in London.

The strength of the SNP case derives from Scotland's national status. It was Scotland (not just the SNP) that was being deprived of political debate and forced to receive broadcasts in which English domestic policies and leaders pre-dominated. In this unionist political era, long before devolution, there was no tolerance of any distinctive Scottish political contribution, separate from that of the Parliament in Westminster. There was no prospect that any Scottish broadcasts would replace those coming from London.

On becoming Assistant National Secretary of the SNP, I brought with me the skills developed by Radio Free Scotland, together with a fair share of the cheek and irreverence with which that organisation had operated. In the fifties, John Smart as National Secretary had used a technique of writing letters to various governmental bodies on current issues and publicising both the letters and any reply received. I decided to follow suit, hesitantly at first since I was new to the job and the SNP did not seriously 'do' publicity. There was little mechanism available. Instant reaction to news stories would have been by post or telephone (in the latter case, the press or news agencies would take material dictated with little chance of it being used). There were no staff members available for telephoning or delivering responses. Telexing was possible, but too expensive. Faxing, e-mailing and texting had not been invented!

Within the Party, there was no expectation that we could win party political broadcasting allocations or achieve for our leaders and candidates appearances on current affairs and political discussion radio and television programmes. I strongly disagreed. Although the SNP was still impressed with Radio Free Scotland, its reach was limited. We needed to penetrate the state broadcasting systems. I decided on a policy of harassment through sending unceasing letters of claim and demand, backed up by publicity. The objective would be to build on Scotland's status as a nation and exert moral pressure.

The immediate aim was to target the approaching General Election and persuade the BBC, the lead organisation, to take a stand for Scotland. I was not operating in isolation since there was sympathy within the National Broadcasting Council and amongst broadcasting news editors who wished to extend their Scottish activities. The more Scottish politics became identifiably distinct, the more the broadcasters would be encouraged to mount separate Scottish election and current affairs programmes. Although concentrating on party political and party election broadcasts (there are separate series of ppbs and pebs), my intention was to use these to persuade the news media to invite SNP representatives on to their shows and newscasts since the volume of time devoted to current affairs and news was vastly greater than for the limited air space given to the ppbs. Again, the more often we appeared on these programmes, the more would our Scottish political profile be visible.

By April 1964, the ice was breaking. I reported to the Executive that I had sent letters to all broadcasting bodies as part of the campaign to secure coverage for the General Election.[1] Since the Leader of the Opposition, Harold Wilson MP had seemed to open the door to a separate series of Party Political Broadcasts in Wales, I had also written to the Prime Minister, Sir Alec Douglas Home and Plaid Cymru.

Additionally, I had received a telephone call from Andrew Stewart, BBC Controller for Scotland, advising that the SNP would get broadcasting time in an election 'hustings' series if it contested 15 seats or more. The Party was also likely to be allowed party political broadcasts, but only after the General Election. This was a major breakthrough. I was also to have a meeting with Mr Stewart and it was agreed that we should send a delegation consisting of Billy Wolfe and me to meet the National Broadcasting Council for Scotland. Billy Wolfe reported that he had been invited by the Scotsman to provide an article on the 'broadcast that would have been if there had been no radio ban'. In preparation for the new era, the Executive authorised 'a mock-up of a hustings' programme and training in radio and television techniques through the medium of Radio Free Scotland. Effectively, this meant Douglas Henderson and I did the training interviews.

The meeting with the National Broadcasting Council took place on 29 May.[2] Billy Wolfe also assisted in the campaign by writing to the Chief Whips of the Westminster parties.[3] No useful replies were received. Efforts were renewed with telegrams to the Prime Minister and Leader of the Opposition and pressure on the ITA. Robert McIntyre and Billy Wolfe, along with Plaid Cymru,[4] held a press conference in London to protest about the delay in awarding party political broadcasting time.[5]

The benefits of pressure trickled through. It was rumoured that the SNP could expect bare parity with the 'British' parties on election 'hustings' programmes in Scotland. In August 1964, the Executive agreed provisional election proposals from STV and nominated Arthur Donaldson to be the SNP representative on the main Grampian TV Election Programme.[6]

The principal barrier to Scottish party political broadcasting was the reluctance of the Westminster parties to give up their control. The method by which the decisions were taken was obscure. The Government referred enquiries to the broadcasters and the broadcasters to the Whips, who represented the parties. For much of the time I was 'chasing my tail'. Over the years by writing constantly, a picture emerged. There was a Committee on Party Political Broadcasting. It consisted of the Lord President of the Council for the Prime Minister, the Leaders of the opposition parties, the Chief Whips of all parties and representatives of the broadcasters.

The Committee met infrequently, usually before elections to agree the schedule of election broadcasts and early in the new parliamentary session after an election to divide the allocation of time offered by the broadcasters in the light of the election results. Non-parliamentary parties such as the SNP and Plaid Cymru were excluded. The Secretary to the Committee, Mr Freddie Warren, my main correspondent, was a career civil servant. He was the official interface between the Government's business managers, the Leader of the House and the Government and Opposition Whips and when eventually, I was elected to Parliament and came across my old adversary, he proved to be helpful once we fitted his criteria!

In early December 1964, the SNP held a meeting with Plaid Cymru in the Lake District, neutral territory, when one of the main discussions centred round broadcasting. It was understood by the Plaid that Russell Johnston, Liberal MP for Inverness, had undertaken to lodge a parliamentary question on the broadcasting issue.[7] At last came the long delayed announcement! We were to receive an annual allocation of 5 minutes on television and 5 minutes on sound. The Executive in January 1965 agreed to accept this award, but disapproved of the manner in which the allocation was made and the amount of time available. It was also concerned about the position in the Borders where the area was covered by transmitters based in England.[8]

The five minute allocation was to last for many years despite a constant stream of letters sent by the Party. But official recognition, however niggardly, had opened the sluice gates, with improved coverage of our 1965 Conference by BBC and Grampian Television for the first time. By April 1965, our representatives were being invited to participate on political discussion programmes. There was even competition on the part of the BBC and STV to produce our first party political broadcast![9] Although the first inroads had been made, parity in elections would extend only to Scotland, with the SNP and Plaid Cymru being excluded to their very great disadvantage from London election coverage. Securing this UK coverage was to prove almost insuperable, and during an election, the SNP was restricted to one nominal UK feature or interview per channel.

Firstly, and unusually, we had to sort out the production of the SNP broadcasts. The London Parties produced their own broadcasts through commercial producers. There were few, if any, independent producers in Scotland who could have tackled this task as well as the main broadcasters and as our initial programme was studio based without film, the public broadcasters were able to make facilities available. It was conceded that the broadcasters would produce, film and edit our programmes. We would provide the scripts and pay for the raw film shot during the productions.

Meetings took place between Rosemary Hall, the Party's National Organising Secretary and David Johnstone of Scottish Television and between her and Mr Stewart, Controller Scotland of the BBC. The BBC offer was accepted in June 1965.[10] Not surprisingly, STV were disappointed. Strange as it may seem, this broadcast for a minor political party had attractions for the Scottish broadcasters. Apart from innate competition between them, they had not produced such a broadcast before. There was a cachet in being selected for the first attempt. Unfortunately, the decision led to antagonism from STV, with the SNP being cut off from news coverage.[11] The position became so difficult that at the September meeting of National Council, I urged the Party to make complaints to the broadcasters and regulators.[12] The relationships with STV were not improved when the first broadcast was interrupted by faulty 'switching'! The ITA apologised for 'human error'.[13] We had our suspicions!

The NEC recognised that the transmissions of our first broadcasts would be news events and planned a mammoth recruitment campaign. Robert McIntyre, supported by Ian Macdonald, launched a programme of action at the September 1965 meeting of National Council.[14] There were to be fly posters advertising the TV broadcast on 29 September and the radio broadcast on 29 November, the issue of 50,000 BRCs, follow-up of membership enquiries and cash prizes for the best performing branches. The first TV broadcast was to be given by Billy Wolfe and the Radio broadcast by Arthur Donaldson.

The TV broadcast was well received by the press and public.[15] Comparing the Welsh and Scottish broadcasts, The Times commented very favourably on that from the SNP. Official ratings provided by the BBC showed an audience of around 1,250,000 (and this in a country of a total population of 5,250,000 – almost one in four tuned in). It also brought in a bumper response of 1,200 membership enquiries within four days. The campaign concluded with the radio broadcast by Arthur Donaldson and a report to December National Council by Robert McIntyre estimated that we had gained approximately 5,000 members over two months.[16] The target had been 4,000. Glasgow Woodside, Dunfermline and Greenock received the prizes for the best showing. Five new branches were recognised in December 1965, two in January and five in February 1966.

With the build up, the SNP was given further recognition. It received an invitation to send a delegation to a Speaker's Conference on Electoral Law, including party political broadcasting. Speaker's Conferences are very rare and are used only to break constitutional deadlock or to discuss changes in the electoral system. The meeting took place in the House of Commons on 25 January 1967, and being Burns Night, should have been auspicious. Ian Macdonald and I along with David Rollo had been chosen to represent the Party. David could not manage. Ian and I had lunch with Gwynfor Evans MP of Plaid Cymru for a background briefing.

The meeting was at night in the Upper Committee Corridor. The select committee room was poorly lit and my first impression was one of gloom with the MPs dimly visible. They were clustered round one of the traditional horse-shoe tables. The Conference was chaired by Speaker Horace King who received us graciously. We had submitted a paper in advance. We made a presentation and answered some desultory questions. There was no real hope of making progress. We were witnesses, not participants and there were too many vested interests in the other parties. It was, however, important to make a reasonable impression as it was one of the first signs of political recognition. Nevertheless, the outcome was more encouraging than expected since the report contained this recommendation[17]:

> 'While the existing arrangements governing the allocation of time for party political broadcasting at general elections are generally satisfactory, the broadcasting authorities should review the arrangements made for broadcasts at election times by the minor parties.'

Outside party political broadcasting, there was continued improvement. The BBC promised better coverage of our Conferences. In line with the Party's growth and improved electoral performance, we were invited to have representatives on the local election results panels on television and radio. Winnie Ewing MP on 14 October 1968 wrote to the BBC and the Independent Television Authority in London regarding party conference coverage. She got no joy from either Lord Aylestone, Chairman of the ITA or Lord Fulton, Vice Chairman of the Board of Governors of the BBC, save that the reply from Lord Fulton contained a table of British and Scottish coverage which emphasised the 'double jeopardy' from which the SNP suffered.This showed the SNP at 24 minutes, Scottish Liberals at 30 minutes, Scottish Labour at 26 minutes and Scottish Unionists at 29 minutes. Although this was notionally fair in Scotland, the British coverage swamped that given to the SNP, all engineered to ensure that any advantage given to the SNP was matched and exceeded by coverage to the others.

British Table

	Special to Scotland	Live on BBC2	24 Hours	Panorama
SNP		24 mins.		
UK Libs			4 hrs 48 mins.	24 mins.
UK Lab			7 hrs 58 mins.	15 mins.
UK Cons			8 hrs 41 mins.	13 mins.

Source: Letter 31 October 1968.

In 1968, our relations with the BBC ruptured. The BBC suddenly withdrew filming assistance and this led to the transmission of a broadcast which we deemed not up to the standard we had come to expect.[18] Helen Davidson, the SNP producer, had borne the bulk of the problems. She and I had a meeting with Alasdair Milne, Controller, Scotland and James Kemp, News Editor on 18 November 1968.[19] We requested an explanation for the lack of co-operation experienced during production and also wished to learn whether it would be possible to repair the damaged relations. We reminded them of the agreement previously made with the BBC, when they had undertaken to provide full production facilities, including filming (on payment of the costs of raw film) and editing. We were particularly incensed with the let-down, having received a letter of 8 August 1968 from the Controller offering 'any help you need with your TV broadcasts'. Despite the prior agreement with the BBC, the producer had refused to provide any filming assistance and had insisted that we employ a freelance cameraman at our expense. We had also encountered resistance, rather than co-operation. Mr Milne claimed that the change of arrangements had arisen from a directive to bring us into line with those in England and that he had been unaware of his predecessor's promise. They undertook to look into the complaint.

Having had many dealings with James Kemp and Alasdair Milne over the years, I had no doubt as to their probity. There remains, however, the question of who had raised the need to keep within the English parameters to our detriment or had failed to brief Alasdair Milne of the deal made by his predecessor or why the BBC had allowed a sudden *volte face* so soon before the actual broadcast. It was a warning of how a major British state institution like the BBC could react to the growing strength of the Party. The failure of the 1968 broadcast to be transmitted timeously in the ITV Borders and Grampian regions heightened our suspicions. Alasdair Milne came back to us with a promise of restoration of the original arrangements. Our trust had been shaken and the production commission was passed to Scottish Television with whom we were by then on reasonable terms.

From this point on, with the election of two Vice-chairmen in charge of publicity matters, both of whom had media experience, I left the broadcasting campaign to the Vice-chairmen, Chairman Billy Wolfe and Helen Davidson who had produced many of the ppbs. Attempts were made to meet Tony Benn, Minister of Trade and Industry who, as holder of the functions of the former Postmaster General, notionally had control over broadcasting. He denied responsibility. Faced with this negative response, we decided to treat it as a campaigning matter. Winnie Ewing held a Press Conference with Plaid Cymru in London, since the Plaid was facing similar obstruction and gained useful publicity. By the mid-eighties, the allocation had been increased to two TV Broadcasts of 10 minutes each. It has only been since the advent of the SNP administration in the Scottish Parliament that the SNP has had the status to achieve coverage in newscasts at UK level.

Chapter 3
The Great Expansion

Naturally, the progress made by the SNP with the broadcasting media was primarily due to the growth in its influence and popularity with the public as its organisation and membership expanded. At the start of 1964, the SNP had been shaken by the reverses of the three autumn by-elections of 1963. The goal of independence seemed as far away as ever. The major organisational reforms had still to be approved, let alone implemented. And while political progress was fitful, the Party had chalked up considerable organisational gains. By 13 March 1964, the number of branches had risen to 80.[1] There were now four area councils although the SNP was far too light on its basic election fighting unit, the constituency association, where only four had been recognised. During the conference year (May to April) 1963/64, branches had been formed in Coatbridge, Liddesdale, Langholm, Lockerbie, West Calder, Dumfries, Peebles, Hawick and Glasgow North leading to a distinct strengthening in the Borders. There was further activity in Dunfermline, Glasgow Partick West and Partick East, Currie and Balerno, Motherwell, Buckie and District, Dingwall, Irvine, Glasgow Springburn and Stevenston. While these filled in some gaps, large swathes of the country remained untouched.

The Conference in May 1964, held in Bridge of Allan, was not well attended. It had limited television news coverage in the Saturday session. When the television lights had been taken away, the hotel ballroom on the Sunday looked dull and dingy by comparison with the previous day. Because of the forthcoming general election, there had been a shortage of resolutions from the branches and the agenda had been cobbled together and naturally was criticised by the branch delegates who had not provided any material. There was only one vote, on a resolution declaring that pacts with other political parties were incompatible with the SNP Constitution, a carry-over from the abortive overtures to the Liberals in the spring.[2] This was carried by a tiny vote of 32 to 20!

There was one bright note to that Conference which went unreported - perhaps just as well. In the dying debates of the afternoon, after the remaining 'stringer' covering proceedings for the news agencies had departed, we reached the final emergency resolution. In the news, there had been a proposal to erect a barrage in the Solway to generate power from tidal movement. This was to be welcomed, but the planners had suggested that the northern bank of the Solway in Scotland would need to be transferred to English jurisdiction. This would have meant parts of Dumfries and Galloway being incorporated into England. When the resolution opposing this transfer went through by acclamation, a delegate, on a point of order, asked the Chairman what action would be taken by the SNP if the scheme proceeded, Arthur Donaldson replied:

'When Scotland's territorial integrity is at risk, nothing can be ruled out.'

The delegates went ballistic, on their feet cheering and clapping. The National Anthem, Scots Wha Hae was sung with increased fervour that afternoon and the delegates went away enthused and excited. Given that the SNP, since it was founded, had steered clear of any form of militarism, this statement by the Party leader was remarkable. If the news had got out, there would have been front page headlines such as, 'SNP to Wage War on Solway Snatch'. It might indeed have led to a great insurge of members or, given the timidity of modern Scotland, a collapse of the Party's steady progress as people took fright. We shall never know. It was, however, an expression of Arthur Donaldson's radical leadership, and his willingness to say the unsayable. Some of the same spirit was missing when 40 years later, Westminster transferred thousands of square miles of Scottish sea to English jurisdiction, so that any fisherman caught fishing as far north as Arbroath could be prosecuted in English courts. Not a squawk of protest came from Scottish and SNP MPs.

With the challenge of gaining election broadcasts, the SNP succeeded in fighting 15 constituencies in the 1964 General Election. The increase in contests was the achievement - the highest number of candidates ever put forward. The overall results did not stack up as progress. The Party lost 12 of the 15 deposits. Bridgeton and Dundee West, scenes of recent by-elections, went uncontested. The only major improvement was in West Lothian where the percentage vote rose from 23.3% to 30.4%. Significantly, the Scottish Unionists lost 6.6% of their vote and 7 seats. Labour gained a small increase of 2% in their vote and a disproportionate gain of 5 seats (heralding the start of their hegemony in Scottish politics). More dangerously for the SNP, the other 'third party', the Liberals doubled their former vote to 7.6% and won three seats. All this compared to an SNP performance of 2.4% overall with no seats gained

In his Election Committee Report, Convener Dr. Robert McIntyre commented on the gap between general support (not always expressed in votes) and the results where we contested through work on the ground and where we knew our vote was located.[3] He also drew attention to the frustrating syndrome where people who supported us would not vote for us because of a perception of our weakness. His message was that there was no political barrier to winning votes provided we had a better organisation than the other parties. Billy Wolfe, now Executive Vice-chairman for Policy and Development, in his report to National Council, paid tribute to The Scotsman and STV for their electoral coverage.[4]

Far from being disappointed, the SNP began a great leap forward on every front. The Party was a very small organisation, run on a shoe string, with an annual income of under £5,000. Yet, in February 1965, it engaged Mrs Rosemary Hall as a part- time, and then shortly afterwards, as a full-time Honorary Public Relations Secretary, operating from the Edinburgh Branch premises.[5] Although there were operating expenses, Rosemary did the work free of charge. Mrs Hall was to be a key administrative figure. Edith and Rosemary had worked together in the Institute of Chartered Accountants without either knowing of the political convictions of the other. Rosemary had been introduced to the SNP by Billy Wolfe.

For the first time, the SNP had a press office. The office itself was tiny and Mrs Hall had her operational difficulties as she mentioned in a letter of 26 March 2007:

> 'In the office we shared a loo off the landing with the other office on that floor, and, unbelievable as it may seem now, at the start we also shared a telephone 'party line' with the occupants of the flat above. Frustration reached its height between 6pm and 7pm on certain evenings. That was the best time to get hold of members on the telephone all over the place, but it was precisely the time when the lady upstairs liked to have long telephone conversations with her friends'.

The new arrangements made it easier for office-bearers to put their ideas for publicity into action. More coverage resulted from the increased output of press releases. As Billy Wolfe reported to the June 1965 National Council[6]:

> 'In the 15 weeks since the Public Relations Secretary took up her appointment (15 February), 25 Press Releases have been issued (5 of them from the Glasgow Office) all based on ideas from office-bearers and others. Of these 25 only a very few received no notice in the National Daily Press or Television news bulletins. Some received notice in Scottish papers and quite a large number of local papers published part or all the releases'.

Earlier, to the Executive in May, Billy Wolfe had expressed concern that there was still a disturbing lack of publicity in some of the more popular papers.[7]

On the organisation front, progress had accelerated. Ian Macdonald reported to the NEC on 11 June 1965 that Branches were still being formed with a spate of enquiries coming in from all parts of the country.[8] There was concern about the development of the party in Glasgow and after a meeting with key activists, Bill Lindsay, Bill Valentine and 15 members drawn from the Glasgow branches, I was able to submit a report dated 11 July 1965, showing that while improvements were taking place, the position was patchy with a general shortage of finance. Poor funding was a perennial problem in the city. Over the years, the Glasgow organisation frequently looked to HQ for assistance, but this was rarely available. In the rest of the country, the message was one of spontaneous growth.

The Party was now on headlong course to contest the anticipated 1966 General Election. This would come too early. There were too few recognised constituency associations. Our allocation of party broadcasts would not be increased and any special election series would likely be on the same basis. Apart from one discussion on a UK BBC Twenty Four Hours programme on a Government White Paper on the Scottish Economy where Billy Wolfe appeared with STUC General Secretary, George Middleton, there was no other UK coverage. STV were uncooperative, firstly refusing a telephoned comment, and after I had complained to the ITA, took a comment, put it over unfavourably and refused to have an SNP representative on the discussion panel. An attempt was made to re-establish relations with STV, who made a peace offering in January 1966, but then had to be the subject of complaints to the ITA for exclusion of SNP representatives.[9] The BBC organised several studio blockbusters over the decade, one majoring on the effects of independence on the Scottish economy. On these, the SNP was now usually represented.

Over the period, the SNP had overhauled its portfolio of leaflets and literature. Billy Wolfe produced a booklet, SNP and You, which set out freshly SNP policy and strategy. It was brilliantly designed by Julian Gibb, a gifted young designer who had worked on West Lothian leaflets and had also created the SNP supporters' badge. This was a tin badge that carried the new symbol of the SNP based on the St Andrew's cross and a thistle. It was used in outline in all SNP leaflets and car badges and was a potent instrument in presentation. In the sixties, the SNP unquestionably held the lead in innovation and presentation.

The SNP was able to contest 23 seats in the 1966 election, achieving 5% of the total vote (up from 2.6%) in 1964. There was also a qualitative improvement as deposits were saved in 10 seats. Significantly, while the

Liberal vote dropped marginally, they won another seat, bringing the number of their MPs to 5. The SNP was very buoyed by the result, even though the Party was not represented at Westminster. Lessons were drawn in different ways.

The National Organiser reported in writing to the 14 April 1966 meeting of the National Executive:

> 'Our increased support in 1966 was not due to the three weeks election campaign - it was due to the steady propaganda of the eighteen previous months. We have five years to build the atmosphere to fever pitch, but we must start now. With this in mind, our 23 candidates should be readopted as soon as possible, and other constituencies should be encouraged to adopt as soon as they are at a reasonable state of organisation. I would like to see 36 candidates adopted by the beginning of 1967.'

In a circulated report, the Convener of the Organisation Committee, J Russell Thomson observed[10]:

> 'The achievement of 120,000 votes was in itself a very good result but with better organisation it could have been improved. From my own observations and from reports of other representatives of the Organisation Committee at the counting of votes, we did best in those constituency districts where we had active branches or groups, and badly where we had no branch or group. Those areas where the candidate was well known were to a certain extent able to overcome the lack of branch organisation.'

In a further written report, Alasdair MacDonald, newly appointed PRO commented that by comparison with previous elections, the Press, save for the Express group, was helpful and that this had continued since the election.

Also looking to the future, in April and May, Billy Wolfe canvassed a change in the Party's name to the 'Democratic Party' and called for a series of fresh, radical policies. He believed we would have to answer two questions to the satisfaction of the electorate[11]:

'1. Will Scotland be prosperous and secure with a government of her own?
2. Can the SNP show that it has the policies and the men and women to govern an independent Scotland in an efficient and democratic way?'

At this stage in its development, the SNP faced a number of identity problems. It had its own philosophy of decentralisation, but compared, say with the traditional conservative and socialist values of the two main parties, this had little resonance with the public who, to a large degree, were ignorant of the policies of the SNP. For many in the sixties, the SNP was a useful vehicle for a protest vote against the Conservative and Labour Governments and their loyalties ended with each vote. This helps explain why support for the Party ballooned and equally suddenly collapsed. The unifying force within the Party was the aim of securing independence. This was the glue that held the SNP together. It was such a radical concept to the voting population that some leaders of the Party, particularly Billy Wolfe, felt that the appeal of the Party had to be broadened if it were to make progress in attracting fresh support. A minority felt that the word 'National' could suggest right wing inclinations and that it would be better to adopt a more neutral term such as 'Democratic' as in the United States. There was certainly no call for a 'Social Democratic Party' which then had European connotations only although this was the direction in which the policy changes turned. Scotland had become defeatist from a combination of industrial run down and emigration. What was uppermost in the minds of the leadership was to develop greater self-confidence in Scotland's future so that independence would give rise to hope rather than fear and also to keep a watchful eye on the way our opponents used the smears of 'nationalism' and 'separatism'

Chapter 4

Victory at Hamilton

Behind the scenes, further changes were taking place. On 6 June 1964, the National Council elected Billy Wolfe as Executive Vice-chairman for Publicity and Public Relations (usually referred to as Policy) and Douglas Drysdale as Executive Vice-chairman for Organisation and Development.[1] Douglas Drysdale was a newcomer to politics as well as to the SNP. Like many of our new office-bearers, he was unfettered by previous political experience and had some interesting notions about how democracy should work in a political party, especially on the peremptory basis his management style favoured. In his fifties, he was dapper and bustling with a crisp personality. He was the owner of an engineering works and brought with him fresh ideas for fund raising.

It took three months for the new Executive Vice-Chairmen structure to bed in. During that period, the standing committees were kept going with their current conveners.

Douglas Drysdale and I had an exchange as to the degree of power to be centralised under the Executive, with Douglas more urgent in his assessment of the need for greater National Executive control. These discussions did not take place in a vacuum. As the Party expanded, the work of the executive office-bearers multiplied, and bearing in mind that they had other work to attend to and family lives to lead, the pressures were onerous. In my own case, I had married and moved to a flat in Pollokshields, Glasgow, where night after night, I sat at my desk, handling the correspondence of the Party and preparing reports, or attended the numerous committees and sub-committees of which I was a member. Although Edith was as committed a member of the SNP as I was and attended the branch meetings and did the canvassing for both of us, the amount of time soaked up by party business was excessive.

Others, too, felt the pressure. Ian Macdonald had married Douglas' daughter, Karen. He was away weekly 'on safari' forming branches. As Douglas Drysdale was now in charge of the organisation brief, I had assumed that this would have made things easier for Ian as National Organiser. Not a bit of it! Douglas was a hands-on 'boss' who got in Ian's way. He expected Ian to phone him every morning for orders.[2] Eventually, Ian had to appeal for operational independence. The pressures did not escape Billy Wolfe and Douglas Drysdale, as they both thrust themselves with vigour into the work of establishing their departments and dealing with committee conveners who did not always see things the way the Vice-Chairmen did.

Although the appointment of the Vice-chairmen was intended to leave the Executive to look after strategy, this did not always happen. The Vice-chairmen and other Committees reported to the Executive which met monthly, and sometimes more frequently.   In his report to Council in December 1965, Arthur Donaldson wrote[3]:

> 'The amount of business now being handled by the Executive Committee has grown to such an extent that the Committee has been sitting until 11.30pm. More frequent meetings will probably be necessary although this will increase the already heavy demands on the office-bearers in particular.'

Nor was it only the administrative work that caused the strain as many of the office-bearers, myself excluded by my own decision, had public duties to perform for the Party as Arthur went on to describe:

> 'I should like finally to say that I have in the past three months addressed a formidable number of Party meetings and have been greatly impressed by the high morale of the Party, the way in which members are coming forward and the very great improvement in public attitude to the Party. We are now well on our way to success on a scale we did not expect quite so quickly.'

As George Leslie described[4]:

> 'I would like to give you a flavour of those early years – the excitement and heat that occupied most of the day. Driving night after night to Lossiemouth, Auchtermuchty, Castle Douglas, and Lochgilphead to speak to packed halls of people who wanted to believe that Scotland could do it. ....Trying to squeeze in a few hours of work to make sufficient money to cover a few bills.'

High morale always makes it easier to bear a greater burden, but sooner or later, there is a physical limit that cannot be crossed. So, only one year after approval of the major changes to the structure of the Party, the whole matter came up for discussion at the meeting of the National Executive of 16 January 1966.[5] Two propositions were advanced. By a vote of 10 to 3, a motion from Dr James Lees calling for abolition of the offices of Executive

Vice-chairmen was defeated and a proposal to increase the number of Vice-chairmen to four was accepted.

Three months later in March 1966, in a further report, Arthur Donaldson added[6]:

> 'Nevertheless, the Executive Committee will require to take further steps to bring its business into manageable compass and this it would seem, must involve delegation of its ordinary administrative functions to the National Office-Bearers individually or as a sub-committee.
>
> These difficulties are the result of the tremendous growth of the Party and the much greater role it is able to play in consequence of all the affairs of Scotland. Our Headquarters organisation as a whole is creaking under what is a welcome strain and much of the Executive's time has been taken in considering ways in which it can be strengthened.
>
> The most important decision is that the Edinburgh Office, hitherto officially only a Public Relations Office, will now be given a much greater role. Records, finance, circularising etc. will in future be the responsibility of Mrs Hall in Edinburgh; organisation, the Secretary's considerable correspondence, and press releases will be handled in Glasgow. These are tentative divisions and will perhaps be modified in the light of experience.
>
> The Executive has also agreed in principle that the staff will soon require to be augmented on the Organisation side as the calls on the National Organiser were becoming impossibly onerous.'

The effect of these decisions was that Rosemary Hall would become National Organising Secretary and start a movement of duties towards Edinburgh. As she acted in an honorary capacity, there was no direct on-cost, but implicit in the changes was that the Edinburgh staff needed to be increased and additional office space obtained from the Edinburgh Branch who owned the premises. Leadership in this reorganisation (which was met with opposition from the National Organiser who advised against the build up of the Edinburgh office) came from Douglas Drysdale who deployed his business experience.

Lack of finance made it difficult to proceed with the recruitment of additional staff. In preparation for the General Election, Alasdair MacDonald had been appointed as a part-time Public Relations Officer. As many a business has found, uncontrolled expansion can cause financial problems. Income always seems to lag behind expenditure. And while the Party was patting itself on the back on its success in recruiting new members, the previous year's income (for 1964) was under £5,000.[7] The overdraft was £2,272 by 1965, running at almost half the annual income.[8] So, even though the position was improving, a decision to spend £500 on the PPB recruitment campaign was an act of faith.[9] There was no crisis, but expansion of professional staffing could easily cause one. A hint of this was given by National Treasurer, Harry (Cunny) Rankin when he complained that the financial position had worsened because of over-spending by the Executive.

There was one piece of brightness in an altogether gloomy financial scene. At the end of 1964, Angus McGillveray had come up with the idea of a lottery. He was a long term member of the SNP in West Lothian and had been part of Billy Wolfe's election team in the important 1962 by-election. He had raised funds for cultural and sporting organisations over many years and when he came up with the proposal for an SNP lottery to be known as Alba Pools, the Party had no hesitation in giving permission for its launch from a base at his home which had been the distribution centre for SNP Publications. All new ideas take time to develop and this was true of Alba Pools. By March 1965, however, Alba was printing 8,000 tickets a week and prize money increased to £120 per week.[10] The brilliance of the concept lay in it providing money for the branches that sold the tickets. They had a vested interest in selling and using the commission to beef up branch income (which meant in turn that they could buy recruitment literature from the Publications Department and build up their election funds).

Progressively, Alba Pools lubricated the growth. From 4 January 1965 to 18 August 1966, the Pools made a profit of £28,000, split between the branches and HQ.[11] This seems small beer by current standards, but it was very real in 1965/66 and cumulatively in current monetary terms, the amount raised by Alba was over a million pounds. Even so, as the Treasurer had complained frequently, it was not enough, in its earlier days, to cover ever increasing expenditure.

The SNP also had to look at its other new resource – new members, most of whom had no experience of political campaigning, and perhaps a shallow understanding of the SNP's policies, chairing or clerking meetings, or basic accounting skills. Beyond that, there were the potential high flyers needing to be trained as local or national candidates, and in radio and television techniques as well as more basic public speaking skills and a deeper understanding of policy and politics. There were substantial problems in acclimatising these members to the goal of independence or the social and economic philosophies of the Scottish National Party. Seemingly, this was a plus for the organisation, but what was not evident was the danger which an untrained membership could constitute. At the time, it was mainly the positive aspects that were considered and Douglas Henderson was appointed Director of Internal Training.[12]

As part of the changes at the 1966 Conference (which increased the number of Executive Vice Chairmen to four, there came a change in executive leadership. Billy Wolfe moved up to Senior Vice Chairman, the deputy to the Party Chairman, and had oversight of research. Douglas Drysdale took responsibility as EVC for Finance, part of his former brief. Dr James Lees became EVC Organisation, John Gair (who had been the by-election candidate in Dumfries), EVC Policy and Provost James Braid Publicity. In terms of personality and outlook, James Lees and Jimmy Braid had little in common, apart from living in Fife. James Lees was a pathologist who did private research into the causes of cancer and was as restrained as one would expect in the days before pathologists acquired the glamour of portrayal in television drama series. Jimmy Braid was an extrovert. He had been a pilot during the War and worked as an engineer. They proved to be a tremendous team, travelling throughout Scotland and building up the Party indefatigably. They were strong exponents of Party decentralisation and were behind much of the drive towards regionalism in the SNP over the next two years. Their field work has been underestimated.

There were also changes in Executive membership with Angus McGillveray, George Leslie, Alasdair MacDonald and Gordon Murray emerging. Angus was also Publications Manager and Alba Pools Promoter, while Alasdair MacDonald held the position of part-time PRO, so at this stage there was no barrier to those holding paid positions from being members of the NEC. Other trends were apparent. The NEC spawned a co-ordinating Committee consisting of the Executive Vice-chairmen, the Secretary, the Treasurer and National Organising Secretary under the Convenership of the Senior Vice-chairman to deal with the business coming before the NEC.[13]   This ran into trouble on 9 December 1966, when the Executive Vice-chairmen were sharply divided as to its use. When it was ruled by the NEC that the meetings were purely for co-ordination and attendance was at discretion of the office-bearers concerned, Messrs Lees and Braid stated that they regarded the Committee as unnecessary and would not attend, while Drysdale and Gair felt that the Committee served a useful purpose.[14]

Membership at June 1966 was 25,000.[15] Already attendances at National Council and Conference were rising. Although Party members had accepted many of the changes concentrating power in the Executive and the office-bearers, there was a growing demand for more diffused power sharing. This manifested itself in proposals, mainly, but not exclusively, at the urging of James Lees and Jimmy Braid for a review of the decision-making power centres. In July 1966, the NEC set up a Committee of Enquiry to investigate the functions of the Annual Conference and National Council with the aim of improving the arrangements for the election of office-bearers and the National Executive as well as looking at the composition of National Council.[16] There was also a wish to streamline the agenda for National Conference.

The first committee, consisting of Cunny Rankin, David Rollo and myself, swiftly reported, but the Executive considered the report along with other representations and made recommendations.[17] National Council accepted some of the proposals[18], but by 82 votes to 15, remitted the proposals for the NEC with a strict request that the NEC provided a scheme for a majority of regional representatives within its number, thus starting a series of cross-referrals and disagreements between Council and the Executive until January 1968.

It was then resolved with a touch of inspiration. The latest sub-committee consisted of Billy Wolfe, Archie Young and me. Like everyone else, we were fed up with the issue. As National Secretary, I felt the proposals for a large regionally elected National Executive Committee of over 100 members, meeting monthly and dealing with detail, was daft. There was no way it could find the time to process business. It would be larger than the numbers attending National Council only a year before. And if more than a few of the members spoke, the meetings, already running past midnight on occasions, would last for ever!

The sub-committee met in my house shortly before Christmas 1967. We desperately wanted to find a solution that would stick. In this third attempt, we broke away from the pattern and concentrated purely on the role of the Executive. We drew attention to the inability of the NEC to manage effectively the proposals emerging from the Party's research and policy committees. With this in mind, the detailed Report stated[19]:

> 'Under the existing framework, there is no spare capacity for it (the Executive) to attend to the preparatory work towards taking over the government of Scotland on Independence Day.
> We have, therefore, decided to recommend that the new Executive be treated as a representative and consultative assembly responsible for policy, that it be termed the National Executive Assembly of the Scottish National Party and that there be also a National

Executive Committee responsible for administration, finance, organisation and immediate work arising between meetings of the National Executive Assembly.

In greater detail, we see the Executive (Assembly) providing:

1. a forum for policy in which all regions of Scotland are represented.
2. a forum where intensive work on the SNP Manifesto for the next General Election will be done.
3. a forum for initial representative discussion of the draft Scottish Constitution and for the preparation for the scheme of administration under which the functions of the government of Scotland will be assumed and carried out by the interim government until the General Election is held.
4. a source of members for departmental committees and sub-committees.'

The paper provided for representation of all constituency associations, thus fulfilling the mandate for regional representation, and with office-bearers, MPs and others, the size of the new body would not exceed 111 members. Despite its name, the National Executive Assembly was not conceived as a policy making body. It left policy making to National Council and Conference which represented the branches. In passing, it provided for continuation of a National Executive Committee (whose administrative duties remained the same), carrying out the humdrum work of running the Party. The NEC retained power of decision making and from a management point of view, with its membership restricted to 24, was able to carry out its functions.

What none of us realised was that the new structure would lead to a creative explosion within the SNP, the setting up of many new committees and the complete reworking of policy that transformed the SNP from a campaigning party to one which had the capacity to compete in the complex territory of government with the long established political parties. Nor did we appreciate that this would soak up too much of the SNP's talent and energies and interfere with campaigning over a period when there were no elections.

Given successive failures, it seemed that the greatest difficulty would lie in persuading the party apparatus to approve these proposals, after most others had been killed off over a protracted period. In the event, whether because the Assembly was perceived as meeting a real need or out of exhaustion, the NEC[20] passed the paper by 14 votes to 6 and the Council unanimously – a miracle in itself![21] Within a few years, the body dropped the name 'Executive' and as the 'National Assembly' has served the Party well for 40 years.

In the meantime, membership and branches grew at great speed, with 26 branches alone being formed at the Executive meeting of 8 July 1966, and many other branches and increasingly, constituency associations forming over the next two years.[22] At times, it seemed that we were careening on the edge of a breaking wave, in constant danger of falling off. No one knew what was in store. When Gwynfor Evans, President of Plaid Cymru won the seat of Carmarthen in the summer, it was taken as evidence that the sky was the limit. Winning parliamentary elections was crucial to the success of a democratic nationalist party. The Plaid Cymru victory ignited further hopes and ambitions.

In his Chairman's Report to National Council of September 1966, Arthur Donaldson wrote[23]:

> 'We were all stimulated by the great victory of Plaid Cymru in Carmarthen. It was a great thing for them but the significance of that victory in Scotland was the way people took it as a portent of similar success to come from the SNP. That this should be the reaction within our own ranks was natural; that it should have roused the same reaction amongst the voters was very significant indeed.
>
> When the Carmarthen victory was followed by the July 20 announcement of the most violent economic squeeze yet, the public reaction was to realise and say that the Scottish National Party had been right all the way through and that it presented the only hope for Scotland of getting out of the frustrating cycle of inflation and deflation to which we are condemned by the fact that we are handcuffed to England.
>
> The Carmarthen victory and the public resentment of the economic squeeze which must soon be blown into flame by the personal suffering of many, have probably postponed for some time the voluntary by-elections which were being planned, but a by-election somewhere is not likely to be long delayed and we shall have a great opportunity, no matter how 'safe' the seat.'

Arthur Donaldson called for renewed vigour by the Party over the winter months and in the course of the next three months, he addressed 23 meetings from as far south as Strathaven and as far north as Tain, also as far west as Lochaline and east as far as Brechin with an average attendance of 100. By December 1966, there were 190 recognised branches. During this period, 10,000 membership cards had been sold and total membership was estimated at 42,000.[24] The television party political broadcast by Arthur Donaldson had produced a response of 600 enquiries immediately and hundreds of others afterwards.

As the SNP observably gained strength, it attracted invitations to give evidence to enquiries. The Wheatley Commission on Local Government Reform requested the Party to make a written response. George Leslie, who had chaired the Committee preparing the evidence, and Robert McIntyre gave oral evidence. George Leslie was soon to be the candidate in a by-election in Glasgow Pollok. George lived opposite me and came across to express an interest in contesting. He indicated that if I wanted to stand, he would not run against me. Being a by-election candidate was not in my mind. My daughter, Margaret, was a baby of 4 months; and in any event, I was happy with my creative role in the background. So I endorsed with enthusiasm his offer to be the candidate. Being in the Pollok Constituency, I did not escape as my ground floor flat became sub-rooms for the Pollokshields area.

George Leslie was a young veterinary surgeon and had ample dynamism and charisma. These qualities were emphasised in highly personalised leaflets. All the same, it was an odd election. Support was extremely polarised. In many of the housing schemes we were picking up between 30% and 40% of the vote, whereas in middle class Pollokshields and environs, the Tory support was rock hard with the canvass for the SNP around the 7% level. In the end we secured a good, if not overwhelming, result. The Tories won, defeating Labour who had held the seat. We came third with over 10,000 votes.

Glasgow Pollok By-election Result (March 1967)

Conservative & Unionist	36.9%
Labour	31.2%
SNP	28.3%
Scottish Liberals	1.9%
Communist	1.7%

This was the best result outside West Lothian five years before. It also had the advantage of thrusting the Liberal candidate into a poor fourth place. For most of us, it was a highly satisfactory result in difficult urban circumstances, but George Leslie is not so kind in his recollections[25]:

> 'The Pollok election was a roller-coaster. The SNP national input was nil other than yourself as chairman of the election planning committee. Those involved brought disorganised mass canvassing to housing schemes like Ardler and Priesthill which are still subjects of conversation with my clients to this day. Certainly the impact of this disorganised canvassing (probably its novelty value) had an entirely different impact on the recipients than our modern day identification canvass and survey cards.
> With the help of Hugh MacDonald and Morris Blythman we raised election music to a serious form of political music. Since Pollok I have never seen people (not just children) dancing in the streets to SNP music. As a candidate I had no serious back-up. We had a series of school meetings (15-20 in all) and they were all packed – usually with no supporting speakers other than Angus McIntosh who chaired almost all the meetings. I took part in my first election panel show with no support from the SNP. I had to drive myself to the studios with no minder after a school meeting. Nevertheless we did achieve certain things, most of all a belief among activists that we were on the move and a willingness to look at new campaigning ideas. We learned almost nothing about organisation. I came to the stunning revelation that Independence was not going to happen overnight.'

The 1967 local elections intervened with a landside performance, showing that we were on the right track. We achieved 24.2% of the votes cast, with 200,000 votes, 69 gains and 170 seats.

Large numbers of delegates and observers were attending National Council at its quarterly meetings. In the election to the Executive, George Leslie topped the poll with 114 votes, and with a new name, Mrs Winifred Ewing close behind with 101.[26] National Council agendas were no longer dominated by Headquarters and had resolutions on both policy and internal matters from constituency associations and branches. In June 1967, there was no change in the identity of the Vice-chairmen. The final places in the SNP administrative jigsaw were almost complete, with arrangements being made for a Research Officer and an Administrative Secretary.

The political dimension was never far from our minds. Over the previous six years, Billy Wolfe, as a an accountant, had been especially interested in proving that Scotland could stand on her own feet. When he became politically active, he helped establish SEISS, the Social and Economic Inquiry Society of Scotland, a non-party think-tank dedicated to analysis of Scotland's position. This attracted experts such as Andrew Hargraves, an industrial journalist and others who could not be associated with the SNP. They did a great deal of valuable research. As the SNP broke through and the attacks increased, the topic of a Scottish budget became interesting to others not directly involved in politics. The Scotsman published on 4 July 1968, a special report that reached two conclusions. One, a major reason for putting control of the Scottish economy into Scottish hands, was the need to strengthen it and accelerate its rate of growth. Two, the available evidence suggested that Scotland had the national income to afford a Budget which would enable this need to be met quickly and effectively. Forty years on, the economic case could not be more cogently summarised.

In the front page article, the Scotsman declared that a self-governing Scotland could afford a Budget which would allow social services to be maintained and industry services assisted on the existing levels. Based on 1966 statistics, Scotland's gross domestic product per head of population came out at about £634, compared with £685 for the United Kingdom. Among small countries in Western Europe, the Belgian figure was £682, the Dutch £600 and the Irish £350. It was a coup for the SNP.

As the Party had foreseen 18 months before, there was to be an election in Hamilton. The candidate Mrs Winifred Ewing, a Glasgow court lawyer, had been in place for a year. Through August, September and October 1967, the SNP was engaged in a titanic election contest with Labour. Winifred Ewing had ability with star quality, and attracted interested audiences in street meetings. Under the direction of John McAteer, her agent, and helped by Ian Macdonald, the National Organiser and Rosemary Hall, National Organising Secretary, there was a taut, well-organised campaign supported by thousands of our supporters. I spoke at local meetings. The turn-out was good and it was clear that people were listening. The campaign built to a climax with an eve of poll rally in Hamilton Town Hall on 1 November 1967. Over 1,000 people attended. Not all were supporters, so it was an old-fashioned public meeting with heckling. Winnie Ewing had the support of the great majority of the audience.

As the SNP had not won a seat for 20 years, we could not assume that we could win. On the Saturday before polling day, I was not sure. Edith and I went out canvassing in Hamilton. In the morning, we were in a good quality council housing estate. We had slim pickings. It was obvious these people with their superior housing were staunch supporters of the Labour council. In the afternoon, it was a different story. We were sent to a run-down part of Hamilton. It, too, had council housing, but what a difference. The houses were poor and uncared for. Most council tenants were unemployed or on benefit. And it was here that the SNP got wide support. These voters had nothing to be grateful for from Labour. By the Monday, the Scottish Daily Express produced a poll showing the SNP was moving ahead. This gave us, and wavering voters, just the boost we needed.

Winnie Ewing triumphed and became our second ever MP (the first MP having been Robert McIntyre for a short period in 1945).

Hamilton By-election Result (November 1967)

SNP	46%
Labour	41.5%
Conservative & Unionist	12.5%

Scotland and the media (including the London and international press and television) went wild. Thousands of enquiries overwhelmed our staff in Glasgow and Edinburgh.

Back in Edinburgh, the day after the victory, Rosemary Hall recounts[27]:

> 'Undoubtedly our most hectic day - and we had many – was the day that the Hamilton by-election result was declared in November 1967. A huge queue formed in the office, snaking its way round the Round Room in 16 North St Andrew Street, of people wanting to join the SNP. There were only two of us in that office (Ray Wallace and myself) and we were stretched to the utmost keeping up with the requests of the people in the queue and with their expressions of delight at Winnie Ewing's election. Meantime the telephone kept ringing insistently. But the queue waited patiently while we coped.'

We decided to celebrate in style. In one of the most complex operations carried out by Rosemary Hall, the SNP hired an overnight train. Tickets were sold to members and the press travelled free. I recall being in discussion with one of the journalists, Neal Ascherson who, like others, was there to sample the atmosphere. We agreed the experience was incredible. After Winnie had been transported to the House of Commons in a Hillman Imp, produced in Linwood, Renfrewshire and supplied by the manufacturers, there was a rally, before we all made our way back to Scotland. Exhilaration was replaced by exhaustion, but who cared. We had made the great break-through at last.

No one knew how our new MP could take her seat. As National Secretary, I recall being nonplussed when asked to make the arrangements. It was quite surreal. I had been to Westminster only once before to give evidence to a Speaker's Conference on party election broadcasting. This was different. We were the actors now, not spectators. A telephone call to Gordon Campbell of the Scottish Daily Express, who was chairman of the Westminster Lobby Correspondents, also provided good background guidance. In addition, I arranged lunch with George Reid, then Head of Current Affairs at Scottish Television and on the background information he provided, prepared a memorandum for Winnie Ewing explaining in considerable detail how the Parliamentary Lobby operated and who were the best contacts for both the Daily and Sunday press.

I also contacted the Serjeant-at-Arms of the Commons regarding a suitable time for Winnie to take the oath. The rules demanded two sponsors. One obviously would be Gwynfor Evans of Plaid Cymru; but there was no way any of the major parties would give any co-operation. We were fortunate that Alasdair MacKenzie, a Highland Liberal MP, agreed to act. He also spoke at the Rally after Winnie had been installed.

For the next six months, the constant activity continued. There was world-wide publicity. London and places further afield sat up and took notice! There was a new dimension to Scotland and the SNP. We had a charismatic Member of Parliament. With exceptional energy and stamina few could match, Winnie Ewing combined her duties at Westminster with those to the Party. In her first month at Westminster, Winnie answered 2,000 letters, made 33 broadcasts on radio and television, gave 400 press interviews, spoke in parliament, dealt with Hamilton constituents' problems, addressed 6 rallies, opened or chaired a variety of functions and asked 61 questions. When the first rush subsided, she operated at an exhausting pace for the remainder of her term. Additionally, she had to cope with another problem. She received competing offers for a weekly column from both the Daily Record and the Scottish Daily Express. It was decided that as the Daily Record had greater penetration amongst Labour voters, it would be beneficial for the Party and the SNP in Hamilton, if she contracted with the Record. The Daily Express did not give up and assigned one of its senior reporters to shadow Winnie and write up a competitive article.

Those of us who were in touch appreciated the huge stress she was under. At Westminster, with a few honourable exceptions, she was harassed by panic-stricken Labour MPs. No mercy was shown. Fortunately, as a solicitor practising in Glasgow Sheriff Court, one of the busiest in Europe, she was well toughened by dealing with difficult sheriffs. There could be no preparation for what she was about to experience. There was constant hostility and abuse, mainly from Labour MPs, whenever she rose to speak. Worse still she had to withstand smears and snide attacks not made to her face. Details of her experiences can be found in her book, "Stop the World" and they do not make pleasant reading.

Every week-end, Winnie would come back from London to face a weighty schedule of constituency surgeries and rallies around the country to squeeze the maximum benefit from her victory. The turn-out at meetings was huge. Hundreds would attend. Winnie had a rare magnetism, plus the novelty value of being completely different from any one else seen at Westminster. She was also at the crest of a wave of national enthusiasm. For many, even new-comers, it appeared that the Grail of independence was within reach. And as pro-SNP fervour grew, so the attacks from the Labour and Conservative Parties intensified. Segments of the media, initially very favourable, began to turn snide. This was particularly true of the Glasgow Herald which ran scaremongering articles that got under the skin of Party activists in the West of Scotland.

An attempt was made by Billy Wolfe, also in January, to initiate discussions with Plaid Cymru for the setting up of a joint parliamentary office, but the project failed to take root, mainly for financial reasons.

The impact on the Party of her election was stunning even on a hyper-active SNP, already experiencing recruitment which took the estimated membership to 120,000. These escalating figures were based upon membership cards sold by the Party Headquarters to branches and not always paid for in advance. As part of its missionary culture at this stage, cards would be made available by Headquarters on the understanding, if not expectation, they would be paid for. Not all would be converted into people joining. SNP membership figures could be difficult to gauge, largely because the Party was decentralised with the cards being sold at local level. Branches were very poor at sending records of members to HQ. By the time we reached the peak, there were over 500 branches with well over 100 members on average. On reflection, Ian Macdonald believes that the true figure would be between 60,000 – 70,000.[28] It did not make too much difference. The SNP was already overtaxed and a substantial series of training courses run by Director of Training, Douglas Henderson could only scratch the surface, leaving the Party open to difficulties if its growth should falter. Although there was a crying need to educate members at branch and constituency level, the priority had to be to induct those members who could be council and Westminster candidates. One of the principal instruments for training of future leaders was attendance at the National

Council. In the period after Hamilton, the number of delegates and observers could be counted in hundreds.

These new members had the opportunity to see the Party's democracy in action, hear about strategy from office-bearers and listen to debates on policy. In tune with the growth of the SNP, the Scots Independent was now a weekly with a circulation of 12,000 and a readership of at least 50,000-60,000. Its coverage helped the Party in its role of political education.

Internally, the Party organisation had to react to the new parliamentary dimension. We had an MP who was overloaded and needed support. The strength of Headquarters was limited. Tours would be organised and publicity marshalled for Winnie Ewing. In particular, there was a need for parliamentary assistance. In the sixties, being an MP was not a 'plum' job so far as pay and allowances were concerned. The salary was low and expenses negligible. As to prestige, it was radically different. MPs were respected and influential; and it is a sad commentary on progress that as pay and expenses for MPs grew, so did their standing decline. Even allowing for the improvement in SNP finances through Alba pools (membership fees were too low to make much of an impact), there was a drive to expand central staffing with a Research Officer, an Administration Secretary, a cashier and a full time PRO. There was not much left spare. However, the Executive recognised the critical importance of giving a service to our MP and providing her with an assistant. It was of help, but did not go close to giving the response that was needed. In turn, Mrs Ewing launched a Club which brought extra money to the Party.

There was a greater political need. Winnie Ewing was under constant attacks at Westminster, where a moment's absence from the Chamber could lead to points of order to record her lack of presence. There were parliamentary questions to be asked and the answers processed and followed up, motions to be drafted and initiatives to be devised. There was no way any one person could do this and indeed, advice was always essential. A Parliamentary Advisory Committee of Messrs. McIntyre, Donaldson, Wolfe and Hugh MacDonald was set up by the Executive.[29] Every Sunday, key people such as Billy Wolfe, George Leslie, Hugh MacDonald, Douglas Henderson, David Simpson and Donald Bain would gather at Winnie's house. I chaired these meetings alternately with Billy Wolfe. Others such as Robert McIntyre and Arthur Donaldson would be available, sometimes in person, but usually by telephone to give guidance and to offer ideas.

As Party Secretary, I found my mailbag expanded. Winnie would pass to me letters from outwith the constituency on all sorts of topics. It was an education figuring out replies on such topics as anti-fluoridation, British Standard Time, decimal currency, the Celtic League, local authority audits and a host of other topics. We tried to give reasoned answers wherever possible, but some letters were obviously from cranks who would never give up. A gentle closure of such correspondence became an art form. The role of the Research Officer, Donald Bain, expanded as he was better able to give the substantial back-up that Mrs Ewing needed.   He helped prepare the 'Black Book on Scotland'. This was a compilation of the information Winnie Ewing had obtained from Parliamentary Answers and for which the Scottish Daily Express offered to buy first publication rights.

The first cloud on the horizon appeared. There had been some bad publicity and Arthur Donaldson commented in his National Council Report for March[30]:

> 'So great is the activity of the party and so keen the public interest that the SNP is at the moment getting the attention of newspapers and newspapermen all over the world and most markedly in our own country. Let us not be surprised or in any way dismayed if at times this publicity may seem unfavourable or if our minor internal difficulties get more attention than even major external successes. It is the unusual that makes news.'

The main piece of bad news arose from the emergence of an elitist splinter group, 'The 1320 Club'. It kept its membership secret and its well publicised views were regarded as extreme. As a consequence, the National Executive Committee placed a resolution before the meeting of Council of 2 March 1968.

> 'This Council resolves that membership of The 1320 Club is not compatible with membership of the Scottish National Party.'

It was moved by George Leslie, and seconded by James Halliday. George Leslie emphasised that the bad publicity being acquired by the 1320 Club would reflect on the Party and our election campaign and pointed out that the Party had no control over the policy or actions of the Club. Winnie Ewing said that her position as an MP made her vulnerable so far as the Press were concerned. The Press had told her immediately of the Executive meeting at which the matter had been discussed and could repeat some of the conversations. She pointed out the necessity of trust.

The Council meeting had been preceded by bad publicity including leaks from the National Executive. The opposition was vocal and the atmosphere tense. The Press were waiting outside the hotel where the meeting was held, for news and comment. The motion carried by 159 votes to 45.[31] Just as interesting as the result was the huge number of delegates voting and the large volume of members attending as observers. Turnout far exceeded attendance at previous Conferences.

The impact of having an MP was phenomenal. Apart from the gain in political credibility and the upsurge in support for the SNP, the election of Winnie Ewing altered the mind-set of the Party itself. Until Mrs Ewing was elected, the SNP was merely a very successful protest movement. It had carried a menace for five years, but this had never been translated into victory. There were, therefore, many members, never mind members of the public, who thought winning a seat was outwith the reach of the SNP. Some of our electoral campaigning did not command conviction. Once we had won, the target of victory in by-elections never seemed so far away – even though winning in many areas could be well-nigh impossible. But with success comes the fear of failure and hanging over our heads during the next few years, especially as the Party drifted backwards, was the worry that Hamilton could be at risk when the General Election came.

It is remarkable that a one-off by-election victory by a fringe organisation should have had the impact it did. But Scotland was stirring and the SNP was an unique outlet for venting the anger and frustrations engendered by our treatment as a nation at the hands of Whitehall. From now on, the SNP was ever present either as a political force or as a potential threat to the Union between Scotland and England.

Chapter 5
Policy Development

The aims and objectives of the SNP have, with one or two minor variations to accord with the times, remained consistent. They were two fold: the obtaining of self-government within the UN and Commonwealth by democratic means and the furtherance of Scottish interests. These were the cardinal principles on which the Party's other policies were based.

These were set out in the Constitution and Rules of the time as follows:

> A. Self-Government for Scotland – that is, the restoration of Scottish National Sovereignty by the establishment of a democratic Scottish Government freely elected by the Scottish people, and whose authority will be limited only by such agreements as will be freely entered into with other nations or states for the purpose of furthering international co-operation and world peace.
> B. The furtherance of all Scottish interests.

In the forties and fifties when the SNP was endeavouring to survive, there was no great pressure to upgrade policy. Things moved more slowly in those days, and in the case of the SNP, there was no influx of members bearing new ideas. There had been some new pamphlets like 'A Hundred Home Rule Questions.'

The principal policy statement was 'Aims and Policy of the Scottish National Party'. The Foreword of the reprint of 1963 tells its own story:

> 'The Policy of the National Party has been created by the resolutions of the Annual Conferences since 1928 but was first brought together and printed as a whole after the close of the 1939-45 War. Basically there has not been much change since that first printing...' and:

> 'Many of the political ideas which are only now becoming the subject of popular discussion will be found in these papers and were thus pioneered by the National Party.'

Changes since 1947 were given in an appendix of one and a half pages at the end of the 1963 reprint.

The ethos of the SNP was decentralist. It tracked the run-down of the great heavy industries as a consequence of loss of Scottish control, accelerated by the two world wars, subsequent nationalisation and the development of company capitalism. The essence of the position is summed up in the Introduction:

> 'The process has been gradual and unspectacular, but its results have been disastrous for Scotland. The responsibility cannot be placed on one political party more than another. During the past two generations all British political parties have fostered the progressive centralisation of political and economic power in the State. With the achievement of over-riding control of all economic affairs by the State and the supremacy of political over economic power, the conflict in society is no longer between capitalism and socialism but between the interests fostering the centralisation of arbitrary power and the movement striving for the decentralisation of authority and responsibility, and the rule of law.
> The Scottish National Party declares that the greatest possible diffusion of political and economic power is essential to the maintenance of the freedom of the individual, and is the only alternative to the development of an arbitrary despotism ruling over an irresponsible proletariat.'

The statement called for reform of local government, with its preferred retention of power at local level, internationalism and support for European co-operation, a special relationship with the other countries of the British Isles, a belief in common defence in Europe (this pre-dated the creation of NATO), control of land planning, access to Scotland's natural resources such as the hills, lochs and rivers, development of coal and water energy and encouragement of agriculture, forestry and fishing. There was a demand for Scottish majority ownership of industry, basic rights for workers and interestingly, well ahead of its day, a call for restrictions on chain stores with local enterprises being favoured. In the important area of transport, the Party was against monopoly and in favour of flat freight rates. Road transport could be diverse. Rail was to be nationalised. Scottish airport services were to be expanded. Utilities were to be transferred from British bodies to Scottish public control.

In the area of social policy, health services were to be public and free of bureaucracy. Improvements in housing were very urgent as the need was of great magnitude. In education, where reform was favoured, there were to be territorial, multilateral schools and ad hoc Education Authorities. Poverty was to be conquered primarily by economic opportunity backed up by adequate social security benefits.

In the appendix containing additions to policy, the Party was in favour of NATO and the European Common Market (provided the terms of entry could be negotiated by Scotland and approved by a referendum), against the nuclear bomb, but not opposed to nuclear power. There was also provision for a statutory right to compensation for redundant workers and local authorities that had provided facilities for a factory closing for any reason other than failure.

Policy formation in late 1963 and early 1964 was held up by the 1963 by-elections, the re-organisation of the party and the 1964 General Election. Not surprisingly, the 1964 Conference Agenda, cobbled together by Edith and me in the absence of the usual number of resolutions from the rest of the Party, was full of re-affirmations of existing policy which were passed by acclamation.[1] A contested motion on health was debated and remitted to National Council where, on my motion, seconded by Robert McIntyre, it was carried. Another resolution on land use, also remitted from Conference, was sent to the Land & Agricultural Committee.

All this was overshadowed by preparation of the Election Manifesto, SNP and You, written by Billy Wolfe and approved by the office-bearers.[2] It was an ambitious work. While not intended to do so, such was the quality of the expression of party policy and the imaginative design (again carried out by Julian Gibb) that it rapidly replaced Aims and Policy as the primary policy statement and became available for post-election sale.

It began by stating that the SNP stood for the nation, not just for prosperity, and dignity. It compared the slum housing conditions of Edinburgh and Glasgow with housing in Stockholm, Copenhagen, Oslo and Amsterdam and attacked the growth of wealth in England to Scotland's loss. It expounded the benefits of democracy, freedom of conscience, equal opportunity and social progress in a free Scotland and outlined the parliamentary route to a Scottish legislature. The economic analysis was updated, but did not differ too greatly from the earlier document. It dealt with industrial expansion, agriculture (where the target was satisfaction of Scotland's basic food demands). Like its predecessor it had a substantial passage on housing which was still in crisis. It savagely attacked the anglicisation of the educational system and its separation from higher education (Scottish Universities having recently been put under the control of the Universities Grants Committee). The document was still against state bureaucracy in social development and outlined a higher social priority to look after those in need, covering unemployment and sickness benefits, fair retirement pensions, minimum wages guarantees and health services for all. There was a section on defence, strongly against Polaris missiles and Scotland being a nuclear nation. The defence needs were to be modest:

> 'An army sufficient to make any invasion or physical occupation of Scotland a very difficult undertaking, and, when required by the United Nations to supply detachments of troops for assistance in implementing decisions.
> A navy planned mainly for effective policing of Scottish territorial waters inside limits of 14 miles from headland to headland.
> An air force coupled with a commercial air organisation.'

All this was costed at a figure less than half of Scotland's contribution to UK defence.

SNP & You had a large section devoted to sport and recreation and undertook to establish an Academy of the Arts; it promised aid to theatre, film, the visual arts, music, architecture and literature, and was well in advance of public thinking on these aesthetic matters.

While SNP & You displayed continuity with the historical policy of the Party, there was a difference in expression. It did not confine Scotland so restrictively in industry or give as much emphasis to decentralisation. It formed an action plan for government, and although it made repeated references to SNP Democrats (in line with a later unsuccessful attempt by Billy Wolfe to influence the Party to change its name to the Scottish Democrats Party), the tone was more 'social' than 'liberal' democratic in outlook.

By the Conference of May 1965, there was still little sign of new thinking emerging from the new policy structure or from the branches.[3] There was a perceptible sign in one resolution of growing opposition to the EEC (especially in reaction to the terms under negotiation by the British Government) and possible membership of Scotland.[4] A month later at Council, Billy Wolfe moved a resolution on behalf of his home branch, Westfield & Torphichen, against segregated schooling.[5] This was defeated by 31 votes to 17.

Slowly, the policy work under the revised structure, headed by Billy Wolfe as Policy Vice Chairman, began to bear fruit, with initial reports from committees dealing with Local Government, Education, Defence, Transport and Taxation, mostly at exploratory level. A discussion paper on defence was presented to Council in September 1965, reconsidered by the Executive and passed by Council in December 1965.[6] It accepted continuation of membership of NATO, agreed to apply for membership of the UN, set the size of forces at a level to deter attack, envisaged defensive armed services on a restricted expenditure basis only and did not tolerate foreign forces in time of peace. Council accepted an amendment that Scotland would not manufacture or store nuclear weapons.

The Agenda for the 1966 Conference[7] displayed traces of proactive policy formulation at leadership level with centrally inspired motions (under the name of National Council) calling for state support for new industrial initiatives involving employee ownership and control of enterprises and for Boards to plan and control our main industries. Branches moved resolutions with radical views on land ownership and NATO. There were more National Council motions than usual and these gave welcome evidence of an upturn in ideas. Glasgow Pollok (probably though the influence of George Leslie) promoted a major resolution on local government and the New Towns. Fraserburgh and Peterhead Branches emerged with a twelve point resolution on sea fisheries.

There was a switch in Executive Vice-chairman for Policy after the 1966 Conference. John Gair succeeded Billy Wolfe who was elected Senior Vice-chairman. On the stocks were a Roads Policy which I had written and a first draft of an Agriculture Policy. The principal external aspect of interest was the Cullingworth Report which had highlighted the deplorable state of Scottish Housing. This led to a motion from John Gair to the March 1967 meeting of Council, giving a detailed plan of action for housing in the light of the Cullingworth Report.[8] This was passed, but not without amendment.

The 1967 Conference Agenda was significantly different from most of its predecessors.[9] National Council proposals predominantly related to internal and constitutional matters. Conference started with a long awaited policy on land use which was passed by acclamation and one of support for Orkney & Shetland services faced with centralised control. Out of 28 resolutions on public or policy matters, only 4 were from National Council. This was undoubtedly because of the upsurge in branches and constituency associations. New people were advancing fresh ideas. There were more debates and votes. The Conference was also very much better attended with the highest votes of 197 to 157 and 236 to 118 respectively. In content, it was also of note, given the SNP's support (2005) for the retention of the Scottish regiments, Conference rejected a similarly supportive motion by 124 to 50 votes. Conference also approved a detailed resolution from Westfield & Torphichen Branch for a Scottish Mergers Board, while rejecting an amendment to give the Board power to take over and run Scottish companies as state owned enterprises Of special interest was the following motion from Larkhall Branch[10]:

'This Conference resolves that the Scottish National Party endeavour to end the scandalous misuse of public credit, and to get the power of credit creation transferred from private banking institutions and placed in the control of the state where all power of credit should reside.'

Seemingly innocuous and reasonable, this motion, if carried, would have revolutionised the economic policies of the SNP: we would have become a social credit Party. The motion did carry by 85 to 84 votes, but on a recount held by a rather anxious Chairman, William Wolfe who was alert to the problem, was defeated on the second vote by 89 to 88, still a very tight margin. It was likewise an indication of the perils facing a political party whose membership doubled every year! Consistency could not be guaranteed. There were, fortunately, more conventional resolutions on housing (although hotly debated on an amendment relating to rent levels), coal and a resolution on the rights of Scottish workers from the Association of Scottish National Trade Unionists passed overwhelmingly with one provision relating to legal recognition of shop stewards and works committees being deleted by 91 votes to 46 and with the addition of a call for a national minimum wage.

In line with the demand for greater membership participation, John Gair established a Land Use and Agricultural Committee and an Education Committee (whose membership included two future MPs Iain MacCormick and George Thompson). A potentially dangerous development lay in the wholesale setting up of Sub-committees on Finance, Industrial Development, Social Security, Transport, Housing, Fuel & Energy and SNP Research under the aegis of the General Committee of the Economics and Information Department and its Convener, William Wolfe, since this could have caused duplication. The Minute was passed without comment in the absence of the Policy Vice-Chairman.[11] No protest from John Gair is recorded and the sub-committees may have had his approval.

In an odd development, the Department of Foreign Affairs and Land Use Committee had large memberships and little output. They behaved more like mini-government departments with bureaucratic structures and took themselves too seriously. The Land Use Committee, which had nine sub-committees, subsequently made a request for its Convener to have membership of the Executive Committee as of right, without undergoing election by the Party as a whole! This request was promptly repudiated by the Executive Committee. Since they had minimal budgets, they were tolerated. Eventually, the Executive asked questions as yet another reconstruction of the Department of Foreign Affairs was rolled out, and had it replaced by an External Affairs Committee with more modest aims.

As if exhausted, the Party gave policy a rest for a few months. More likely, its members directed their energies into winning the Hamilton by-election and maximising the recruitment drive. In December, resolutions on Vietnam of a mutually conflicting nature were remitted into the long grass by a 'next business' motion which carried by the narrow margin of 95 votes to 84.[12] Because of an outbreak of foot and mouth disease in England, there was an unusual preponderance of resolutions on agriculture.

With over 1,200 delegates, observers and party members attending, the 1968 Conference, now three days long, was the biggest ever.[13] The SNP was on a roll and everyone wanted to be present. There was a mood that the Party was unstoppable, summed up by Arthur Donaldson's exhortation in his Chairman's address; 'On them. On them. They fail. They fail.' The Agenda echoed this sense of impending victory. Independence appeared to be close and the mechanics of negotiating with Westminster were of dominant interest. So there were official resolutions emanating from the Economics and Information Committee on such topics as Scotland's share of the national debt, the setting up of a Scottish Central Bank, future economic policy (targeted by the social credit supporters) and transfers of the National Insurance contributions already made by Scots. Old favourites such as health, the nationalised industries and defence figured amongst a wider range of resolutions from the branches and constituency associations. There was also a major debate on the Scottish Constitution policy. Conference saw the election of George Leslie as an Executive Vice-chairman who inherited the Policy portfolio.

This was to be the year of policy production on an unprecedented scale, thanks to the acceptance of the National Executive Assembly by Conference, whose sole task was the processing and development of Party policy. But first the old system had to play out. The Foreign Affairs Committee produced a statement of the principles behind SNP foreign policy in these terms and considered at the June 1968 meeting of Council[14]:

> 'Scotland will play a significant and constructive role in world affairs through her own diplomatic initiative and co-operation with other nations.
> Scotland should avoid such political, defensive or economic entanglements as might lead to a loss of essential sovereignty (which) might force Scotland to adopt policies inconsistent with the wishes of the

Scottish people or might prejudice her future trading position and interfere with her ability to control and develop her own economy.
Scotland will uphold the right of self-determination of Nations and the principle of non-intervention in their affairs.
Scotland will give as much assistance as possible – consistent with her own resources - to developing nations.
Scotland will support the principles embodied in the ILO.
Scotland will play a full part in the UNO and affiliated bodies.'

This, not unnaturally being close to a 'motherhood and apple pie' formulation, was passed by acclamation. But a different fate awaited a further resolution on behalf of the Foreign Affairs Committee – this time on Vietnam. It was remitted back to the Committee for further consideration and in December, a play-off between two resolutions – one from the Committee calling for peace and another requesting the Party not to be involved in 'meaningless political posturing' led to the Committee version being approved by a large majority.[15] In what was to become a pattern, other branch resolutions were remitted to the Assembly.

While little policy had emerged from the new system as yet, the following committees were set up or reconstituted:

Constitution, Local Government, Finance and Taxation, Industrial Development, Agriculture and Horticulture, Fisheries, Forestry, Fuel and Power, Natural Resources, Transport, Health Services, Welfare and Community Services, Manpower and Employment, External Affairs, Defence, the Arts, Broadcasting, Recreation and Sport and Tourism. Many of the Conveners were new and some like Provost Gordon Murray, Tom McAlpine, Hamish Watt, Helen Davidson and John McAteer were destined to play a prominent role in the next decade. Behind the scenes, Prof. T. B. Smith, Scotland's leading jurist, had agreed to give advice on legal policy matters.

The Oban Conference in 1969 was even larger in attendance than that of a year before and required a video linked over-flow to a nearby hall.[16] It was also a Conference of a Party undergoing stress. The euphoria of 1966-68 was over. There had been a great deal of adverse publicity from innocent, if not naive, inexperienced councillors, resignations and branch and constituency disputes. The local election results had shown a slow down since 1967 and 1968. There was also a leadership challenge from Billy Wolfe against Arthur Donaldson.

In policy terms, it was the culmination of work from the new National Executive Assembly. Conference commenced with a five page draft statement on Manpower Policy with large votes of 202 to 117, and 203 to 125. It was approved in principle by 203 to 159, but was agreed to be reviewed so that the observations of delegates could be considered. I thought that the resolution was unrealistic in places and strayed by calling parts of the resolution 'codswallop'. This led to journalists scratching their heads and consulting about shorthand outlines, and on the following morning, unwelcome headline reports of splits. There followed a detailed, but less controversial, policy statement on forestry and an impressive, though controversial, four page statement on welfare and community services. This cast doubt on national insurance schemes, preferred financing out of taxation and dealt with the whole gamut of the welfare system. There was no direct opposition, but the resolution faced the inevitable motion to remit back. Scarcely had the delegates digested their lunches than they faced a mega-resolution (seven pages) on industrial policy. After a fierce debate, this was defeated by 339 votes to 269. On the Sunday, Conference debated a four page resolution on the Scottish Constitution which it passed, having rejected all the amendments.

What this Conference achieved was an ability to debate detailed resolutions, with many amendments, in a high quality manner. Because of vociferous contributions by major figures (not just me) and the leadership election won by Billy Wolfe, the press had a field day in portraying splits and highlighting differences of opinion. What they did not appreciate was that the SNP had come of age as a mature political force. It no longer relied on simple assertions of opinion or policy (although with the longer conferences, these were there in plenty). It had the facility to discuss complex matters, to select from amongst the proposals and to reject or remit back for further consideration aspects that needed reworking. In future years, the Party would benefit from these new found skills.

From 1966, there was a genuine and strong demand for the development of policy since much of it had been preserved in aspic from 1947 to 1963 and also because new members were enthused with their involvement in politics and wished to contribute. But the whiff of another reason appeared in a Kilbirnie Branch resolution before the meeting of National Council of 6 September 1969, which expressed concern at accusations of the Party's lack of policy and the need for members to speak with one voice.[17] It called for a series of policy schools to train candidates, constituency association officials, branch officials and members. Although heavily amended, it substantiated that policy was not an end in itself or purely an intellectual exercise.

At this time the Party was under incessant attack, and the initials SNP were deployed by Labour Secretary of State, Willie Ross, as an acronym for 'Sorry No Policy' Party. So there is ground for believing that the Party's great rush into policy was a reflex response to the accusations being levelled against the SNP from all sides. Policy can be a preparation for government; however, in a small Party with one MP, policy should also be used as a weapon for campaigning. Like many weapons, it could be double edged as the SNP not infrequently found to its cost. There was sensitivity within the Party that the policy making had gone too far and might be anti-productive. Nine months later in April 1970, Council rejected a Hamilton Constituency Association motion[18]:

> 'This Council deplores that policies are being decided by narrow margins in the voting. These policies are often controversial and though possibly appropriate for an Election Campaign after independence are detrimental to the unanimous policy of all members, Self-Government for Scotland.'

The direct negative was moved successfully by Mrs Margo MacDonald, one of her first influences on the future of the Party.

As the SNP entered the vortex of the approaching General Election, these issues came to the fore. With the election of George Leslie as Senior Vice-Chairman, Douglas Henderson took responsibility as Policy Vice-chairman. He began by tightening the Assembly policy committee structure, introducing a steering committee, clustering the 23 committees into subject groups and drafting a General Election Manifesto. Another of his tasks was to chair a special committee deputed to prepare the Party's evidence to the Royal Commission on the Constitution, and this was an instance where the adoption of the Party's policy statement on a constitution for an independent Scotland moved from a matter of almost academic concern to one of great practical value.

For a good part of the year, National Council was involved in tidying up resolutions which had been remitted to the National Executive Assembly and its constituent committees. So on 6 December, Council agreed a statement on post independence intra-British Isles arrangements[19]:

> 'This Council resolves that after Scottish Independence has been secured, the Scottish Government should seek to establish an association of states of the British Isles, while seeking to further international understanding and co-operation by participation in all

appropriate international bodies; and that the object of the association should be co-operation between the member states in economic, social, cultural and scientific fields, provided nothing in the Constitution of the association would derogate from the national sovereignty of the member states; and that the institution of the association should be so arranged that the consent of all member states would be necessary for the implementation of any political decision of the association.'

It was passed by 104 votes to 31. This concept of co-operation was not new. What was new was the remarkable coverage it received from the media, especially from the Daily Record on 11 December 1969. In front page banner headlines, it said, 'SNP DECIDE: WE WILL NOT GO IT ALONE!' And followed with; 'The Scottish Nationalists dropped "separatism" from their official party line in an amazing about-face yesterday. From now on, separatism is a "dirty word". Instead the nationalists will fight for an independent Scotland linked with the rest of Britain in a Common Market type of economic and political tie-up.'

The same meeting also approved, with amendments, a Health Policy and with no amendments, a policy on Transport. In April, the Manpower Policy Statement which had been remitted for reconsideration reappeared with amendments and was unanimously accepted, as was the Welfare Statement. The External Affairs Policy was also tabled, amended and approved, leaving the policy on NATO expressed as:

'... consider membership of a suitably revised North Atlantic Treaty Organisation while forbidding the stationing of nuclear weapons on Scottish soil or in Scottish Waters.'

The National Council Meeting of 11 April 1970 continued the tidying process by approving amended versions of policies on Manpower, Welfare and External Affairs.

Although the Assembly had processed a number of policy statements over the conference year, only one appeared on the agenda of the 1970 Conference.[20]

This was a revised statement of the Constitution with new paragraphs for approval. There was a resolution at the outset from Glasgow Govan Constituency Association, also sponsored by National Council, which set out the prime objective of the SNP and committed the Party to participating in government. As it encapsulates the attitude of the Party at the end of the decade, it is worth quoting[21]:

'This Conference fully recognises that the Scottish National Party has two distinct objectives:-

(a) as a national movement whose aim and purpose is to restore independence to Scotland by rallying the support of the Scottish people, so that a Parliament and a Government be established in a sovereign and independent Scotland;

(b) when the objective is achieved the Scottish National Party will continue to participate in the political life of the nation by contesting elections and forming governments if successful at the polls; and to this end and to ensure that an effective choice will be available to the Scottish people, is actively engaged in forming policies suitable to the needs and priorities of an independent Scotland.'

The Agenda was amply packed with resolutions from the grass roots for the forthcoming election and the Conference was designed to be the launch pad for candidates. Scheduled for the Sunday session was the General Election Manifesto, 'The New Scotland - Your Scotland.' The Election was called for June and the Conference was postponed to the autumn!

In many ways, The New Scotland Manifesto echoed SNP & You, without emulating the quality of its design.[22] It did, however, incorporate updates on policy, with some summaries which had not yet been approved by Conference or National Council. The document posed questions, such as: what will the new Scotland be like? What sort of action will be needed to put right the years of neglect by Westminster? What sort of country will it be like to live in, and what opportunities will there be? To all of which, the booklet, with a libertarian flavour, set out to provide answers in terms of the Party's policy ideas. The preface to this read:

'This is why we have set out an outline of some of the action the Scottish National Party would like to see taken to build Scotland in the future as an independent country. Many of the ideas are new, but they are all based on the old Scottish principles of democratic participation, personal independence and initiative, compassion for the sick, the aged and the deprived, and a mature sense of responsibility and practical common sense in the affairs of government.'

Later in the statement, in the section on local government opposing the Wheatley proposals (setting up the Regional Councils), it said:

> 'More democratic participation in government is wanted, rather than less. The future of local democracy for Scotland is inseparably associated with the prospect of democratic self-government. Support for one is support for both these principles.'

And in a final section on - The Future - it continued:

> 'We must go forward on the best of our traditions – freedom and respect for the individual, proper control of the state, protection against the over-privileged and the lawless. We must care for the people who need care; but we must not have authority and bureaucracy being allowed to do things because 'they' think they know what is best for us. We must create an atmosphere in which the active and the enterprising are encouraged and not frustrated; in which we have social co-operation and the lowering of social barriers.'

In other parts of the booklet, there was a hardening of attitudes against the Common Market with a statement that an independent Scotland would not be bound by any signature of the British Government to the Treaty of Rome. There was an uneasy compromise between the 'No Voice. No Entry' line and hostility to perceived European centralisation. There were passages on technology as the way to an industrial future. Instead of restriction on foreign ownership and control of Scottish industry, there was a welcome to foreign investment – a reversal of the position in Aims and Policy. The Party was still against English students driving out qualified Scots from entry to our Universities and there was an attack on the anglicisation of our education system whereby excessive emphasis was placed on English history, geography and habits. Forty years later, much the same criticism may be made!

In essence, the Party over the ten years of growth had not lost its decentralist traditions in experiencing the influx of new members. It had balanced the previous libertarianism and drive for decentralisation in Aims and Policy with stronger support for social care and compassion, the building blocks of social democracy. It was also still a nationalist party whose goal of Scottish independence, sometimes disguised with the more gentle terminology of 'self-government' was front-ended.

After a General Election, financial, organisational and strategic reviews always take precedence. Conference had been postponed. In the strategic review, 'The Next Four Years', presented to the Council meeting of 5 September 1970, there was not a single mention of policy.[23] On 5 December 1970, Council debated a resolution on the Common Market remitted from Conference and after a messy debate, approved a version which pledged the Party to lead the opposition to Scotland being taken into membership as part of the UK without the consent of the Scottish people in a referendum.[24] Policy papers on technology and fishing were approved by acclamation, while one on housing was remitted back by 60 votes to 47. The reduced voting was a significant reminder of the impact on membership from a disappointing General Election.

A special meeting of Council on 30 January 1971[25], called to discuss a paper on education - another policy hangover from the previous year, was largely hijacked by administrative business, including the sale of Glasgow Headquarters at 59 Elmbank Street, but did manage to pass, with the support of Winnie Ewing, proposals for local legislative devolution for Orkney and Shetland (something which had resonance five years later when the islands were cynically used by Westminster in one of its many efforts to deflect Scotland from benefiting from oil and gas in the North Sea.[26] Eventually reaching education, the Party's teachers mustered for battle and proposals for creation of a middle school were defeated by 32 votes to 21 before time ran out and the rest of the resolution was lost.

Chapter 6
Electoral Setbacks and Reverses

The local elections in May 1968 produced another landslide with over 30% of the vote and the election of 107 councillors. In Glasgow, the margin was greater, with 35.5% of the vote and 13 councillors. Elsewhere, there were major gains. In Edinburgh, 8 SNP councillors were elected. We all knew that it was going to be a good night.

It was also a night of one of the BBC's greatest bungles. I was in the BBC studio as the SNP representative in the results programme. Throughout the country, the SNP gains were stacking up, though there was silence from the Kelvin Hall in Glasgow where the multiple counts for city wards were taking place. To my side, there was a whispering radio monitor, suggesting we were winning. As time dragged on, Magnus Magnusson in the chair commented on the lateness of the results. Then, Bill Lindsay was ushered in to be met by the question: 'How does it feel to be the only SNP councillor?' Bill looked at him as if he were daft, and replied: 'But there are 13 of us'. Crimson BBC faces all around. What I had distantly and indistinctly heard was commentary from BBC radio which BBC TV had not thought to tap. In the Kelvin Hall, someone had cut the direct line for the reporter to phone the TV studio and he could not get through on other lines which were engaged.

It was a moment of triumph to savour and I paid for my joy in many subsequent results programmes where we did less well. The momentum appeared unstoppable. With 500 branches, there was less scope for expansion and the rate of branch formation slowed. By contrast, the second phase - the formation of constituency associations - speeded up. These were the key organisations that fought parliamentary elections and as the Party got into shape for the next General Election, it was necessary for them to have the framework in place to allow the adoption of candidates.

It was about to turn. Arthur Donaldson announced his retirement from the Chair. And while pressure from branches and constituency associations caused him to change his mind, by then Billy Wolfe had announced his candidacy and subsequently won at the 1969 Conference. During the year, there were personality and organisational disputes, leading to public resignations. In Edinburgh, the SNP Group of eight Councillors was a disaster with public disagreements and resignations. In other areas, dirty washing was constantly being put into the press. A great deal of time was spent in fire-fighting. As there were appeals to National Council, it got sucked into on-going disputes. Morale suffered, effort was distracted and the forward impulse was lost.

After Hamilton and the landslide local election results, our opponents had woken up to the nightmare of impending defeat. Aided and abetted by the newspapers, principally the Glasgow Herald and the Daily Record, they seized on every blip. Labour produced a Scottish budget to show how independence would be disastrous for the Scottish people. Under pressure from Labour, the Record dropped Winnie Ewing's weekly column.

The SNP was suffering in other ways. Some of the Councillors proved to be fair weather friends. Some had stood to help the Party or were carried along by the SNP euphoria. Many did not expect to be elected. They had received no training. They were inexperienced, allowing their Tory and Labour counterparts to trick them into embarrassments or political errors for which they were duly lambasted. A good number lost their jobs and could no longer claim expenses for loss of pay. Being a Councillor also disqualified them from social security benefits. They were faced with the choice of financial ruin or resignation from their Council. Resignation created an impression of SNP instability. In Edinburgh the Group started in disarray and soon fell apart. George Leslie had become a Glasgow City Councillor and elected Leader of the Group. He says of the period[1]:

> 'My first stint as a councillor gave me enormous admiration for my fellow councillors (not just in Glasgow) who got landed as councillors and abandoned by the SNP. Our Group held a balance of power for one and a half years, yet no single councillor did anything to disgrace the Party.
>
> You will remember that 5 of our Group lost their jobs and since councillors' expenses were loss of earnings that meant that they lost everything. Not one broke ranks. As you know I was one of those affected. I never drew unemployment benefit. I slept rough for 8 weeks. Absolutely nobody helped. Arthur Campbell, who unlike me had a young family, drew his loss of earnings expenses after he was sacked and (was) eventually sent to Barlinnie for a year. I appealed to the Party for the £600 that would have prevented his imprisonment but the SNP said – 'no'.
>
> Despite all of that the SNP Group in Glasgow managed to achieve:
>
> *   a streamlining of the city's massive committee structure

* the saving of Glasgow's subway system which was going to be closed
* a recognition that council house rents could not be imposed on council properties lacking basic amenities
* recognition that Glasgow Airport development should not continue at the expense of Prestwick
* a cessation of Glasgow's comprehensive destruction of the city and its replacement with comprehensive rehabilitation (the first site being the Old Swan in Pollokshaws)
* agreement that the first ever Community Council in the UK would start in Glasgow
* a priority to bring more shopping, pubs and recreation facilities to the big peripheral housing schemes we had taken over from Labour.'

With a sardonic comment that 'maybe they should have done more to achieve independence' – despite the difficulty, George concluded by paying tribute to the importance of fellow Councillors; Bill Lindsay who was dependable and constructive, Tom Brady who was erratic and occasionally brilliant and Isobel Lindsay who was as sharp as a knife (and just about as sympathetic) as well as to the others who had played an important part in the team.

I recall shortly after the election getting an agitated telephone call from a Glasgow Councillor who wanted an immediate meeting. He had been having a drink in a pub near the City Chambers after a meeting and had had a social chat with someone who worked with Crudens, a construction firm. When this man left, he had handed him an envelope. He had gone before our councillor could gather his wits and discover there was £30 in the envelope. Not surprisingly, he was very concerned about the implications and wanted my advice. I asked him to leave the envelope with me and wrote to Crudens' Head Office to ask what the sum was for. I received a very quick reply to say it was nothing to do with them, but represented a personal gift to the Party from an employee. As the company would have had to declare the gift to the SNP in their annual accounts, there was a potential embarrassment to them as they were in the public construction market and Labour local authorities would have penalised them for being benefactors to their feared rivals.

As the year progressed through the autumn and winter, the SNP appointed John McAteer as National Organiser, Peter Gormley as National Organising Secretary, three field organisers and an administrative secretary. In addition to an earlier appointment of Donald Bain as Research Officer and Douglas Crawford as Director of Publicity, the Party had a substantial full time staff capable of managing the growth of the Party. With the sales of Alba Pools running well (as at July 1968, it was providing, in one quarter, a profit to branches of £14,455 and to central funds, £3,173)[2], there was just enough to meet the monthly outgoings on staff although the Party had £10,000 invested in short term loans as a reserve.

The administrative structure at national level was completed with the formation of a General Business Committee (1967) to which much administrative and financial business was delegated and an Appeals Committee, elected by National Council and independent of the Executive, to take care of appeals against suspension or expulsion of members which were becoming common - and decisions on organisational disputes. With multiple challenges for national office, the Constitution was changed to permit election to single offices by transferable votes. To meet the growing attacks and smears, a Campaigns Department was established under my convenership. Campaigning leaflets, 'Independence and Your Job' (1969) and a later one on Emigration (1970) designed to combat the smears of separatism spread by the unionists and to take the offensive were produced by the Campaigns Department.

By June 1969, there were worrying indicators.[3] Alba Pools sales were falling. The credit in the bank had gone and the loans account was to be tapped to meet salaries. The National Organiser reported that the branches were not pursuing the recruitment drive with their customary enthusiasm. Sales of leaflets from the Publications Department were dropping substantially. As a consequence the Party Treasurer, Prof. Joe Gloag, was looking to a national appeal and taking a higher proportion of membership dues. The SNP failed to make headway in the May local authority elections, with 22% of the vote and only a sprinkling of wins. There was every sign that the 1968 charge had petered out. The National Organisation Committee of 17 May 1969 gave as its reasons – too much detailed policy, not enough emphasis on the basic aim of independence, not enough canvassing, bad national image and poor quality of candidates.[4]

Changes in office-bearers resulted from the 1969 Conference. George Leslie was now Senior Vice-chairman. John Gair ceased to be in charge of Policy and James Braid had left Publicity. Douglas Drysdale had resigned from Finance earlier in the year from ill-health. The only Vice-chairman remaining was James Lees in charge of organisation and he resigned in the spring (1970) to be a candidate, when he was succeeded by the former National Organiser, Ian Macdonald. Incoming at this time were Douglas Henderson for Policy and Hugh MacDonald and Michael Grieve who both specialised in publicity and were allocated campaigns and media respectively, an awkward division of responsibility. Finance returned to the

National Treasurer. Helen Davidson had assumed Internal Training from Douglas Henderson and was able to report that in the course of the last 10 years (but really within the last 4 years), over 500 people had attended SNP training courses).[5] For a party with few resources and no full-time trainers, this was a remarkable achievement. Nevertheless, with the huge increase in membership, it had only scratched the surface. With the personnel available, it is difficult to see how the numbers processed could have been higher.

There was a rare meeting of the office-bearers and elected members of the National Executive Assembly on 10 June 1969 to discuss strategy. It was decided to divert a higher proportion of HQ income to public relations. To free the resources required, the current part-time PRO Alasdair MacDonald and the full time Administrative Secretary were to be made redundant.

Strangely, despite these signs, Party activists, toughened by events, had continued to work. Great effort was thrown into the Glasgow Gorbals by-election where the SNP candidate was Cllr. Tom Brady. Tom Brady was irrepressible, and, with the media skills of Michael Grieve, managed to win considerable newspaper publicity. There was a long lead time into the election: but one evening sitting at my desk with some particularly tedious paper-work, I idly glanced out of the window to see the Secretary of the Labour Party in Scotland enter the close of the tenement across the road where the Labour candidate, Frank McElhone lived. It did not take the deductive powers of a Sherlock Holmes to work out that the election was about to be called, and my arm stretched out immediately to the telephone to alert the Party organisation.

Gorbals, notorious as a slum, was now almost derelict. The Council was knocking down the old buildings and the place was full of gap sites. My wife, Edith who was the active canvasser for the family while I was a pen-pusher and minder of our two young children, Margaret and Katie, would tell me when she got back of how she would enter these tenements in the dark unaccompanied, listening to the rats scurrying around, as she tried the doors, only to find that the tenants had decamped to the 'paradises' of Castlemilk, Drumchapel and Easterhouse. The outcome of the election for that constituency, which is one of the last we would have chosen, was creditable, but as Party Chairman Billy Wolfe highlighted in his Report to National Council on 6 December 1969[6]:

> 'To many in the SNP, the result, 25% of the vote, was a disappointment. It was not a great victory, like Hamilton. There are many reasons for the difference, including the preparedness of our unionist opponents, and the scale of their campaigns. We have learned lessons in Gorbals. Gorbals would have been won by

the SNP IF there had been a much larger committed local membership throughout the constituency three months before the poll; and we could have enrolled sufficient, had we had the manpower to do it and the foresight. The latent support was there, as it is throughout Scotland, <u>from a clear majority of the voters.</u>'

In these circumstances, it was the Chairman's view that we did well to secure second place.

Gorbals By-election Result (October 1969)

Labour	53.4%
SNP	25.0%
Conservative & Unionist	18.6%
Communist	2.5%
Other	0.5%

Hard on the heels of Gorbals came another by-election – again in a place we would have preferred to pass by, South Ayrshire. South Ayrshire had some affluent housing areas and farming, so the Tories had a nucleus of support. Its main industry was coal mining and it had been a seat under Labour control since the beginning of electoral time. We had good notice of the coming contest, but, unfortunately, the area was one where some of the branches had fallen back over the previous few months and were in semi-collapse. It was also too far from the areas where the SNP was strong and logistically it proved difficult to bring in help from outside.

Canvassing visits made reluctantly to the desolate mining villages of South Ayrshire became something to dread as there was great hostility mixed with disinterest. Part of this was due to our choice of candidate, Sam Purdie, who had been election agent to the former Labour MP, Emrys Hughes. Sam Purdie had left Labour to join the SNP and this was regarded as treachery by diehard Labour activists. The other factor was that the Labour candidate, Jim Sillars, launched a series of hard, personal (vicious, might be a more accurate term) attacks on the SNP candidate. Jim was not in the habit of taking prisoners, and on looking back at the campaign, it is no consolation that, in due course of time, he had a Pauline conversion to independence and eventually became an SNP MP. The result was down again; still respectable at 20%, but not good enough to give a boost to the party for the local elections, where our support dropped off badly to 12.6%.

South Ayrshire By-election Result (March 1970)

Labour	54.0%
Conservative & Unionist	25.6%
SNP	20.4%

While this was depressing (and it <u>was</u> since the loss of hope is worse than having no hope at all), other events were taking place which had a longdelay time-fuse ultimately beneficial to the cause. The first break-through came when Edward Heath made a speech as leader of the Opposition at the Conservative Conference in Perth in 1968, called the Declaration of Perth, when he appeared to accede to demands for a Scottish Assembly. He appointed Sir Alec Douglas Home MP, a former prime minister, to head up an enquiry into whether such a parliament was desirable. The Douglas Home Review eventually recommended the creation of a weak Scottish Assembly. In making this gesture of a Commission, Edward Heath was conceding nothing. When he became British Prime Minister in 1970, there was not a sliver of action during the four years of his premiership. We expected nothing better. It was, however, the first crack in the unionist firmament. The announcement came as a bombshell to the Tory faithful gathered in Perth. They had not been consulted and a concession to the nationalists caused consternation.

Although calculated to take electoral pressure off the Conservative Party in the oncoming General Election and do harm to the SNP, it had the effect of changing the balance of politics in Scotland. Until the mid sixties, Scotland was a unionist nation tied tightly into the British two party system. In the UK as a whole, the Liberals had huffed and puffed, winning the occasional highly publicised by-election without showing any sustained attack on the big two. With the SNP winning Hamilton and impacting on the Tory vote as well as that of Labour, the Tories had been stampeded by the suddenness and scale of the SNP advances. By giving way, however slightly and however fraudulently, Edward Heath had unwittingly opened the devolution door. If he had delayed for a year, then the pressure from the SNP would have been off and no announcement on devolution would have been made, giving encouragement for Labour to do nothing.

But Labour, too, could not be seen to be dragging its heels. Prime Minister Harold Wilson followed suit - with an official Royal Commission on the Constitution under the chairmanship of one of his reliable Yorkshire cronies, Lord Crowther. As a sop to Scottish opinion, the Vice-chairman was a Scottish judge, Lord Kilbrandon. The SNP had quickly decided to ignore the Conservative declaration and treat it as an empty political stunt. Even although the political purpose of the Crowther Commission was clear – to buy time and hope to win over any flagging Labour support on the issue – just as cynical a move as that of Edward Heath – it was not possible to give the Royal Commission the cold shoulder. And from another point of view, it permitted the SNP to present its case for Scottish self-government. On receipt of an invitation to present evidence to the Commission, the NEC set up a sub-committee consisting of Arthur Donaldson, Robert McIntyre and myself under the leadership of Douglas Henderson.[7]

The sub-committee, meeting on 3 August 1969, decided that the structure of the report would be[8]:

'(a) General preamble describing the SNP, its aims and philosophy and stressing the irrelevance of the Commission in relation to the right of the Scottish people to independence.
(b) Declaration of Rights – general philosophical discourse on the principles of self-determination, their compatibility with international unity etc.
(c) 'The Crisis facing Scotland'. An outline of the various threats facing Scotland:
    (i)   Centralisation;
    (ii)   Imposition of unsuitable policies;
    (iii)   Isolation from the international community;
    (iv)   Lack of development of human and natural resources;
    (v)   Emigration and employment trends.
(d)   Conclusion - re-affirmation of sentiments in the preamble.'

There would also be appendices dealing with the constitutional alternatives to independence, with commentaries on housing, the constitutional background to independence and the EEC, the lack of parliamentary time for Scottish affairs, emigration statistics, instances of unsuitable policies and the issue of land ownership
On 10 October 1969, reporting to the Executive, the leader of the delegation Robert McIntyre drew attention to a statement by Lord Crowther that a UK government would not necessarily accept a majority of Scottish seats at a General Election as a mandate from the people of Scotland. There had been considerable hostility to the delegation from Lord Crowther who had hogged the discussion. He went so far as to question whether Scotland was any more of a nation than Yorkshire. The Executive decided to pursue the mandate question at Westminster and to send a delegation to a further smaller meeting of the Commission to give oral evidence on the SNP's constitutional proposals. The SNP's evidence, and the arrogance and anti-Scottish sentiments of the Commission's Chairman had produced a good media response. The Executive was very happy with the outcome.[9]

The next meeting of the Commission took place in Glasgow on 4 May 1970. It was chaired by Lord Kilbrandon and was a much more civilised affair. The SNP delegation consisted of the Director of Research, Dr David Simpson, Cunny Rankin and me. Lord Kilbrandon took our submission respectfully, but nonetheless dissected it. We were mostly able to answer the questions and as a rather junior solicitor, I had it pointed out to me by a Court of Session Judge, rather more charitably than I deserved, the legal differences between domicile and residence as standards for entitlement to Scottish citizenship.

After the successive blows of Gorbals and South Ayrshire, the headlong momentum of the Party had halted. There was still the unfinished business of the 1970 General Election which was called for June. It was a blazingly hot May and June. I was serving for the third time as Director of a General Election Campaign and along with my assistants, Rosemary Hall, Douglas Henderson and Archie Young, was trapped inside Party Headquarters in Glasgow. Douglas Crawford, Director of Communications, masterminded the media aspects from Edinburgh with John McAteer, National Organiser, frequently active in Hamilton and having three Field Organisers to deploy. This gave us much more strength and resources than before.

Disregarding the political disappointments of the last year, the SNP was mounting a more substantial challenge with 65 candidates out of Scotland's 71. There were many constituencies, especially rural ones, where the SNP had good organisation and finance. There was a lot of new blood amongst the candidates, some of whom were in the first rank of political talent. And, compared with 1964 and 1966, we had a Member of Parliament, so that we had crossed the political threshold.

During the Campaign, we ran into the problems of British television coverage which persisted for years to come. We did, for the first time, have an electoral broadcast. This was only for 5 minutes, welcome but submerged by the superior allocations to the Labour, Liberal and Conservative Parties (who also received a 'regional' broadcast within Scotland to top up their main British time).

This time, there was a number of multi-party Scottish election programmes in which our leaders and candidates could participate and also a great deal more press coverage - not that the leading articles and political scientists gave us much of a boost. Where we did lose out was in the UK panel discussion programmes on which we were unrepresented and worse still, there was a black-out of mentions on BBC and ITV network news programmes day by day. So far as many Scots voters were concerned we were non-existent. Again, too, UK issues trumped Scottish issues. This was after all a UK parliamentary election designed to elect a UK Government, besides which the question of having a Scottish parliament seemed irrelevant. Had the election taken place two years earlier when we were peaking, the curiosity aspects might have enabled us to force our way into the UK media.

Once again, I had the dubious task of serving on the BBC results programme, on both the Thursday night and the Friday morning in two separate sessions. It was a job normally done by an office-bearer who is not a candidate and who usually gets shunted off by leading MPs as and when they are elected. I was not in this situation and it was a long and exhausting haul, through the night and back in the morning.. The urban results came through first and it was generally a tale of lost deposits. After a while, you get fatalistic and accept the personal disappointment and the jibes of triumphant opponents on the panel, gloating at our expense. But when the result came in from Hamilton, it was as if the ground had opened up under my feet. We had lost Hamilton. Winnie Ewing, our star performer, had been defeated by Labour. It was no consolation that she had put in a magnificent campaign and obtained what in other circumstances would have been an excellent result with 16,849 votes (35.1%).

My line that night was that we expected our best results from the rural counties for the following day. But the following day was little better. True, some results were encouraging. There were second places: Aberdeenshire East (29.8%), Angus South (23.1%), Banff (22.9%), Galloway (20.5%), Kinross & West Perthshire (18.6%), Moray & Nairn (27.8%) and West Lothian (28.2%) but no victories. Saturday dawned with the results due from Argyll and the Western Isles. We had had little campaign news from the Western Isles and some reasonable expectation of Argyll. Argyll returned 29.9% - a wonderful result and a good second place. It dashed our hopes of remaining a parliamentary party. We stood on the brink. There was only one result to come. There was little expectation; the reverses had taken their toll.

That Saturday morning, Edith and I were in our Glasgow flat at the kitchen table. The gloom was palpable. With us were Douglas Henderson, Angus McIntosh (a Glasgow candidate) and Sheila McIntosh. After Argyll, Douglas looked up wearily and observed: 'Do you think prayer might help! If so, it did, for half an hour later, Billy Wolfe phoned to tell us that he had received a call from Donald Stewart, our candidate for the Western Isles. He had just been elected!

Donald Stewart, who had been elected MP for the Western Isles, had an entirely different personality from Winifred Ewing. He had served in the Navy during the War, had been Provost of Stornoway Burgh Council for three terms and was Sales Director of a Harris Tweed firm. He was well travelled and widely read. He was given a ceremonial send off at Glasgow Central Station. As he leaned out of the sleeper train to London to wave to the crowd, Robert McIntyre came up and said, 'Sorry, Donald. You should have been on an earlier train. Yours has just left'. This meant that Donald and Chrissie had to sit up all night and the story was not recalled fondly by either of them!

With his wife Chrissie, he soon settled into Westminster and with their cordial interest in the lives of other MPs and their families, established a warm rapport with Members of Parliament of all parties and the staff. Donald was a wonderful man with complete recall from memory and a rich source of anecdotes. He had well-defined, unalterable principles. Although amiable, he was quietly strong and if slighted, his highland spirit would emerge to the discomfort of his enemies – and occasionally his colleagues! Like Robert McIntyre, he had been a member of the Labour Party in his youth, but soon after shifted to the SNP.

With that saving news of Donald's election, the results looked that bit better. Overall, the Party had won 306,854 votes (11.41%) compared with 128,467 (5.04%) in 1966. In 1966, we had fought our strongest seats and in terms of average votes calculated on the basis of seats contested, the SNP vote was 12.2% in 1970 as against 14.3% in 1966. And the SNP, again being represented in parliament, could come back to the fray another day. And there were all those second places!

Yet, the overall result was nothing of which to be excessively proud. Donald Bain, the Research Officer, reported to the Executive in July[10]:

'Despite the gain in the Western Isles, the General Election Results are a major disappointment. No statistical juggling can conceal the fact that the present rate of progress is unlikely to lead to self-government in the immediate future.

The Party will have to take a very hard look at its overall strategy in the light of the new situation facing Scotland and in terms of its failure to make headway in the Central Belt. Results from the Highlands, South West and North East are encouraging but scarcely compensate for the fact that we have tended to fall back in the centres of urban population. We saved only 10 out of 46 deposits in the cities and the industrial belt, compared with 12 out of 19 elsewhere. I need scarcely catalogue our depressing record in the industrial seats nor remind you that 51 out of the 71 Scottish constituencies come into this category.

If the SNP is to achieve its objectives it must gain seats in the industrial belt. This is going to be increasingly difficult following the Conservative victory since the

Labour Party can now cast itself once again in the role
of a radical party. While in terms of pure rationality, we
might expect the Labour Party to recognise the lessons
of the election and opt for self-government, there
seems little prospect of this happening, for as long as
centralist elements remain in control.'
And later:
'We must assume that there will be no lucky breaks, no
inevitable turning of the tide in our favour if we simply
sit tight and continue as before. The Party will simply
have to face the fact that the present strategy is not
producing the necessary results.'

Drawing on the evidence that many urban constituencies had fought the
election with organisation and finances inferior to those of local election
contests in previous years, Donald Bain raised the provocative issue of
whether it would be better for the SNP to pull back from local council
participation until self-government was achieved.

John McAteer, the National Organiser, gave his view that the campaign
had been damaged by the squeeze-out by the mass media as it was a TV
election aimed successfully at Left/Right polarisation, the mauling of the
Party in the local government elections, shortage of cash and workers and
unfamiliarity amongst the electorate as to the nature and purpose of the
Party.[11] He also felt that the Party had been bedevilled by bad publicity from
local government involvement and an intrusion of Northern Ireland religious
disputes into some central belt constituencies such as Hamilton, West
Lothian and Airdrie and Coatbridge.

Billy Wolfe, as National Chairman, launched a series of enquiries which
involved two full day meetings of the National Executive and this resulted in
a paper entitled 'The Next Four Years' being presented, with resolutions for
action, to National Council in September. On review, the proposals were
lacking in originality; perhaps there was no 'silver bullet' after all! The paper
contained restatements of the aims of the Party, recommended continued
contesting of local elections and internal changes in the constitution and
organisation. There were some valuable points on the need for political
training and propaganda campaigns and strategic involvement of Party
activists in places of employment to persuade workers and their trade
unions to give support to the Scottish National Party. Most of the resolutions
were exhortatory only, although there was a call for the Chairman to have
powers, subject to NEC approval, to appoint 'shadow' departmental
spokesmen. There was also an appreciation that the Policy Committees
should take more of an interest in current affairs for publicity purposes. The

Report was debated at the September National Council, amended in some minor respects and approved.[12]

Significantly, Douglas Crawford, the Director of Communications, in his Report had taken a different tack. In the 1970 election the SNP had at last bested the Scottish Liberal Party in terms of votes cast overall.[13]

> '1. The Liberal Question will loom large in p.r. terms over the next few weeks.
> 2. I would like to say at the outset that I am as anti-Liberal – on the self-government question as anybody - but that what I am concerned with is not what the SNP does but with what it is seen to do. Jo Grimond (Liberal MP for Orkney & Shetland) out-manoeuvred the SNP brilliantly in 1968/69, saying one thing one day and another thing another day but – and this is the point – enjoying the image of being a man more sinn'd against than sinning. I suggest that we have it in our power now to do likewise.
> 3. However tough we are behind the scenes it is vital for us to appear reasonable in public. We have in p.r. terms the ball in our court and again in p.r. terms the Liberals are defending desperately. This means that we can drive a very hard bargain indeed but appear to be magnanimous at the same time. We don't need to drive a bargain at all but it is important for us to appear to be conciliatory etc'.

Douglas Crawford believed this gambit would keep the self-government question to the fore and be a peg for building up confidence and our image. It also spotlighted the constant battle to take the third place slot after the Labour and Conservative Parties – a battle which would continue and have consequences in the future.

After a series of press statements, there was an exchange of letters between David Steel (Liberal MP for Roxburgh, Selkirk and Peebles) and Billy Wolfe, where the Liberals wanted press coverage to cease and the meeting to be exploratory only with no agenda. The meeting took place in Edinburgh on 30 July 1970.[14] It was attended by Billy Wolfe, Robert McIntyre, James Halliday and Douglas Crawford for the SNP and by Russell Johnston, David Steel, Donald Gorrie and Bill Mackenzie (Liberal Secretary) for the Scottish Liberals. By this time, the Liberals were into the act and had told the press of the location of the meeting, and there was a good attendance of journalists.

A joint press statement was issued in note form:

'i   A useful and amicable discussion had been
       held
ii   Agreed on the right of self-determination
iii   Agreed on the primary importance of self-
       government for Scotland though a difference
       in approach recognised
iv   Difficulty of making pacts was recognised and
       the subject was not pursued
v   Agreed to co-operate where possible on
       current issues affecting Scotland, e.g. at
       parliamentary level.'

Following the meeting, the Executive resolved to continue the current approach of giving constituency associations the right not to contest against the Liberals if they were agreed that such a course was in the best interest of Scotland. The Chairman summarised the position to the September 1970 meeting of National Council[15], adding that we continue to welcome the active support of all those who want to work with us towards achieving self-government for Scotland, that it was made clear to us that the Scottish Liberal Party did not recognise that the survival of Scotland was a matter of paramount importance and that we should keep the matter under review.

After the election, the SNP was almost bankrupt. It had sustained a cataclysmic drop in income and membership in the preceding year and yet had taken on high levels of staff in preparation for the election. Douglas Henderson and the Treasurer, Michael Murgatroyd had to juggle court writs and persuade the bank and creditors to give time for payment. Inevitably, tough action was required and the three field organisers were made redundant. Douglas Crawford moved from being fully employed to a contract to give the same service through his newly created PR firm, Polecon, at a lower cost to the Party. In the Research Department, it was agreed to look for outside work to offset the employment costs of Donald Bain. Steps were also taken to sell the basement and ground floors of the Party's Glasgow Headquarters at 59 Elmbank Street. The gloom did not persist. As the year progressed, gentle signs of recovery became apparent. Membership had dropped to between 20,000 and 30,000, a far cry from the notional peak of 120,000 or the realistic one of 70,000. Cash flow was improving. Bingo Alba Pools sales were increasing by the spring of 1971.[16] Once again, the officebearers changed. Douglas Henderson became Senior Vice-chairman and Provost Gordon Murray of Cumbernauld (then controlled by the SNP) was elected Vice-chairman for Policy. In the Executive elections,

Isobel Lindsay topped the list. Mrs Margo MacDonald just failed to be elected.

Times were changing for me, too. I had been re-elected National Secretary in 1970 and had come to the conclusion that I could not go on indefinitely. I had been running at top speed for ten years through my involvement with Radio Free Scotland and as Secretary of an organisation undergoing a bewildering roller-coaster of change. I had been very fortunate also coming into a position of influence at a critical time. The post of National Secretary gave me the opportunity to take a public stance on behalf of the Party and these initiatives, usually by letter, brought a surprising amount of publicity. Some, like a letter to the Secretary of State, Gordon Campbell MP on 20 October 1970, were prescient. In this case, I called upon the Government to ensure that oil royalties must be credited to Scotland and used for development, and for oil servicing work to be concentrated in Scotland.

Now in my early thirties, I could not keep up the pace for ever. My family were growing up and needed more attention. My workload was increasing as I took on new legal posts. I was also tired. I had been National Secretary too long for my own good and that of the Party. A more appropriate time to have gone was immediately after the General Election. This would have been irresponsible, since the SNP was in a financial crisis and it would have been unfair to colleagues to pull out my expertise at a very difficult time. In the last two years of my stay in office, partly as a response to fatigue, I became autocratic. It was a signal that I was stale. It was time I made room for others.

I announced my intended retirement at the next Conference to the NEC on 13 November 1970 and to National Council in December. It is fair to say that I felt light headed. A tremendous burden had been lifted. A phase of my life was over. I had no idea of whether I would return to national leadership or what I would do if I did come back. The Party I had joined in 1959 and in which I had held office since 1963, was a completely different body now. In 1959, it had been only the largest of the groups in the nationalist movement. The late fifties had seen the SNP come from nowhere through the leadership of people like Robert McIntyre, James Halliday, Arthur Donaldson and David Rollo who had stuck the course. When the SNP had hit rock bottom in 1955, the injuries seemed fatal. In practice, rid of the dissidents, it began to grow. This unity brought in new members and their enthusiasm, married to the experience of others, led in time to the rapid growth that caused the SNP to transform the politics of Scotland.

The progress was uneven – more like snakes and ladders, as the growth was frequently stunted by adverse election results. Members shared a burning vision of a free and equal Scotland. In these days, when the SNP has become the largest party in the Scottish Parliament and in government, it is easily forgotten that the pioneers expected neither any political benefit nor had any expectation of personal success. There were no career paths to elected office or as parliamentary researchers.   It was the vision of independence that carried them forward.

The SNP had gained little support and the Scottish people acquiesced in the union with England. The Party was seen to be eccentric and not in touch with the times. When, therefore, in the sixties, the SNP gathered strength, the political establishment both underestimated and overestimated the phenomenon. The SNP, they thought at first, was having a brief positive blip, based on protest votes. Like minor eruptions in the past, its support would swiftly vanish. True, the popularity of the SNP came and went during the sixties. It was also evident that when the Wilson Government became unpopular after 1966, the SNP was an ideal vehicle for protest voting.

Scotland, too, was changing. Its heavy industries were in decline and the more modern consumer industries like cars and electrical appliances had been established in the Midlands and South of England. At the turn of the 20th century Scotland was a world industrial leader. Its disproportionate man-power losses in the First World War and the effects of the great depression had combined to hit national self-confidence. The loss of the Empire had diminished jobs overseas.

The end result was huge emigration and increasing unemployment. In 1965, 45,000 more people left the country than entered it. On average the net loss between 1954 and 1964 had been 30,000 a year. Between 1954 and 1964, England and Wales had a net addition of 1,805,000 new jobs; and Scotland a net addition of 17,000. England and Wales grew at over ten times their equivalent share of new employment. In England and Wales, the new jobs were equally divided between the sexes, with 903,000 for men and 902,000 for women. In Scotland, there were jobs for 34,000 fewer men and 52,000 more women. In those 10 years, Scotland lost 60,000 jobs in the primary industries (coal mining, agriculture etc. and 30,000 jobs in manufacturing). The country gained 17,000 jobs in construction and 81,000 in services (retailing, offices, teaching etc). Scottish industry, itself lacking in confidence, was particularly open to take-overs and the resultant factory closures, with the jobs going south, created bitterness.

Initially, the Conservatives took the blame. They had been in power since 1951 and the slogan of 'You have never had it so good' of the fifties rankled as it contrasted a successful England with a struggling Scotland. Of course, during this period, the fortunes of the North of England, also heavily dependent on heavy industry, likewise turned adverse. The first political effect in both areas was to see large scale migration of the working class Tory vote to Labour. In Scotland, the growing feeling of alienation in industrial areas had another outlet – the SNP. In rural areas, there was a minority Labour vote, sometimes sizable, which was anti-Conservative and this, the SNP and the Liberals found it easier to divert and retain.

When Labour came into power, the feeling of disappointment after 1966 spilled over to the industrial areas and helps explain why the SNP had such landslides in the burghs, cities and counties in 1967 and 1968. But it would be wrong to look at the sixties purely in Scottish terms. Plaid Cymru, the sister party of the SNP in Wales, was completely different in outlook from the SNP. Whereas the nationalism of the SNP was rooted in Scotland's civic institutions such as separate legal, education, health and local government systems, Plaid Cymru had a special dedication towards the survival of the Welsh language and culture. In contrast, Wales was served by institutions common to England, legislated for in the same way by the British Parliament at Westminster, with only local administration devolved to Wales. Scotland and Wales were two countries entirely separate from each other. Yet, the movements of public opinion in each nation were similar, if not manifested in exact time-scales. Plaid Cymru also developed and attracted new people during the sixties. Nor was it the SNP that made the vital parliamentary break-through. In 1966, the President of the Plaid, Gwynfor Evans was elected in a by-election in Carmarthen and thus became the first nationalist MP to be chosen since the short-lived service of Robert McIntyre as MP for Motherwell in the interregnum between the ending of the war in Europe and the 1945 General Election. In succeeding times, it was the SNP that took the lead, only for the baton to be passed in turn to Plaid Cymru. The Parties were both hard dealt with over broadcasting, and with electoral success, they began to work together in these fields and to exchange speakers and Conference delegations.

The sixties was also a decade of radical change throughout the world. In Quebec, the Parti Quebecois, encouraged by the endorsement of General De Gaulle's controversial cry of 'Vive Le Quebec Libre' emerged into the limelight to the consternation of the Canadian Government. In Paris, General De Gaulle in turn got his come-uppance when the students and workers took to the barricades during the 1968 riots. Nationalist activity intensified in the Basque Country and Catalonia. There was unrest in Eastern Europe. And through Africa, the wind of change was blowing strongly. So it would be parochial for Scots to divorce their progress from world-wide trends. The decade was a time of struggle against authoritarianism, from which many political movements, including the SNP in Scotland, were beneficiaries.

What kind of organisation had the SNP become during the sixties? In policy terms, it had flirted with social credit economics. By and large, it believed in de-centralisation at local and national levels and as the decade progressed, especially during the 1968/69 eruption in policy creation, it developed a stronger social democratic tinge, believing in state intervention for industrial development, workers' rights and relief of the endemic poverty that had bedevilled Scottish society for so long.

In April 1968, the Glasgow Herald carried out a survey based on interview of 81 out of 309 candidates to identify the make-up of the SNP. It discovered that 67% had joined in the previous three years, 38% in 1967 and 23% in 1965. The majority were new to politics with only 13.5% of the sample having previous political affiliations. Of these 64% were ex-Labour, 36% ex-Liberal and 9% ex-Conservative. In terms of employment, 27% were skilled tradesmen, 13.5% small businessmen, company executives, management and supervisors, 15% clerical, 7% salesmen, 7% technicians, 16% professions, 2% academic, and 4% students. These are classifications only but the prevalence of inexperience over experience predicted some of the problems and the bad publicity that lay ahead.

While the collapse of SNP votes in the 1970 election brought severe disappointment, the achievements of the movement were not ephemeral. Even at the height of the SNP's decline in 1970-71, there were 20,000 to 30,000 members, compared with 2000 in 1962. There was large scale branch coverage, weakened certainly, but having a strong base. These were the building blocks for the future. Constituency Associations were providing cohesion to what had earlier been anarchistic growth. Those members who remained were tougher and more experienced. Many of them had developed political skills through involvement in policy formation, candidacy and council work. There could be no comparison with the small, struggling SNP of the fifties. There were also new leaders emerging to take up an active role in the SNP of the future.

While the counter-attacks on separatism had immediate adverse effects on the SNP's fortunes, the impact of the Party on Scottish politics had been major – and as it was to prove - lasting. The shape of British politics was also changed. From being a safe regional backwater, Scotland now had to be watched. British Governments did not understand the SNP and the Scottish people.

The SNP was still represented at Westminster. Not much was expected of the Crowther Commission on the Constitution, whose Chairmanship was to pass to Lord Kilbrandon on the death of Lord Crowther - and it had still to report. In 1970, news of a find of oil in the Forties Field off the coast of Scotland had been announced. Nobody paid much attention. The SNP quietly regrouped and I retreated to the law and my garden!

Chapter 7

It's Scotland's Oil

The Party found my departure eminently sustainable. The leadership of the Party was experienced. Party Chairman, Billy Wolfe had taken a less prominent role initially after the 1970 General Election, having put future Party strategy to bed. As the best performer in the 1966 Election and with the stupendous step-forward of the Party after Hamilton, he had had realistic ambitions of winning his fourth contest of West Lothian. With the turn down in the Party's fortunes in 1969, this was not to be and it would be surprising if he were not depressed at this failure and the fall-back of his vote. During this period, Billy was not the creative spirit of the sixties who had modernised the Party's image and policy. I was to receive approaches to stand for the Chair and had no hesitation in turning them down. Gradually, Billy Wolfe resumed the exercise of his national leadership with close involvement in the workers' fight to keep the Upper Clyde Shipbuilders from being closed down by the Conservative government. This was the iconic campaign of the era and brought Billy Wolfe into close proximity with trade union leaders who had hitherto little contact, and certainly no sympathy, with the SNP. While the Labour Party and SNP were mortal enemies, problems in the car and steel industries made it necessary for shop stewards at local level to welcome the numbers that the SNP could provide for protest meetings and demonstrations. The closer involvement of the SNP in industrial campaigns was not welcomed at higher levels of the union movement which was closely allied to Labour. In 1972, there was a spat over a public complaint by James Jack, General Secretary of the STUC that the SNP had misquoted the views of the STUC on support for a Scottish Parliament.

Soon another challenge emerged. In the spring of 1971, Malcolm Macpherson, the Labour MP for Stirling and Falkirk Burghs died. In his Research Bulletin, Donald Bain was under the firm view that this election offered the SNP an exceptional opportunity and continued[1]:

> 'The Financial Times has described the seat as potentially another Hamilton but a better analogy would be Carmarthen, the seat won by Gwynfor Evans in July 1966. Both are constituencies in the respective heartlands of their two countries. Both have a long record of nationalist activity at national and local government levels.

The Labour Party is riding high at the moment, with by-election success in England and sweeping victories at the local elections behind them. Yet they are far from invincible. What people forget is that Carmarthen was won only months after Labour's greatest-ever General Election victory and at a time when Labour was riding very high in the opinion polls.'

Commenting that the SNP had won 14,500 votes in the 1968 local elections and gained 14.5% in the General Election, he was optimistic that a well fought campaign using exploitable local issues such as Oceanspan (a scheme to link the Atlantic bulk carriers with Europe through entrepot facilities) and North Sea oil could lead to victory.

The SNP chose one of its best candidates, Dr Robert McIntyre, the Party President and former MP for Motherwell. Robert McIntyre was the well respected Provost of Stirling Burgh and a popular chest specialist. Labour took no risks and selected Harry Ewing, an able, hard-hitting trade unionist as their candidate. It was also the first election when the issue of North Sea oil became an issue. It was hoped also to make the Common Market a campaigning feature, but in the event this was not possible because the Labour candidate was also vehemently opposed to the Market.

It was not a pleasant campaign. Incidents like the smashing of an SNP bedecked plate glass window of a public house opposite Labour's campaign headquarters, intimidation of shopkeepers who had premises displaying McIntyre posters, the slashing of the tyres of an SNP car on election day, the removal by the Presiding Officer at a Falkirk polling station of an abusive Labour agent and the presence outside the count of a swearing Labour supporter, wearing no fewer than three SNP badges. Another incident was the post-declaration caller, claiming to be SNP Director of Communications, Douglas Crawford, who telephoned the local press with an inflammatory and Anglophobic 'official comment' on the scenes outside the count.

Stirling & Falkirk Burghs By-election Result (September 1971)

Labour	46.5%
SNP	34.6%
Conservative & Unionist	18.9%

Given the disappointing General Election, the result was a major boost to the SNP. In his analysis, Donald Bain felt that the low key coverage by the media made it difficult to project Robert McIntyre's qualities. There were also deficiencies in organisation where outside help was resisted locally, slow appearance of workers from outside the constituency and defeatism amongst the Party as a whole.

During this period of abstinence from national responsibilities, I was not inactive in the Party. I became Chairman of the Paisley East Branch and a delegate to Paisley Constituency Association. It was an eye-opener. On the ground, the Party was weak and demoralised. The optimism of members, however misplaced, had been dashed. Members had left in their droves and the organisation had imploded. But there was left a group of people who had been toughened by the reverses and were keen to make up ground once more. Efforts were made without much success to revisit members who had left to attempt to sign them up again. From my own attempts, I came to the view that it was easier to recruit new members than persuade former members to renew their subscriptions. I concluded that only populist national campaigns mounted by the Party at the centre would revive the Party's fortunes.

I was not alone in coming to this opinion. There was also internal Party disaffection. In September 1971, a resolution to National Council from Stirling St Ninian's Branch, proposed by Helen Davidson, a very influential Party member, criticised the slowness and lack of co-ordination of campaigns, instructed the NEC to amalgamate the publicity and campaigns departments, to hive off responsibility for leaflets to the Executive Vice Chairman for Policy and to issue action packs containing materials on employment, oil and underinvestment. I was attending the meeting as an observer and supported the resolution vigorously. At this time the Party was involved in a number of industrial issues as Scotland's heavy industry base crumbled. There was no concerted push of a single theme and steel, shipbuilding, the automotive industry and oil took turns for precedence.

And then there was the oil issue! I felt strongly that something more should be done and sent a detailed letter to the National Executive on 20 August 1971. After the Stirling Burghs By-election, Robert McIntyre was appointed Oil Spokesman; otherwise, there was little co-ordinated national response. Nobody, other than the Research Officer, seemed to realise what a potent issue this could be in influencing the hearts and minds of the Scottish people if properly presented. Yet, the NEC took the important step of sending Donald Stewart MP and Donald Bain in April 1972 to the Headquarters of OPEC where they met Dr. Nadim Pachachi, Secretary General and Dr. Rafael Macia-Jerez, Chief of the Technical Department. The SNP set out Scotland's claims and our representatives were very pleased with the tenor of the meeting. Looking at it retrospectively with Donald Bain, further involvement with OPEC at a sensitive time for oil prices and supply was not envisaged as this could have spurred the Western intelligence community to adopt a more radical strategy of opposition to the SNP.

My mind was stimulated and one response was to send a detailed resolution to the National Executive suggesting that there should be a single oil campaign committee composed of the Publicity and Policy Vice-chairmen, the Oil spokesman and senior members of staff with the following tasks:-

1. Encouragement of claims for the oil revenues and control of development;
2. Assurance of Party members that the establishment is divided on the question of oil revenues and vulnerable to public opinion when pressure is applied;
3. Encouragement to use action packs and to write to the press;
4. Revision of the Scottish budget account to reflect the inclusion of oil wealth and to pursue the Prime Minister on what were the benefits of the Union exclusive of our use of Oil;
5. Encouragement of Local Authorities in the light of unemployment to write to the government supporting the demands of the Scottish Council (Development & Industry), the SNP and the Scottish Liberals for control of the oil and use of the revenues;
6. The holding of a national Poster Campaign; and
7. The use of demonstrations to highlight the benefits of oil and the problems if we did not have control.

The NEC took up many of these points, but referred some for consideration by sub-committees. For me, there was a creative leap forward. Apart from business pressures, I was trying to get a wilderness of a garden into cultivation. This involved much digging. The main problem was that I did not have the stamina or inclination to dig vigorously, so there were plenty of breaks and during those periods of reflection, there stole into my mind the details of a campaign based on the discovery of oil in the North Sea opposite the coast of Scotland. Soon, these gardening breaks became more directed as I noted on paper the ideas as they came freshly to mind.

Post war, oil had been dirt cheap with the international oil companies able to pick off the producing countries. The user countries stamped down hard on any nation that showed signs of independence. So, when in the early fifties, Dr Mohammed Moussadeq, the Prime Minister of Iran proposed the nationalisation of the oil fields, Britain and the USA objected and the USA with British connivance organised a coup to replace the democratically elected government by the Shah. By the sixties, the oil producing countries had begun to organise under the umbrella of OPEC and to negotiate with the petroleum companies for the partial nationalisation of their oil resources. None of the countries opted for complete nationalisation as they were reliant on the exploration, production and marketing expertise of the oil companies. Nevertheless, the pendulum was beginning to swing from the users to the producers, although the price of oil kept stable – and cheap – in the interim.

There were problems with exploration for oil and natural gas off-shore. The three mile limit was generally in force and efforts by individual nations to expand off-shore could conflict with the interests of neighbouring countries. The legal position was resolved when a United Nations Conference in Geneva in 1958 agreed a Convention on the Continental Shelf. Ratified by the UK in 1964, this established that states had sovereign rights over mineral exploitation and development in parts of the Continental Shelf adjoining their territory. The Convention established rules for determining rights in areas of conflicting interest.

In 1968, the UK government set boundaries between the different legal jurisdictions of the United Kingdom, which in the case of the North Sea, was between England and Scotland. In the course of early exploration, substantial discoveries of natural gas had been made off-shore of England. There were rumours that seismic tests had located possible oil and gas fields in the northern sector of the North Sea off Scotland, but the process of exploration was slow and news of possible discoveries so guarded, the possible existence of oil did not impact on Scottish politics during the late sixties.

In a move that they came to regret, the UK Government promoted the Continental Shelf (Jurisdiction) Order which stated that responsibility for oil and gas found north of parallel 55 degrees 50 minutes, along a line jutting from Berwick on Tweed, would fall within Scottish legal jurisdiction. There was a slight difference between boundaries drawn under the rules of the Convention and those under the Jurisdiction Order and as most of the oil and gas field fell north of the Convention line, in practice, there was little argument against 90% of the discoveries being within the Scottish sector. Only the small oil fields of Auk, Argyll and Josephine, the first to be discovered, might have been debateable. But in politics – and propaganda - simplicity is everything and the existence of the boundary Order gave an undisputed opportunity to the SNP. The unionist response that the oil would be British since the UK was a unitary state was, of course, also arguable, but to do so would be to lay the foundation that the oil resources could only be Scottish if Scotland were an independent country. A further counter argument that the jurisdiction order was wrongly defined would be easily dismissible. After all, it was the Westminster parliament that had made the concession and in any case, in its absence, an independent Scottish Government could rely on the rules set out in the Convention.

Meantime, I was out of office and the Party was pre-occupied with the common market and industrial campaigns. In January 1972, Michael Grieve resigned as Executive Vice Chairman for Publicity. Michael was a working journalist and there had been a demarcation dispute between him and Douglas Crawford, the Party's Director of Communications who tended to work through the Chairman over publicity initiatives, some of which were made without consultation with Michael. Conversely, Mike believed that all press releases and conferences should be approved by him as the elected office-bearer – and approval of routine press releases would have cut into the role of Douglas Crawford.

The ensuing vacuum in direction worried me and I pressed as an outsider, mainly by letter, that something should be done. I also promoted a key resolution for an oil campaign through Paisley Constituency Association to the 1972 Annual Conference.[2] It was intended to deal with the questions of taxation and development and above all to link the economic aspects with delivery of a Scottish Assembly. The resolution ran:

> 'In the knowledge that the discovery of the large oil deposits within Scottish territorial waters has made self government inevitable and that the Government is aware of the new pressure from the Scottish public to ensure that Scotland benefits fully from the oil fields, this Conference demands solely as first steps:-
>
> (a) that the government implement its election promise to establish its directly elected Scottish Assembly before the next General Election
>
> (b) that all royalties, revenues, duties and taxation arising from the exploitation of Scottish oil resources be administered by a Minister in charge of Scottish economic development answerable to the Scottish Assembly
>
> (c) that in order to control development of the oil and to ascertain more readily the Corporation Tax which will be paid to the Scottish Exchequer, the companies now exploiting the Scottish oil fields be instructed to establish subsidiaries incorporated in Scotland and that all relevant exploration and development contracts be transferred to the Scottish companies

(d) that the Scottish Assembly be empowered,
     if it considers it desirable, to require the oil
     companies to employ a reasonable proportion
     of Scottish citizens in their enterprises within
     Scotland and to allocate a reasonable proportion
     of service contracts to Scottish companies or
     citizens

(e) that the Scottish Assembly establish an
     inspectorate to make regulations to reduce the
     possible incidence of spillage or leakage of oil
     which might give rise to pollution

(f) that the Scottish Assembly set up a Pollution
     Contingency Fund to indemnify the fishing
     and tourist industries and others proved to be
     affected by oil pollution, from any loss which
     they have found to have sustained.

As the resolution set out the future basis of SNP policy, apart from regulation of the pace of development and quantum of desirable oil production rates, this was the first serious attempt to establish a sound policy structure and, although the delegates were unaware of this, it was to be the platform for a major campaign that I had in mind. I had expected it to go through without difficulty and told Conference that oil was the political issue of a generation. I should have known the SNP better. It ran into severe opposition from SNP ultras such as Alex Ewing of Rutherglen who attacked it as "low octane" and "dangerous and defeatist". George Leslie wanted to be professional and take more time to formulate a proper policy. Others saw the resolution as an admission of defeat for the self-government platform and reduction of the Party to the role of a pressure group.

After a hard debate the motion was accepted by 93 votes to 76 and a hard line amendment on Scottish oil jobs was defeated by only 6 votes. It was not an auspicious beginning. The debate was a source of some merriment to journalists. As Stewart MacLachlan of the Daily Record put it[3]:

> 'The Scottish National Party yesterday found itself in
> utter confusion over North Sea Oil. A seemingly simple
> motion which opened the annual conference in
> Rothesay caused the trouble by calling for control of
> North Sea oil to be put under the Tory proposed
> Scottish Assembly.
> In the muddled debate that followed, the Nationalists
> looked like ending up with NO policy on oil at all.'

Notwithstanding this uncertain beginning, I had already drawn up a detailed programme for an oil campaign. The proposals were ambitious. They formed a battle plan for the development of the Party's campaigning effort and a focus for its political relevance at the next General Election. As I told Robert Crawford, ten years later[4]:

> 'I reckoned that the emergence of oil was a new factor in Scottish politics, and covered a multitude of dimensions not just political; economic, psychological and so forth. And the question then was whether the Party would just kick the ball about the park, or whether we would try and build up team-play on it.'

The oil campaign was to be founded on good research. It was intended that the Party become a respected authority on the subject of oil development, on-shore exploitation and taxation. This was so that the political initiatives would be treated as serious and from an organisation that had real expertise. Already, Donald Bain in 1971 had published articles in the Party's Research Bulletin, looking into the economic and political implications.[5] Assisted by two academics, Dr Malcolm Slesser and Nick Dekker, he had touched upon the future international price upon which any future benefits to Scotland could be secured, and was one of the first in the UK to hint that the oil price could move up to $5 a barrel.

The campaign schedule[6] backed by a Memorandum on Finance[7] outlined a number of political initiatives, such as providing a draft letter for local branches to send to their Councils. This urged support to be given to a resolution which the SNP controlled Cumbernauld Council was to place before the Convention of Royal Burghs, highlighting the benefits of oil to the Scottish economy. A letter was to be sent to oil companies advising them that their licences might have to be renegotiated by a Scottish Government with changes in oil taxation, depletion controls, observance of fair manpower conditions and use of Scottish goods and services. It was hoped that an Oil Bill would be presented by Donald Stewart MP in the House of Commons, with letters being sent to Scottish MPs soliciting their support or reasons for not doing so! And so on. Driving all these proposals was the vision that oil had a crucial role to play in Scottish and UK politics. It was a one-off opportunity to command the political agenda and to arrest Scotland's economic decay by using the wind-fall benefits for the future generations as well as for the present.

Theory is one thing. Putting it into practice and projecting the issue was another. The SNP had only one MP and was perceived to be in decline, with the earlier impetus of the sixties having run into the sand. It was going to be very difficult to persuade the media to cover the political dimension, although specialist energy correspondents were beginning to make their mark. Credibility was the key. It was hoped that a stream of press conferences taken by Party leaders, on innovative topics, and developing fresh ideas on how oil could benefit Scotland, would provide part of the answer.

But I reckoned this was not enough. The issue had to be brought before the Scottish public visually and on the ground. Thus, there was to be a bill board campaign, using twenty large 16 sheet commercial sites and fly-posting of double crown posters, through the Party organisation. In addition, there was to be large scale leaflet distribution along with membership business reply cards used for recruiting new members. For the first time, the leaflets were personalised to the extent that interested members of the public could write to a named person to seek a free action pack from HQ.

In the run up to the proposed campaign, it was by no means sure that I would be in charge, except perhaps as a Director or Oil Spokesman under the tutelage of the EVC Publicity. I had not submitted a nomination for election to the Publicity Vice-Chairmanship at the Conference held in May 1972. Still, coincidence had its way. George Park who had been elected to the post of Executive Vice Chairman (duties to be allocated) resigned and this allowed me to stand for the vacancy and, on election, to present the oil campaign proposals to the National Executive. This unspecific vice-chairmanship had been used at various times for campaigns, finance, administration and guidance of the youth wing. In view of its approval of the campaign, the Executive agreed that it be named EVC for Scottish Oil[8] and to give me full responsibility for the campaign.[9]

I had anticipated that one of the major problems would be to persuade the Party to spend what little cash it had. In the run-up, and as delegate for Paisley Constituency at National Council in March 1972, I raised during the National Treasurer's report the advisability of spending the General Election reserve on an oil campaign, since the same expenditure during a three week election campaign would have little effect on the election outcome. I was also helped by the Conference resolution instructing the NEC to do something about the oil finds. Nevertheless, funds were short with HQ income dropping and expenditure exceeding income.

Proposals were made for a sharing of major costs of the poster campaign with Constituencies, with HQ providing posters and the constituency associations choosing the sites they would fund. In an attempt to make the campaign as self-financing as possible, the leaflets and other materials were to be sold, not given, to the branches and constituencies. Doubts were expressed about tapping into the election funds, and it was agreed to have a special levy on branches and to organise an appeal for funds. Given the circumstances, the commitment of expenditure of a high magnitude, whether locally or at centre, was an act of faith by the Executive and the approval of the levy by branches which were financially weak themselves, extremely courageous.

I convened meetings of a special group consisting of the Publicity Committee under EVC Publicity, Isobel Lindsay, EVC Policy, Margo MacDonald, Tom McAlpine, Stephen Maxwell, the Research Officer, Donald Bain, and Director of Communications, Douglas Crawford (and others on an ad hoc basis). Our first action was to commission graphic designer Julian Gibb to assist. Julian had been responsible for the design of the Party symbol and the artwork for the policy document, SNP and You. The sessions were creative and eventually the Committee approved the message, 'It's Scotland's oil – with self-government'. At first, we called it 'Scottish Oil'. Then Julian Gibb who was very keen on semantics and looked at the tone as well as the meaning of words, suggested the slogan, 'It's Scotland's Oil' as this had more emotional timbre and conveyed the right of the country to ownership. He was also responsible for the design of the poster, a roundel with a gush of black oil pouring from the white O of 'oil',. Many of these ended up on bedroom walls, and samples were requested by Wood Gundy, an international oil consultancy firm, for American clients taken with the design. There was also a leaflet printed white on black with magenta colouring entitled, 'To London with Love', based on the title of the James Bond film 'From Russia with Love'. While many people might be willing to put up with British oil, few would countenance 'London's Oil'. There was a suite of accompanying campaign materials.

The Campaign had an internal launch at the September 1972 National Council and was enthusiastically received. Substantial publicity was reaped from the public presentation. The results were impressive. By the end of December 1972, there had been 196 x 16 sheet posters on display.[10] 787,000 'To London with Love' leaflets had been sold to branches. Also produced were 1,840 double crown posters, 210,300 lapel badges (stickies), 2000 window posters and 2000 car banners. 2,318 action packs had been issued in response to requests. 200,000 business reply cards had been sold and 1,400 returned to HQ. The Research Department reported that there had been many enquiries from the public (including stockbrokers) for information on oil. Along with Alex Ewing, Donald Bain prepared visual aids and maps for use in the campaign and also by candidates. By the spring, a second action pack had gone to branches and Nick Dekker's booklet, 'The Reality of Scotland's Oil' had been published and well received. Orders were made by local authorities and other public bodies.

During the autumn, there were frequent press conferences taken by Party leaders and a featured visit by Party Chairman Billy Wolfe to Norway, a start to many comparisons that the SNP drew between that independent nation enjoying the North Sea oil bonanza, and the benighted nation of Scotland, with its deep poverty, giving its oil away to London.

Significantly, during this period, the Party's reputation with economic agencies grew and its pronouncements were treated with growing, though not uncritical, respect by the media. The initial response of the opposition by our unionist opponents was one of disarray. They had expected the SNP to exploit the finding of oil but not on this scale. The massive offensive in the press, on radio and television and on the ground through the SNP organisation gave them shell-shock. It took them time to recover. When they did, the same arguments were wheeled out by Tory MPs (then in government), the Labour opposition and the Liberals. Partly they were the same as those used in the sixties, for example, Scotland was too small. Now there were fresh arguments: the oil belonged to the oil companies, the boundaries excluded the major oil fields, the northerly Shetland basin fields were the property of Orkney and Shetland (which, of course, and for the purposes of blackmail were assumed to want to stay with England), the oil fields really belonged to Norway and would not be available to an independent Scotland and the revenues were over-estimated and not enough to meet the subsidy given to Scotland by England. There was not much oil, anyway and it would all run out soon!

No argument was silly enough to preclude deployment. They all had one thing in common and that was to undermine Scottish self-confidence. Repetition was the key, in the hope that the unionist command of the media would eventually seep into Scottish consciousness. Then there was the claim that the SNP was selfish and materialist and that Scots had a duty to look after the poorer parts of the UK such as Northern England. This was meretricious and avoided the reality that the City of London and the British government would be prime beneficiaries if Scotland were to continue to be part of the UK. But, given the essential gullibility of the Scottish people, there was no reason why this naïve view would not be swallowed. Even some members of the SNP were swayed by it.

This did not stop the SNP onslaught. Membership was increasing, new branches were being formed or old ones reformed. The Party's support was expressed in the Dundee East by-election (1 March 1973) and in the local elections in May, when the SNP vote rose overall from 14% (1972) to 21%. The average in county council seats was 31.3%. All in all, it was highly satisfactory.

By the autumn of 1973, the economic picture changed to make the SNP case irresistible. Whereas the SNP had deliberately given conservative valuations in phase 1 of the campaign, the outbreak of the Arab/Israeli war in October 1973 led to a fourfold increase in world oil prices. Since this would give an independent Scotland a hard currency, internal discussions were commenced to determine the likely impact of this on the future Scottish economy.

By now I had been elected Senior Vice Chairman and was responsible for the strategic planning of the General Election as well as exercising oversight of the oil campaign. This was no problem as the oil message was an integral part of the election strategy. Phase 2 of the campaign featured a new leaflet, 'England Expects Scotland's Oil' - based on the Nelson signal at the battle of Trafalgar. It carried an illustration of the Union Jack – never before portrayed in an SNP publication. Like its predecessor, 'To London with Love', it sold extremely well. There was also an Oil Slide Show much in request and it is interesting that when I made presentations in Inverness and Dumfries, there were representatives from commerce, the development agencies and councils. With an eye to the imminent publication of the Report of the Royal Commission on the Constitution, expected to recommend some form of Scottish Assembly, phase 2 linked the asset of oil to the issue of self-government. There was also to be a focus on the social and economic consequences of oil development and on conditions of employment in the oil industry. Phase 2 was a great success with 4000 requests for action packs flooding into Party Headquarters.

After the General Election, much of the emphasis switched to oil legislation and devolution, and interest in the oil campaign on the ground was diluted. Under the influence of Margaret Bain MP and Janette Jones, EVC Publicity, the Party developed particularly fine posters showing pictures of old age pensioners, workers, children etc, tying in a social and economic message in terms people could understand and personalising the benefits of the oil revenues. The oil became 'Her Oil' or 'His Oil'.

What then was the success of the oil campaigns? I reject the notion that they were solely responsible for the rapid advance of the SNP. The Stirling and Falkirk Burghs By-election had already demonstrated partial political recovery. But there is equally no doubt that the oil campaigns accelerated that progress. The parliamentary break-through on the scale of 1974 would not have occurred without the presence of the theme of 'It's Scotland's Oil'. It was also the gambit that brought international recognition to the SNP.

On my election to Westminster in 1974, I was invited, as if I were the Oil Minister of an independent country, to deliver a paper, helpfully drafted by Donald Bain (while I was laid low by a bad attack of flu') to a Financial Times Conference in Oslo and had the pleasure of hearing vocal dissent from English bankers during the speech and a protest at the end as to why I had been invited! The SNP's policy of claiming the oil for Scotland and setting out a slower depletion policy was considered provocative and damaged the interests of the City of London. The visit was accompanied by a BBC crew.

The same speech was delivered by Douglas Henderson shortly afterwards in Canada. In 1975, Donald Bain and I visited OPEC in Vienna when we were accompanied by the British Ambassador on a tour of the Austrian parliament and had dinner at the Embassy when we were discreetly pumped for information on what had been discussed on the OPEC visit. To boost interest in London, suitably evasive answers were given!

Billy Wolfe was feted by senior executives of the American oil companies on their visits to Scotland. As subsequently transpired, Washington was acutely interested in the position and during the oil taxation debates of 1975, brought heavy political and financial pressure to bear on the financially weak British Government to secure a benign taxation policy that suited the US majors active in developing the North Sea. In Scotland, there appeared a new United States Consul General, Richard Funkhouser. Mr Funkhouser was very experienced for such a junior post. He was a high profile diplomat who tried to influence Scottish businessmen at dinners and on golf-courses. His specialty was to argue against policies for slow development and low depletion on the basis that these would harm the creation of jobs in Scotland.

He had a number of meetings with Billy Wolfe. I was happy to keep my distance as I had suspicions that he might have connections with the CIA, then active in its meddling in the affairs of foreign governments. It is always better if the opposition is kept tantalised! I had the impression that Funkhouser viewed me as a hard man, behind SNP intransigence on development and extraction rates and dangerous to the interests of the United States. It was not true. It was the policy of the Party that I projected.

If the SNP made an impression on the US government, it certainly impacted on a British Government that was lurching towards bankruptcy. London had to get the oil on stream swiftly to retain its credit rating with the international banks and this was why it opted for pell-mell development at the expense of building up an oil related industrial infrastructure which would have provided world wide expertise to the benefit of British industry from Birmingham to Tyneside, as well as in Scotland.

The immense advances made by the SNP in the two General Elections of 1974 rang alarm bells and the convention that the civil service was above party politics was discarded as all the resources of the British state were thrown into the battle against the SNP. There was no way England was going to allow Scotland to secede with what it regarded as its oil resources. George Reid, SNP MP for Clackmannan and East Stirlingshire overheard Edward Heath, then Leader of the Conservative Opposition standing ahead of him at a Downing Street reception observe that there was no way the oil would go to Scotland. Mr Anthony Crosland, the Foreign Secretary inadvertently gave the English game away when quoted in the Daily Telegraph of 8 October 1976:

'Mr Crosland, the Foreign Secretary, asked at a Washington Press conference yesterday why Britain refused to give Scotland its independence said in an aside heard distinctly over the microphone, 'because they have got a lot of oil'.

The same Anthony Crosland told the Prime Minister James Callaghan in 1977 that he was being advised by officials that the government should make a more robust case to counter the threat the SNP then posed to Britain's international position. He recommended 'confidential briefing of selected opinion formers and seeking to inspire articles'. Information released in 2005 under the Freedom of Information Act showed that civil service officials provided the Labour Party in Scotland with return ammunition against SNP propaganda on oil revenues and, on Labour advice, helped a Tory MP attack the SNP case. Bernard Ingham, the Energy Department's Director of Information said that undermining the SNP and its claims about North Sea Oil belonging to Scotland was 'part of my standard sales patter'.[11] He went on to advise that foreign diplomats should be prepared to take on Nationalist arguments in parts of the 'old Commonwealth' - Canada, Australia and New Zealand – with large quotas of Scottish blood. In Scotland, a senior Scottish Office economist, Gavin McCrone, warned Ministers in 1975 that the SNP case for independence with oil revenues was very strong and criticised the SNP estimates of revenue as being too low.[12] This did not stop Labour and the Scottish Office arguing that Scotland could not afford to be independent.

The McCrone report was hidden from public view. Just to make sure, the economic returns from oil which would have figured in Scotland's balance sheet were spirited away to a newly created offshore province so that they could not easily be prayed in aid of the SNP case for independence. Labour Ministers also leaned on the BBC to stop a series of programmes on oil and the Scottish economy.

Ultimately, the SNP oil campaign failed. When the first oil came ashore, it was landed in a secure base in England. Logistically, it was not possible to organise a mass demonstration large enough to shake the British establishment. Inside the SNP, a new group of leaders was frustrated that other worthwhile issues such as poverty and Scotland's declining heavy industries were not receiving the attention they deserved. Donald Bain is also of the opinion that my election to Westminster hindered the oil campaign as I became trapped in the intricacies of oil legislation and other parliamentary distractions. It is a moot point. Without election, I would not have had the exposure or authority to advance the Scottish oil case in the media and without undue modesty, my expertise would have been difficult to replicate in the Commons.

As the decade progressed and devolution dominated the legislative and political agenda, oil became a side show and by 1978, the Party's single-minded focus that had challenged the might of the British state had been thrown away. With the poor performance in Glasgow Garscadden and other elections that year, the Party lost its commanding grasp on Scottish politics and any chance that Scotland would benefit from ownership of oil, the oil revenues, an industrial development fund financed by oil and a heritage fund for future generations and jobs from oil industries built up to serve the world had gone. The pressure was off. Scotland had indeed ended up as one of the few countries to discover oil and be poorer as a result.

Despite the passage of time, with an asset of this magnitude, ownership is still an issue. Oil in the North Sea belongs to Scotland under international law – but only if the Scots claim it through self-government. The remaining reserves are massive and more than enough for a country of 5 million people to transform its economy and society. The key in 1973 and now is 'self-government'. Without Scottish independence, it's England's Oil! So far as London is concerned, independence is not on the table until the oil runs out. Catch 22, I believe.

Chapter 8
Making the Breakthrough

While the Oil Campaign continued full-tilt, the Party had little time to be pre-occupied with its normal run of activities. Most of the leaders were caught up with the demands at the 'grass-roots' for public meetings or as candidates. It was a voluntary organisation where those in charge held down jobs, managed their family life and coped with their local commitments, as well as serving at national level. It was a feature of the SNP in the sixties that while new people came and went at National Executive level, there was a core, composed of Robert McIntyre, Arthur Donaldson, James Halliday, William Wolfe, Douglas Henderson, David Rollo, Helen Davidson and me, who were elected year upon year. In addition, Rosemary Hall and Ian Macdonald added to the pool of experience in organisational or administrative matters. This gave consistency and experience at a time when the SNP was careering up and down on a switchback of popular support. Nevertheless, at key times, the 'old blood' was refreshed by new people who brought in ideas for change. In the sixties, these were James Lees, James Braid and Douglas Drysdale.

By the late sixties, a more permanent infusion became evident. First amongst these were Isobel Lindsay and her husband Tom McAlpine. Isobel Lindsay was a lecturer in sociology at the University of Strathclyde who was significantly to the left of the Party. She first came to prominence when she was elected on to Glasgow Corporation in the great landslide of 1968 and remained until the equally large defeat of 1971. In that role, she was very capable and deserved to stay, but she was ousted by a Labour candidate who was one of my cousins. She was particularly active in policy formation and had produced a major policy on social benefits.[1] This policy sought to link the benefits and tax systems and was well ahead of its time and the technology available. It also simplified the benefit structure in ways that could still be put into practice with great advantage. She was elected Executive Vice Chairman for Publicity in 1972.

Tom McAlpine, her husband, also of the left, had been active in the Iona Community and had been Chairman of the Church of Scotland's Youth Assembly. Before joining the SNP, he had been a Labour Councillor in Hamilton for three years. He was the Managing Director of Rowan Engineering, a company formed on co-operative principles. In due course, he and Isobel were to found an alliance with Billy Wolfe that had considerable sway within the National Executive during the mid-seventies.

Also emerging in 1968 was Margo MacDonald, a teacher of physical education. She was finding her feet in the run up to the 1970 General

Election and made considerable – if not meteoric - progress thereafter. She was destined to play a major role over the next four decades. She joined the National Executive in 1971 and in 1972, became Executive Vice Chairman for Policy. Margo was a charismatic personality who had under-played her professional family origins by adopting a broad Glaswegian patois. This woman of the people image was enhanced, maybe not entirely to her taste, by the press calling her the SNP's 'blonde bombshell'! She was always a politician to be reckoned with.

By this time, the policy making forum, the National Assembly had recovered from the tsunami of policy making produced by its formation and was largely given to tidying up some of the areas where agreement had proved difficult to achieve, such as education where most of the policy was approved by National Council on 4 March 1972. In 1972, there were no National Assembly policies placed before Conference which, to an unusual degree, allowed space for resolutions from branches and constituency associations. In 1973, the Energy and Land Policies had been drafted for National Assembly. With Britain going into the Common Market in 1973, resolutions on this theme were ever present.

In late August 1972, I received an invitation from Ian Macaulay, Chairman of Dundee East Constituency Association to have a chat over coffee. Being intrigued, Edith and I accepted. It was interesting. Ian Macaulay explained that there was a by-election in the offing as the MP, George Thomson, a Labour government minister was likely to be offered the position of a Common Market Commissioner. In those days there were two Commissioners, drawn equally from the main British parties. If that happened, George Thomson would resign as an MP and a by-election would result. For business reasons, Ian who had been the candidate for the seat in the 1970 General Election was unable to stand. He invited me to put my name forward. I agreed to think it over and certainly did not react too enthusiastically.

There was a lot to consider. Despite my prominence in the Party for the last 10 years, I had enjoyed my back-ground leadership. I was happy as a lawyer and indeed, was beginning to reap the financial benefits of partnership as I had grown in seniority. My family was settled in Paisley where my children attended school. The idea that I should change my role to being a candidate was quite revolutionary.

Nor was Dundee seemingly much of a political 'catch'. In the 1960s, it had been one of the least responsive areas, even during the great upsurge. It had experienced poor leadership and was the source of innumerable organisational complaints. In my role of National Secretary I had taken the rare step of suspending a branch and its office-bearers in the midst of the 1969 local elections. Admittedly, this had happened in Dundee West where most of the trouble had existed, but Dundee East was not immune as it had spilled over into a branch in the Hilltown area. Three of the Branches set up in the sixties were no longer functioning.

The seat was also not promising. In 1945, Arthur Donaldson had fought the combined Dundee seat (two MPs), encountering much hostility. A contest of a by-election in Dundee East in 1952 proved similarly discouraging, while the Party gained less than 9% in the 1970 general election. Political support was also tightly polarised between Labour and Conservative and although Labour had held the constituency, the 1970 election had seen it become marginal – always difficult for a third party to crack. Dundee was also going through a bleak phase with the jute and mechanical engineering industries, the main stays of the local economy, in decline.

Looking at it objectively, it was a constituency to avoid. My political contemporaries thought I had lost my senses by considering a contest. My law partners also expressed little signs of anxiety about a future victory. For strategic reasons, I saw it differently. I had launched the biggest political campaign Scotland had seen in decades. It was new and exciting. It was making an immediate impact, including in Dundee which was in the top three areas of response to the BRCs, used for recruitment. Politically, I sensed an opportunity. The adverse factors of decline could be turned by concentrating on the positives of Scotland's oil. Dundee was a city of high unemployment and social deprivation. The arguments about using the oil finds to create local jobs through servicing the oil industry and building up precision engineering for long term growth could make their mark. The creation of an atmosphere of hope through use of the oil revenues to up-grade housing and improve the quality of life could also impact on how people voted. In addition, the stranglehold of the two party system was there to be broken. The Labour controlled Dundee Corporation had a whiff of corruption to it, while the local Tories had no dynamism or new ideas.

Having taken the essential precaution of obtaining my wife's agreement – something she and my children probably lived to regret - I put my name forward. I was not the only candidate. Margo MacDonald had also been invited and having heard both of us separately, the Constituency Association was split and asked the NEC to choose. The Executive decided unanimously to approve my contest[2]. From then on my life was not my own. My candidature as a 'national figure' and leader of the oil campaign was published at a Dundee Press Conference in late November and received good coverage in the press and on Grampian TV. The National Council in early December was relocated to Dundee to allow a series of office-bearers to speak in relays in City Square and also to familiarise delegates with the 'road and the miles to Dundee'. This was essential to get the Party campaigning before the by-election was formally called.

So, regularly, I travelled every week to the city, sometimes to do industrial visits and mainly to loud-speak around the shopping centres and canvass people in their homes. The campaign was based on getting me known, so taped music with lively campaign ditties composed by one of our active members, John Dryden, was played from cars festooned with 'Gordon Wilson' posters. Unexpectedly, given the pessimism which had existed over the Dundee organisation, I found that I had stumbled on treasure. The Election Agent, Alan McKinney was exceptional. He and his assistant, Dave Keddie were backed up by a team of enthusiastic and dedicated volunteers, some battle hardened from a tough time in the sixties and others brought in by the rolling success of the oil campaign.

For once the Party rallied swiftly after the election was called. Hundreds of Party workers surged in and two weeks from polling, the Saturday turn-out touched a thousand. The campaign was run by a committee (consisting of the National Organiser, John McAteer, Director of Communications, Douglas Crawford and Isobel Lindsay, EVC Publicity in charge of publications and local representatives) which devised new electoral techniques. I was not involved. I was the front man spear-pointing the campaign and always to be kept in action. In a rural constituency, candidates get time off while travelling. In a city seat, you are in action all the time. So it was not surprising in the last three weeks, Edith and I were so tired that on the way back to Paisley, we had to draw into a lay-by for a cat-nap as we were unable to drive with safety. The SNP did not supply candidate support outside the field of battle!

The SNP did a full canvass, but did not have enough time to complete a second round. The battle raged fiercely. The Labour and Conservative candidates refused to participate in a television debate, so as not to give me an advantage and television coverage was small. Outside professional agents were brought in, with Labour having 10, the Conservatives 9, and the Liberals 2 compared with 1 for the SNP. A principal feature was a contest of window posters from which it was evident that the SNP was in the lead as the main contender to Labour. Some houses even sported rival posters, showing a domestic division of opinion!

In the event, Labour had a narrow victory with a majority of 1,141.

Dundee East By-election Result (March 1973)

		(1970)
Labour	32.7%	(48.3%)
SNP	30.2%	(8.9%)
Conservative & Unionist	25.2%	(42.4%)
Liberal	8.3%	(0%)

Support for Labour dropped 15.6% and for the Conservatives by 17.2%, giving a good platform for a further contest. On the day of the election, Parliament published the Report of the Public Accounts Committee that was fiercely critical of the performance on oil policy of both Governments. Billy Wolfe believed that publication of this Report had been delayed so as not to put it into play during the campaign. It certainly would have given a final nudge towards an SNP victory.

The by-election was followed shortly after by the local elections which showed a huge growth of support for the SNP, especially outwith the cities.

SNP Local Election Results, May 1973

	1972	1973
Overall	14%	21%
Cities	9%	13.8%
Burghs (non-cities)	25%	32.7%
Counties	-	31.3%

After a successful Conference, several changes took place. I was elected Senior Vice Chairman and given the tasks of co-ordinating the planning of the campaigns for the autumn and spring, direction of the Oil Campaign and appointed chief spokesman for Oil. Tom McAlpine as Executive Vice Chairman for Administration assumed responsibility for the General Business Committee, previously the job of the Senior Vice Chairman. Michael Murgatroyd was Treasurer, while Rosemary Hall was Secretary.

The steady progress of planning for the General Election was interrupted by by-elections in Edinburgh North and Glasgow Govan Constituencies. In October 1973, the National Executive approved Billy Wolfe and Margo MacDonald as candidates. Neither constituency fell into the winnable bracket. Edinburgh had long been sticky territory for the Party and it was anticipated that, with its social orientation and history of Conservative and Labour conflict, winning Edinburgh North would be an uphill task, even allowing for the overall progress of the SNP. Govan was different. True, Labour had a large, entrenched majority but the Labour organisation had declined into a small activist base, and in the late sixties, of all the cities, it was Glasgow that had seen the SNP triumph with the election of 13 councillors.

Both contests faced a common hazard. The elections were to take place on the same day and this would lead to a split in the SNP travelling support. My home in Paisley was close to Govan, and it was there that I mainly canvassed, with Edith helping in the office. As a senior office-bearer, I also went to Edinburgh and after canvassing, came to the judgment that there was little hope of break through. By contrast, Govan was doing well and imperceptibly, party workers recognised this and transferred their attentions to Govan. Margo Macdonald was the ideal candidate for the seat. She had a cheery, outgoing 'gallus' personality that went down well. She was a first class speaker and spoke the same language as the voters.

As the election in Govan progressed, there was a high profile defection from the Tory party. Baillie James Anderson, election agent to Teddy Taylor, MP for Glasgow Cathcart, declared his support and came over. I was in the election rooms that night. In the legendary meeting between David Livingstone, the African explorer and missionary and the American journalist, Stanley, Stanley is alleged to have extended his hand and said, 'Dr Livingstone, I presume'! In this case, James Anderson came face to face with veteran nationalist, Provost Gordon Murray of Cumbernauld. It was a case of a rather stiff, 'Hullo, James' and 'Hullo, Gordon". Baillie Anderson did not remain a member for long and there were rumours, never substantiated and always denied, that he was there to provide a possible bridge for the highly populist Teddy Taylor to cross over and given Teddy's strident unionism something most unlikely to transpire. Intriguingly, in the early thirties, Cathcart Unionist Party had defected in numbers to join the newly formed Scottish Party which shortly afterwards merged with the National Party of Scotland to form the Scottish National Party. In this case, history did not repeat itself.

In the closing stages, both campaigns received a boost. The long awaited Report from the Royal Commission on the Constitution (the Kilbrandon Report) was published. It had taken over four years. It came out in favour of an elected Scottish Assembly with restricted powers and satisfied no-one. For the SNP, it was a 'Godsend'. It brought the issue of a Scottish Parliament to the fore and raised questions as to its powers and what, if anything, Labour could deliver. The end result was that the SNP's Margo MacDonald swept to victory in Govan and William Wolfe achieved a respectable result in Edinburgh North. It is difficult to imagine the impact. The SNP had gained another MP to join Donald Stewart in the House of Commons and enough to cause the SNP to be recognised as a political party at Westminster. Margo MacDonald became a spectacular political super-star as had Winnie Ewing before her.

Glasgow Govan Result
(November 1973)

SNP	41.9%
Labour	38.2%
Conservative	1.7%
Liberal	8.2%

Edinburgh North Result
(November 1973)

Conservative	38.7%
Labour	24.0%
SNP	18.9%
Liberal	18.4%

As with the election of Winifred Ewing in Hamilton 6 years earlier, a large number of members, including Edith who had missed the Hamilton - London trip, travelled to Westminster to see Margo take her seat. There is no doubt Margo made an immediate impact. Apart from her own personality, there was the novelty value of a further surge by the SNP with senior members of the Labour Party, like Denis Healey, seeking her out to learn what was happening. Donald Stewart was perplexed and disappointed. He had expected another SNP colleague and found that Margo was more in company with Labour MPs than with him. But Margo did not consort much with Scottish Labour which was in a panic. One of their fortresses had fallen and if the Govan swing was repeated throughout Scotland, many Labour MPs stood to lose their seats. And where seats are perceived to be at risk, there come fear and bitterness.

Hardly had the Govan victory been absorbed than I circulated a memorandum depicting the failure of most of the SNP office-bearers to carry out their responsibilities under the election battle-plan.[3] I had responsibility for planning the General Election. Although the election was not due till 1975, I was alarmed to find that no progress was being made. It was timely. The Heath government was involved in a major dispute with the miners and the UK was placed on a three day week due to electricity cuts. In February, things came to a head and in order to buttress a weak political position, Edward Heath, the Prime Minister called a spot general election on the issue of 'who governs Britain'. He procrastinated before announcing the election and lost credibility through his hesitation.

The issue of who governed was on the face of it a distinctly unhelpful topic for the minority parties who had no chance of forming a government. The ground was particularly damaging for the SNP since the prospect of us governing Britain was in the realms of fantasy. More than ever, this election would be about government – something that favoured the big parties. Also, a fight between the Conservatives and the unions would harden working class voting in favour of Labour.

With the SNP's long running oil campaign, the victory at Govan and the Kilbrandon Commission Report favouring a Scottish Assembly, circumstances had changed in our favour. For the first time in its history, it was the SNP that was relevant and had forward momentum. We found that Scottish voters had lost faith in the ability of Westminster to govern and were willing to consider Scottish choices. The media coverage reflected the SNP's increased profile, and some of it extended into London coverage

Apart from sharing Press Conferences, I was able to concentrate on Dundee East. Rosemary Hall took charge of the national election arrangements, with help from John McAteer and Stephen Maxwell who had become the Press Officer.   Unlike the by-election, the General Election contest in Dundee East had to be fought locally although some financial assistance was available from HQ and Edinburgh in particular sent in troops. In the course of the year, Dundee East had built up its membership to close on 1,000 which was phenomenal and the organisation could deliver the 'last-minute' leaflet in one and a half days. Alan McKinney and his team were on top. During the year, I had diligently read Hansard and had discovered that, apart from his maiden speech, the Labour MP, George Machin had hardly spoken in the House or asked many questions. The SNP literature saw to it that he was duly exposed. On 28 February 1974, I was elected MP for Dundee East, a constituency that I had come to love. Over the years, my Scottish nationalism was almost equalled by my Dundee loyalties. Dundee was a neglected city, described before the building of the Tay Bridge and the new road to Aberdeen as being on the 'road to nowhere', isolated as it had been before the building of the Tay and Friarton Bridges on a corner of Scotland, and by-passed by those travelling from the central belt to Aberdeen. It badly needed championing.

On that same date, the SNP surged through to its biggest ever victory, holding the Western Isles with Donald Stewart and with Winifred Ewing ousting the Secretary of State for Scotland to win Moray & Nairn. Douglas Henderson won East Aberdeenshire, Hamish Watt the constituency of Banff, Iain MacCormick, Argyll and George Reid, Clackmannan & East Stirling. In all, the SNP had seven seats, three from Labour and four from the Conservatives. We were still a minority, but after such a landslide, no one was caring. The electoral landscape of Scotland had changed.

February 1974 Results

Party	Percentage Votes	Seats
Labour	36.6% (-7.9%)	40
Conservative	32.9% (-5.1%)	21
SNP	21.9% (+10.5%)	7
Liberal	8.0% (+2.5%)	3

The Conference in Elgin was triumphal.[3] I was in process of moving house from Paisley to Dundee and could not appear until the final day. My constituency delegates were disappointed that Dundee East's success had been eclipsed by my absence. My new parliamentary colleagues had, however, spoken too frequently so that my popularity with the delegates was commensurate with my enforced silence.

The election break-through was marred by the loss of Glasgow Govan and Margo MacDonald. Dundee East remained the only city seat and we had lost our tenuous out-post in the West central belt. In some ways, I was surprised. One of my last tasks before leaving for Dundee had been to help out at Margo's weekly surgery. There were over 50 constituents crowded into her rooms. I was sure that the impetus of the Party, combined with her profile and the concentration of Glasgow activists in Govan would have been enough to carry her through.

Ever present in our minds in the months following was the expectation of another General Election as Labour formed a minority government. If we were not careful, the gains of February might be wiped out. An analysis of the votes showed that while we had won support from all parties, we had done better against Labour. If there were to be another early General Election, then Labour had political problems in Scotland. Their February manifesto had been weak as it promised neither a parliament nor dealt convincingly with answers to the SNP's oil campaign. Labour in Scotland was resolutely unionist and did not want a Scottish Assembly. Labour Headquarters in London read the runes and perceived the peril. It published a Green Paper setting out five alternatives for devolution. It further instructed Scottish Labour to hold a special Conference in August and demanded that the Scottish Party reverse its opposition. Reluctantly, the Scottish Party fell into line. The manifesto for the October election promised an economic powerhouse for Scotland. It undertook to deliver a Scottish Assembly, the creation of a Scottish Development Agency, financial support for the Scottish economy and the head office of a British National Oil Corporation it intended to form. Trinkets for the natives, perhaps, but it had been forced to concede an Assembly and Labour appeared to tie in Scottish aspirations to benefits from the oil industry, although there was no concession on any of the oil revenues being dedicated to Scotland or Scotland's industrial regeneration. But it could be enough to sway a desperate people and allowed Labour ground to fight the nationalists, especially in the seventeen seats where the February result had promoted the SNP to second place.

Fortunately, other more promising trends were in play. In the seven months since the February election, there had been an explosion in membership and in the recognition of new branches. The Executive recognised 22 branches in June[4], 16 in August[5], and 12 in September[6]. The MPs fanned out throughout Scotland during the summer recess to stir up support for SNP candidates. For finance, apart from the usual limited resources, there was an anonymous donation of £10,000 and release of £3,000 of the capital from an earlier donation, previously restricted to income. For the first time for a General Election, the SNP was invited to attend a special meeting of the Committee on Party Political Broadcasting to allocate time for election broadcasts. The Party was represented by Chief Whip, Douglas Henderson MP and me as Deputy Leader of the Parliamentary Group. I had sent letter after letter to this Committee in the sixties and it was revealing to see how it operated. The broadcasters, BBC and ITA, made an offer of time that all Parties agreed was inadequate, though this ritual complaint did not lead to any increase and in a naked exercise of self-interested political power, the major Parties divided up the spoils. Although we were able to argue a case for additional time based on performance, there was no change to our share.

In September, Douglas Crawford, by then Executive Vice Chairman for Publicity, outlined the election themes which included the next phase of the Oil Campaign and the Strategy and Tactics Committee set the political agenda.[7] The election was to be fought on the SNP's continuing success, devolution, proposals for a wealthy Scotland to bail out England, the mortgaging of oil and its theft, agriculture, the London wage/salary weighting (whereby public servants in London received higher rates of pay) and support for an Association of British States to counter attacks of 'separatism'. The Strategy Committee proposals were broadly similar, but envisaged setting out conditions under which we would support a minority British Government. This latter theme was rejected by the Executive as being too definite. The broad strategy was to be based on the slogan 'WE'RE WINNING', to re-inforce the advances previously made.

In the October election, the Conservative vote crumbled. In Scotland, the Labour vote held. For the SNP, it was as close to a landslide as could be expected. We emerged with 4 new MPs, Andrew Welsh in South Angus, Douglas Crawford in Perth and East Perthshire, Margaret Bain in Dunbartonshire East and George Thompson in Galloway. We had also come very close with 42 second places.

October 1974 Results

Party	Percentage Votes	Seats
Labour	36.3% (-.03%)	41 (+1)
SNP	30.4% (+8.5%)	11 (+4)
Conservative	24.7% (-8.2%)	16 (-5)
Liberal	8.3% (+0.3%)	3 (0)

With a large Parliamentary Group, the SNP held considerable influence. The beleaguered unionist parties, faced with further losses, would become vicious in their attacks. Internally, within the SNP, there were to be problems over future strategy and direction between the MPs and Party leaders who had not been elected. But for the moment, all was happiness and light!

The SNP continued its surge in membership and 58 new branches were recognised, 23 of them in December 1974 alone.[8] As a consequence of this dramatic growth, the Party budgeted for the employment of additional staff, including a further administrator, an industrial liaison officer and research assistant. Since the Party was cramped in a basement in Manor Place, Edinburgh with an outpost for publications and research in the West Calder Publications Dept., the ill-fated decision was taken to finance larger HQ offices in Edinburgh.[9]

In the UK, the main preoccupation was with the European Common Market which Britain had entered in 1973. The Labour Government was hopelessly split at all levels, including the Cabinet. Over the last five years the SNP had gradually taken a harder line against the Common Market, flimsily clad as 'No Voice, No Entry'. Senior figures like Donald Stewart, Isobel Lindsay and Stephen Maxwell, the Press Officer were utterly against on principle. The Party's opposition to the Common Market had been strengthened by the disastrous loss of Scotland's exclusive fishing grounds since the Heath Government had not sought an opt out from the Common Fisheries Policy. Feeling was also heightened by European centralisation that was anathema to SNP members who had been fighting London control and saw little benefit in exchanging that jack boot for a European model.

Stephen Maxwell saw great advantages to the SNP in campaigning hard in the forthcoming referendum. In a memorandum to the NEC meeting of February 1975, setting out proposals for an election type campaign, he stated[10]:

> 'In spite of the scale of the resources available to the European Movement, the referendum provides the SNP with a tremendous opportunity. The SNP will be the only political party in Scotland speaking with one voice. The issue lends itself to grass roots campaigning of the sort at which the SNP, with its decentralised branch structure, excels. And the SNP is in a position to appeal to both the gut anti-EEC vote in Scotland and to that section of opinion, (which) while broadly sympathetic to the 'European' idea is sensitive to Scotland's lack of political status in European affairs.'

The Executive accepted the proposal for a campaign committee but reserved a decision on the political line till National Council had been consulted. After a confused debate arising from a stalemate vote at National Assembly in January, Council contented itself with a simple formula of advising the Scottish people to vote against remaining in the EEC in the UK referendum.[11]

This was the first ever referendum in Britain. There were two umbrella groups, Britain in Europe and the National Referendum Campaign.

Effectively, the SNP was unable to mount a distinctive Scottish programme. Television and radio broadcasts went to the umbrella groups and the anti-case was drowned out by a huge insurge of funding from industry. There was little co-operation between the Parties on the anti-side and this contrasted with a sophisticated and unified presentation by Britain in Europe. There were alarmist warnings about the threat to jobs if Britain pulled out. SNP branches did not act as if it were an election and the SNP campaign proved ineffective. It was no surprise when Scotland voted to stay in the EEC. Nevertheless, the rebuff came as a shock and the SNP was no longer seen as invincible as the Scottish people had reacted on a British basis. The Scottish card of 'No Voice. No Entry' did not register with the electorate. It also introduced suspicion within the Party that a referendum on either devolution or independence would be open to manipulation as in the case of the European referendum and under a year later John McAteer, the National Organiser, reported a fear of this at branch level and counselled that the SNP be psychologically prepared for one on the constitution.

But that was later. There was an urgent need to grasp the thistle of Europe and the MPs authorised Douglas Henderson and me to propose an emergency resolution to the 14 June meeting of National Council.[12]

> 'This Council, acknowledging the democratic decision of the Scottish people in the EEC referendum, resolves that the protection of the national rights and the living standards of the people of Scotland now requires full independent representation of Scottish interests at all levels of the EEC including particularly the right of veto in the Council of Ministers and calls on all Scots to unite with the SNP in demanding the immediate achievement of the objective and asserts the rights of a future Scottish Government to determine its exact international relationships with the EEC and other world bodies.'

An attempt was made by the anti-EEC camp to amend the resolution. All amendments were beaten off, one by 148 votes to 80 and the unamended motion carried by a large majority.

Internally, control of the Party had altered. The 'big beasts' on the Executive - Billy Wolfe, Robert McIntyre, Margo MacDonald (who since her victory in Govan had emerged as a strong presence), Isobel Lindsay and Tom McAlpine – were still present and influential. Amongst the Vice-chairmen, out had gone Ian Macdonald (Organisation), Arthur Donaldson (Policy), Douglas Crawford (Publicity) and Tom McAlpine (Administration). Into office had come other personalities, Brian Innes-Will (Organisation), Isobel Lindsay (Policy), Janette Jones (Publicity) and William McRae (Administration). Brian Innes-Will was a technocrat who sought to strengthen the constituency associations at the expense of the branches, Janette Jones was a Party loyalist with great support from members and William McRae was a brilliant Glasgow lawyer with a colourful, larger than life personality and a huge capacity for spell-binding rhetoric. The National Secretary was Muriel Gibson who had been detained briefly as a nationalist during the War and had subsequently risen to the rank of Lt. Colonel, the second highest rank for a woman in the British Army.

After the triumphs of 1974 and the continuing popularity of the Party (averaging around 32%) in the opinion polls and the Government on the back foot over devolution, the SNP believed that the Scottish Assembly was in the bag and that independence was inevitable. There was not much the Party could do about tactics – that was the preserve of the Parliamentary Group - but it could prepare for the Scottish Assembly. Part of this preparation was a wholesale expansion of the list of approved candidates so that there would be 150 candidates in place for the Assembly elections (based on the SNP constitutional proposals until the government could firm up their proposals). This entailed a large output of time by senior office-bearers and MPs serving on the Election Committee that was responsible for the approval of candidates. Under the urging of the Party Chairman, Isobel Lindsay (who needed no encouragement) re-invigorated the policy formation process so that the SNP would have a fresh Manifesto for the Assembly Elections and ready for a possible General Election. By November 1976, five policy statements on new and upgraded policies on Housing, The Democratic Road to Self Government, Defence, Financial Management after Self Government, Transport, and External Affairs were queuing up for discussion by National Council. After these came policies on the Environment, the Structure of Local Government and Crofting. At the 1977 Conference, for instance, there were full statements on Education, Taxation and a statement of principles for a draft Scottish Constitution.[13] These Policies were intended to be published in a series of pamphlets and made available to the public.

Writing in 2007, Isobel Lindsay justified the policy-making processes of both the sixties and the seventies[14]:

> 'Conventional Left/Right divisions were not as prominent as has been suggested. There was both considerable agreement on a fairly centre/left, social democratic agenda and also cross-cutting alliances. Positions on EU issues cut across (gradualism and the

role of the Party as a non-political movement for independence) and Left/Right

There was continual tension around whether the SNP should focus solely on independence and not be 'distracted' by involvement in specific policy areas unless they involved a Scottish 'rights' dimension or whether seeking to be a major political party required a coherent policy programme both to guide candidates and elected members and to give an ideological identity that the public could understand.

The early 70s saw a move in the latter direction actively promoted by the national chairman through the recently established National Assembly. The Assembly did provide a valuable opportunity both to develop policy ideas through its committees and to debate them in some depth and as a source of political training for potential candidates. The policy committees were encouraged to involve experienced people who were not necessarily party members. David Hamilton, convening the Health Committee, had a very distinguished group – I recall among others Prof. Watson Buchanan and also the professor of general practice at Glasgow University. The Industrial Development Committee actively went out to seek ideas from people in industry, the development agencies and the Scottish Council. People like Malcolm Slessor helped to encourage some (at that time) fresh thinking on environmental issues. After 1974 when it looked as if there could be a Scottish Assembly within a few years, there was added urgency to prepare for this whether in opposition or in government. Had the Scotland Act been implemented, I think there would have been an appreciation of how well the party was prepared. Post-referendum there was an understandable view that this had been wasted time, a distraction.

My own view (predictably) is that the policy work that was done at the very least helped to avoid the pitfalls of 'a policy in every constituency' which opponents were always looking for, contributed to the political development of a generation of core activists and helped to give the SNP a reformist, social democratic identity. The process itself was very open and often quite creative unlike the policy process that characterises most political parties today controlled by a small appointed group around a leader.'

In the approach to 1977, the SNP opened its new Headquarters at 6 North Charlotte Street, Edinburgh. With alterations, the total cost was around £60,000 met by a loan from Noble Grossart Bank, and although the loan was guaranteed by Sir Hugh Fraser, the rate of interest was a disturbing 2.5% over LIBOR (the London Inter-bank Lending Rate). As Britain was going through horrendous inflation and interest rates were high, at one time the Party was paying around 17% per-annum. The building had been purchased to meet the additional staffing envisaged for post Scottish Assembly operations and for much of the time was wildly excessive to requirements. It reminded me of the HQ of the Utter Hebrides Council in the cartoon strip 'Angus Og' in the Daily Record which Angus Og described as 'Prodigality House'. As the Party's fortunes waned, it became a millstone.

The Party had also relied heavily on experienced senior staff and in one year between 1976 and 1977, lost John McAteer through death and Donald Bain and Stephen Maxwell through resignation. They were succeeded by Alan McKinney, my former election agent, as National Organiser, Duncan McLaren as Press Officer and Robert Crawford as Research Officer. Oil had receded as a campaigning issue and been replaced by industrial campaigns on steel and factory closures. In the forefront of everyone's mind was the implementation of the Government's policy on the Scottish Assembly.

Chapter 9

The Magnificent Seven and Scotland's First Eleven

Most of the February 1974 SNP victors were experienced politicians. Donald Stewart (Western Isles) was the first SNP MP elected at a General Election. His majority showed a ten fold increase from 1970. Being so far from his constituency, Donald found it necessary during the parliamentary term to live in London, save for a mid-term week spent on tour. During his four years, he had built up a good reputation in the Commons and he and his wife, Chrissie, were extremely popular. He was one of life's individualists, socially conservative and surprisingly radical at times. He had served in the navy during the war and apart from a short stay in the Labour Party as a youth, had been a longstanding member of the SNP. He was a nationalist through and through and had little time for the conflicts of the notional left and right. Before his election, he had been widely travelled as Sales Director of the main Harris Tweed firm in Stornoway.

Winnie Ewing, former victor of Hamilton from 1967 to 1970, had won Moray & Nairn, ousting the Conservative Secretary of State for Scotland in the process. Her unwillingness to accept the humiliations heaped on her by Scots Labour MPs and her feisty nature had made her earlier stay in the Commons as the sole SNP MP a very tempestuous affair. She was probably the best known nationalist and was an obvious candidate for the leadership of the new group, along with Donald Stewart since both had had experience of Westminster.

Neither Donald nor Winnie had undertaken administrative leadership within the Party, but Douglas Henderson, MP for East Aberdeenshire, had been Director of Internal Training, Executive Vice Chairman for Administration and Policy and latterly Senior Vice Chairman (or deputy Leader). He was a management consultant and law graduate and had the experience of having been expelled from the SNP as a young man. He had the reputation of being a right winger. This was unfair as he fought in parliament for the rights of workers. He was certainly a firm nationalist and his caustic wit did not spare fools or back-sliders.

Of the remaining three MPs, Hamish Watt (Banff) had served on the National Executive Committee and had been Convener of the influential Land Use Policy Committee. He was a farmer and live stock dealer, with a sound knowledge of agriculture. Before joining the SNP, he had been a Conservative candidate in Caithness & Sutherland. Whether the leaving of the Tories and the joining of the SNP had had a direct effect, he now loathed the Tories and, unusually for an SNP representative, he had an affinity with Labour.

Nevertheless, in the SNP pantheon he could be properly regarded as a gradualist and devolutionist. So it is not surprising that he and I never saw eye to eye on strategy and tactics. He was open to doing deals with the Government. To me as a nationalist, it was anathema that we should ever collude with any of the London parties.

Iain MacCormick had won Argyll with a large majority. He was a son of John MacCormick, one of the founders of the Party. Iain had been a member of the Glasgow University Scottish National Association and had developed as a strong debater in the furnace of the Debating Union. He had a flair for rhetoric. Some observers believe his views had been of the left or liberal brand. The truth was that he was too colourful to be easily pigeon-holed although he did eventually leave the Party to join the SDP.

The last of the seven had no experience of the Party. George Reid had won a landslide victory in Clackmannan & East Stirling in a whirlwind campaign that had ejected Labour. He had joined the SNP in mid 1973. George had been Director of Current Affairs at STV and employed earlier with Granada Television. He brought much needed skills in media and television to the Party and did occasional lecturing to the civil service and police colleges. He also had a tabloid newspaper column. George Reid described himself as a social democrat. He was on the gradualist wing of the Party. He and I were room-mates – sitting back to back in a tiny room so small, the backs of the chairs, if in line, would have touched. There were complaints from our secretaries that when we were dictating, one voice mingled with another.

These, then, were the SNP MPs. They all faced a mammoth challenge. The SNP had never had a parliamentary group, let alone one potentially holding the balance of power. There were to be many lessons to be learned by the MPs and Party leaders in Scotland. We were working in a completely new environment. Few had been confident of being elected and were suddenly torn from jobs and families, without preparation for the transition. Westminster also did not know what to expect from this new grouping. It had not had to deal with dissident members who wished to break up 'Britain' since the Irish Nationalists of the nineteenth century. For many MPs with experience of Donnie and Chrissie Stewart's warmth and courtesy, there was hope that the new SNP group would be politically and socially agreeable. Others, influenced by the tabloid press and the strength of SNP campaigns expected the arrival of SNP revolutionaries who would be noisy, brash and disruptive. Given the suddenness of the SNP victory to those in England, there was no limitation to their imagination. The English press analysed the group and accredited them with left-right affiliations to fit British politics. In an article in New Society (18 April 1974), William Rankine commented:

'It is a happy coincidence for the Scottish National Party that it has emerged as a credible political force at a time when a handful of votes at Westminster could make or break the Government. Robert Mellish, Labour's Chief Whip will have to live with the fact that even if the SNP is more civilised than the Loyalist alliance from Ulster, the two groups have much in common. Deep down, they both feel a burning sense of grievance against the English and the Westminster parliament. Both are sustained, indeed obsessed by a single idea. While the Loyalists hark back to the Union as it used to be, the Nationalists attribute almost all Scotland's ills to the English connection. Their ambition is to win a majority of Scottish seats in the House of Commons so that they can then walk out and establish an independent, sovereign government in Edinburgh.'

In this perceptive article that was not always flattering about historic divisions within the SNP, he further observed:

'It can be argued that, in most of the seats they won, the nationalists skilfully exploited local issues or personalities. It can be pointed out that North Sea oil has weakened the economic case against Scotland going it alone. But to leave it at that is ungenerous to the SNP. The party has now shown that it can win votes in significant numbers in all parts of Scotland, from all classes of people. They now hold four former Tory seats and three former Labour seats. We have to start to think in terms of genuine nationalist voters, rather than disappointed former Tory and Labour supporters.
On the other hand, however, there are questions to be asked about the character of this nationalist support. Although the SNP is an independence party, all the available evidence from polls and surveys suggests that most of the people who vote for it, want nothing more than old-fashioned home rule. It may be that the SNP would have advanced faster in recent years, if it had not taken the separatist road in the 1940s. Nationalist leaders freely acknowledge that their policies are more radical than most of their supporters want and they have already identified the problems this could create for them in the current parliament.'

The first question thrown at the MPs immediately after their election, was who will you support? As William Rankine had stated, there was no clear outcome to the General Election. Edward Heath's outgoing Government had won the highest number of votes. The winner on seats was Labour. Labour did not have a majority over all other parties. If they were to govern, it would be as a minority administration. In the immediate aftermath of the election, the Conservative Prime Minister did not surrender his seal of office immediately and endeavoured to forge an alliance with the Liberals. The Liberals were reluctant and so Harold Wilson became Prime Minister for the third time. Before all this happened, both Winifred Ewing and I were quoted separately as saying that the SNP were elected to look after Scottish interests and although we would act reasonably, would not give our outright support to either of the British Parties.

After the poll, I returned to Paisley to allocate my accumulated workload to my shell-shocked partners, and generally, to clear my desk. Douglas Henderson convened the first group meeting at the Caledonian Hotel and HQ organised the press conference and photo-calls at Edinburgh Castle. I did not campaign for office in the new Group. The contest for leadership would have been between Donald Stewart and Winnie Ewing. Donald Stewart had the edge, having current experience of Westminster. I nominated Winnie Ewing for the Deputy Leadership. She refused as she wanted to concentrate on her constituency of Moray & Nairn. Donald Stewart was duly elected, with me being appointed Deputy Leader and Douglas Henderson as Chief Whip. What I did not know until Winnie Ewing published her memoirs was that Hamish Watt had canvassed her for the leadership!

In the division of responsibilities the following allocations were made:

Energy and Oil	Gordon Wilson
Finance, Trade & Industry	Douglas Henderson
Common Market, Home Affairs, Defence & Foreign Affairs	Winifred Ewing
Agriculture, Forestry & Fishing	Hamish Watt
Education & Highland Affairs	Iain MacCormick
Housing, Health & Social Services	George Reid

It was accepted that Donald Stewart as parliamentary leader would have over-riding rights to speak on any topic. After a convivial lunch with the Party President and Chairman, Douglas Henderson asked those who had not been elected to leave. There had been no prior consultation with me about this unconstitutional declaration. The Chairman was an ex officio member of every SNP Committee and Billy Wolfe was visibly shaken although it is fair to say that he has no recollection of the incident. It was a gesture of independence by some of the MPs, but was a poor beginning to what was going to be an entirely new relationship with office bearers of the Party. A quick glance round the room indicated that this was seemingly the will of colleagues. Either Douglas was acting on his own initiative or I had been excluded from any discussions. As a former National Secretary and stickler for the Constitution, I could have been expected to object. Many years later, as National Convener, I made sure I presided over the first meeting of a parliamentary group of which I was not a member!

Billy Wolfe maintains (as at 2008) that at this session, he called upon the MPs to respect the collective leadership of the Party. He reminded the Group of this appeal in July 1978, when relationships were strained although a subsequent Group minute records that the MPs had no recollection of his claim.

The next few weeks were a whirl of activity. Westminster treated the SNP members shabbily over accommodation. In those days, there was little space and members were crammed into whatever crannies could be found. We were each entitled to a locker. The traditions of the House did not expect MPs to carry out constituency work. For preparation of speeches, there were desks in the Library and cubby-holes and banks of public telephones in the corridors. Only a few years before, there had been no free telephones – let alone installed at desks in offices. MPs were poorly paid, and those who had no private means had to phone home in the evenings when calls were cheaper. Being an officer of the SNP Group, I was fortunate to obtain a shared room.

For the next two months, I was in a constant commute between Westminster, my home in Paisley, with part of Fridays spent at my law desk soon after arrival by sleeper, journeys to Dundee, back to Paisley, and off again to London, again by sleeper. But if it was tough for me, my wife, Edith had to manage the family and sell the Paisley house. We moved to Dundee in May. With changes of schools near the end of the school term, this was not good timing. My own children, Margaret (7) and Katie (5), having been dragged round 'boring' SNP public meetings in early childhood, were now marked out as the children of the local MP. Being young, this did not expose them to too many problems at primary school. They found the experience less comfortable at secondary level. It is hardly surprising that, although loyal to the SNP, the last thing they were ever to consider was a political career.

The first session of Parliament was unusual. It was light on legislation. There was not much time available for it. With the government short of a majority, it was obvious that a second General Election was scheduled for the autumn. So apart from the Finance Bill, the government set out to win support with a series of populist statements and general debates. We made our maiden speeches early and ignored the tradition that we should not ask oral parliamentary questions until these speeches had been made. Those making their first speech are protected from hostile intervention on the basis that this speech should follow certain conventions, be about the constituency, contain a kind mention of their predecessor and above all be anodyne. Suffice it to be said most SNP MPs naturally covered their constituency, and did not keep to the convention of being inoffensive!

The principal items of legislation were the Finance Bill and the Trade Union and Labour Relations Bill. Douglas Henderson was the SNP representative on the Standing Committee of the latter. He held the balance of power. He was in a difficult position. His problem was nothing to do with having won East Aberdeenshire from the Tories. The SNP vote came from the fishermen operating from Peterhead and the fish processing workers. The fish processing workers were unionised whereas the fishermen had left Aberdeen after a bitter dispute with the dockers. Naturally, they were not favourably disposed towards trade union liberties. Effectively, during the Committee Stage, Douglas voted with the Government. The one exception was to support the Conservatives on the retention of the Code of Industrial Conduct which protected against unfair dismissals and established good procedural arrangements in disputes. But he said not a word – a rare discipline for a politician. So the Tories who tried to tempt him into speaking received no quote that could have been hung round his head in the coming election. From then on, Douglas had a good relationship with Michael Foot and Albert Booth, the Ministers who were in charge of the Bill. Of Douglas Henderson, Michael Foot said at the outset of the Committee Stage:

> 'He made the most notable contribution to our debate and we should approach this Committee Stage in the spirit of (sic) speech....I think the Committee will be carrying out the will of the House as expressed on Second Reading if we proceed along the lines he suggested.'

In the votes on the floor of the House during the later stages, the SNP voted with the Government.

Apart from this legislation, the contribution of Douglas Henderson as Chief Whip was immense and has been underrated because of his withdrawal from office two years later through personal difficulties. When we went to Westminster first, no one had experience of how a group should operate. Both Winifred Ewing and Donald Stewart had been largely on their own, and when we won Govan, there was insufficient time for Donald Stewart and Margo MacDonald to gel as a group before the election.

The rest of us had no mentors. For the first few weeks, the 'usual channels' involving government, opposition and Liberal Whips did not extend to the SNP with the practical result that we did not receive notice of the following week's business until its announcement on Thursday by when it was difficult to have a full turn out of SNP MPs to discuss speaking and voting arrangements. Firstly, Douglas managed to get an advance copy of the business for next week on Wednesdays from the Liberal Whips who had been given the task of liaising with the 'odds and sods' such as the SNP, Plaid Cymru and the various brands of Northern Ireland loyalists and republicans. He then gained recognition for the SNP so that the notice of business and advance copies of ministerial statements were available direct. He also attended a meeting of the Liberal Group and regaled us with stories of their leader, Jeremy Thorpe, conducting the meeting with his feet on the table amid general anarchy. At last, the SNP received an invitation to be represented at a meeting of the Committee on Party Political Broadcasting. Although I had a fair idea of how the committee worked, from years of correspondence, this was the first time one of the smaller parties was represented.

Both Donald Stewart and Douglas attended (Plaid Cymru were not invited) and Douglas recounted what happened. There were two representatives from each of the political parties and the Directors General of the BBC and ITA with their political liaison assistants. The meeting was chaired by Lord President of the Council, Ted Short and the Secretary was Freddie Warren.

As soon as the meeting was convened, Edward Heath as Conservative Leader intervened. Looking distastefully at the SNP, he said, 'Why are these people here?' Ted Short looked round. There was a silence. He obviously had not been consulted. Then, the quiet, confident voice of Mr Warren was heard. 'The Secretary, Sir.' 'And who is the Secretary?' boomed the voice of Heath. And Warren, whose main job as a civil servant was to be the facilitator between government and opposition, rejoined, 'I am, Sir'. At this point, the fait accompli was accepted.

These were the days before MPs and the political parties were well funded. The individual secretarial allowances for MPs were small and the parliamentary salary meagre. MPs had their secretary, either shared or part-time, at Westminster or in their constituencies. Additionally, there was no funding for research and administration, so that the Group had no assistance. The Party in turn was desperate to be kept in touch with the activities of the MPs. The Party constitution had not envisaged the implications of a large and powerful group of Members of Parliament, most of whom had constituencies away from the central belt and Party Headquarters in Edinburgh. In turn, the MPs who were seeking re-election very shortly were anxious to be involved with Party business. George Reid, for example, who had been elected 'out of the blue' and had no previous role in party business, brought professional media and political experience and joined the Strategy and Tactics Committee and the Party Political Broadcasts Committee responsible for producing the broadcasts. By contrast, I became a poor 'attender' at meetings of the National Executive Committee, relinquished the post of Senior Vice Chairman and had difficulty in managing the Oil Campaign, causing the NEC to patch in substitute arrangements.

In the meantime, the SNP MPs had much to live up to if their sudden explosion on the Westminster scene was not to be extinguished. The Press had labelled them, 'The Magnificent Seven'. A quiet settling in period was impossible. The experienced MPs gave a lead. Donald Stewart spoke in the first day of the Queen's Speech on 13 March 1974 setting out Scotland's case, complaining about the short-changing on election broadcasting and mentioning oil and our support for a directly elected Scottish Assembly. Winnie Ewing began with an intervention in the speech of the Prime Minister and kept up a barrage thereafter.

I joined in with a maiden speech, apparently offending by breaking the courtesies of the House by not paying tribute to my predecessor. Instead, I concentrated on Dundee's problems and the claims to Scotland's oil. Each day of the Queen's Speech was devoted to particular aspects of the government's programme, but maiden speakers were given considerable latitude. Hamish Watt showed his mastery of Scottish agriculture when speaking on 14 March. George Reid followed the next day with comments on poverty and oil, the need for social justice and support for devolution. Douglas Henderson waited till after the Queen's Speech before tackling finance in the Budget Resolutions Debate. Before that, SNP MPs had their first taste of the manipulation of procedures by the 'big two' when an amendment proposed in conjunction with the Liberals and the Plaid Cymru was not called for voting. In retaliation, the Liberals forced a vote on a procedural motion, supported by the Plaid and the SNP. On the main vote, only the SNP and Plaid voted against and this gave rise to Labour accusations that the SNP had voted against the socially just aspects of the Queen's Speech. The SNP had intimated prior to the vote that if the Conservative Opposition threw its weight against the Queen's Speech, the SNP would support the Government. As it was, we had to find a way to register our disapproval of the omissions relating to the EEC referendum, action on the Kilbrandon Commission Report and oil.

The main debates for the Party were on devolution. Iain MacCormick made a fluent maiden speech in a debate on Kilbrandon on 20 March and was joined by Douglas Henderson who called for economic powers and oil revenues for the Assembly and supported independence. On 20 March, I had a disagreeable experience of general work in the Commons when I was called to speak at 12.44 am!

In all, the SNP was kept fully extended in Westminster and had to fit in Party work whenever possible. Although the SNP Group was involved in the Committees dealing with the Trade Union and Industrial Relations Bill, Land Tenure Bill, Broadcasting Bill, Young Persons Bill, Expenditure, Independent Broadcasting Authority Bill, Scottish Select Committee and the Select Committee for Statutory Instruments, attacks were made by Labour and Conservative alike that we were not pulling our weight because we had not volunteered for service on the Committee considering the uncontroversial Housing (Scotland) Bill (worth only £6 million and a measure inherited from the outgoing Conservative regime).

My parliamentary career almost came to a premature halt on Monday, 17 June 1974. As usual, I had travelled from Dundee to London by the night sleeper, as had my Labour colleague for Dundee West, Peter Doig. Peter was faster in getting off the train and I saw him getting on to an earlier 'tube'. When I arrived at Westminster, I was met by smoke wisping from the facade of Westminster Hall. An IRA bomb had gone off eight minutes before, injuring eleven people. As the cloister to the members' entrance to the Commons passes close to the Hall, it was a near miss for me, and even more for Peter Doig who had been three minutes ahead.

On 11 July 1974, there was a government statement in the Commons on oil policy. As the main plank of the February 1974 election and as the Party's continuing propaganda effort had been oil, it was critical that we performed strongly on the issue. On the day, the House was packed and the SNP MPs in strength on their section of the green benches of the Commons. The Statement was made by Eric Varley, the Secretary of State for Energy and set out the government's policy for oil. Amongst other things, the Statement called for the setting up of a British National Oil Company. Little heed had been paid to Scottish criticisms, apart from a throw-away reference to the Scottish Development Agency that Labour intended to establish, and my question was forceful.

> 'Is the Secretary of State aware of the tremendous and widespread anger throughout Scotland over the sequestration by England of Scotland's principal natural resource? Is he aware that the absence of any specific reference to the oil revenues coming to Scotland will cause concern to our people? If it is his intention to make a direct allocation of oil revenues to Scotland, will he state categorically what proportion

will go to the Scottish Development Agency? In view of
the failure of the Parliamentary Undersecretary, (Gavin
Strang, East Edinburgh) to defend Scotland's interests
and in view, too, of his selling of the Labour Party short
in Scotland, will he ask for his resignation?"

Both government and opposition benches were barracking every word. I
kept my 'cool' and stopped in mid-sentence to enforce silence. The SNP had
united the House in opposition and our profile remained intact. Not that
there was much joy from Eric Varley's reply. The SDA, he said, was not to wait
for the oil revenues and was to be financed immediately. Labour never made
any revenues available for industrial development and their much vaunted
operation, The British National Oil Corporation (BNOC) was established as a
brass plaque front organisation in Scotland. It had its Chairman working with
senior staff from an office, inappropriately named Stornoway House in
London, long before the Glasgow HQ was leased, let alone manned.

The SNP had induced panic amongst both the Labour and Conservative
Parties. With an election looming, the SNP had 17 second places. This put
the jobs and careers of many Scottish MPs at risk, so that it became the
pattern that the SNP Group were mocked, derided and insulted at every
turn. It was especially interesting to see how both the Labour and Tory MPs
united to exude bile on the SNP MPs. This was particularly evident during
Scottish Questions.

As to how the MPs performed, the SNP research bulletin for October
1974 (Vol. 4 No. 3) read:

> 'In a recent edition of the B.B.C. radio programme, 'The
> World Tonight', Stewart MacLachlan, Political Editor of
> the Daily Record and P.R. Adviser to the Labour Party in
> Scotland, said that a major reason for expectations of
> further S.N.P. gains was the impressive way in which
> our M.P.s had conducted themselves in the Commons
> and their outstanding record as constituency
> representatives.'

And he further commented on tactics:

> 'In the Commons, the aim of the SNP members has
> been to support the Labour Government to the point
> of allowing it to govern but seeking to modify the more
> extreme and centralist of Government proposals. This
> has meant that, unlike previous parliaments where

opposition M.P.s of all parties have tended to vote against the government than for it, (albeit) for different reasons, this particular session has seen more SNP votes for than against the government. Such support has not been given unconditionally, and there have been notable attempts by the Government to accommodate Scottish opinion in order to win SNP support.'

The parliament meandered to a close. On the day of its adjournment, the Commons rose early, the place emptied, the lights dimmed and I was left hanging on till the time came to take the night sleeper. By chance, I met Walter Harrison, the deputy Government Chief Whip who told me that if I had time, I should go to the Lords as something of interest would take place. So, having nothing better to do, I went to the Lords which unlike the Commons section was in session and brightly lit. In came a number of Lords in robes and wearing antiquated tricorn or bicorn hats. They sat on chairs laid out before the throne and listened to the reading of their commission from the Crown. Then, the principal clerk read out the name of each parliamentary bill ranging from the Finance Bill to the Lochmaddy Harbour Confirmation Order Bill. At each listing, the commissioners doffed their hats to intimate the royal assent and the clerk intoned in Norman French – 'La Reine Le Veult'. At that point, and only then, in this quaint ceremony did a bill become an act of parliament. Little had I thought as a law student lectured on the theory of the Queen in Parliament that twenty years later, I would see it put into practice.

During the session, from 6 March to 31 July, 1974, the SNP participated in 67.9% of the divisions (the Group did not usually vote on English and other non-relevant measures or attend for private business on Fridays). In preparation for the election, we had drawn up a record of voting patterns. The MPs knew they would be accused of voting for one side or another, regardless of the facts, and sure enough, the main plank in the Labour attack at factory meetings in Dundee in the October election was that I always voted with the Tories!

Analysis

SNP Votes

with Government	66.2%
with Conservatives	21.6%
with others only	6.8%
free vote	5.4%

The real work began after the October 1974 election when 11 SNP MPs were returned. No seats were lost and there were four new members to share the work load and form 'Scotland's First Eleven' – or so they were described by the Press. The new arrivals were an interesting bunch. Senior amongst them in Party terms was Douglas Crawford (Perth & East Perthshire). Douglas had been an industrial correspondent with the Glasgow Herald and associated with the Scottish Council (Development & Industry) as Editor of their magazine. He had served as Director of Communications to the Party and was Executive Vice Chairman for Publicity. His specialty was economic and industrial affairs. Douglas could be excitable, but when it came to amendments, he was indefatigable and ingenious.

Margaret Bain's election with a majority of 22 was a bolt out of the blue – although when her husband, Donald had claimed that East Dunbartonshire was winnable, I had exercised my usual lawyer's disbelief. She was the youngest of the Group and if Margo MacDonald had been the SNP's 'blonde bombshell', she was immediately displaced by 'the dolly-bird' tag placed on Margaret by the tabloid media. Margaret had one of the keenest political brains in the Group. She kept indifferent health and she was one of the most courageous and least self-interested people I have met. She was sympathetic and kind – and a natural for the brief of social services. Soon after she was elected, I met her parents at Westminster and was rocked back on my heels by a request that I should look after her. At the age of 36, I had not regarded myself as particularly avuncular. Happily, Margaret was well able to look after herself, although she encountered personal distress during the parliament with the break-up of her marriage. With a tiny majority, she never let personal considerations get in the way of doing the right thing by the Group.

Another unexpected arrival, with a small majority of 30, was George Thompson who won Galloway from the Conservatives. I had met George at Edinburgh University where he was a member of the Nationalist Club. He had been a mature student who had a brilliant record. He spoke around seven languages and, indeed, I once met him on a visit to Paris where he was studying Russian through the medium of French! He came as a shock to the Commons. With his slow delivery in a broad Gallovidian accent, George Thompson sounded as if he was 'from the sticks' and easy meat. Very shortly, the Tory MPs, in particular, were confounded by his erudition and wit. George played a special role in the Group. Like Margaret, he was not in fear of his small majority. He was the epitome of the reasonable man. Whenever the Group divided equally on some contentious matter, George had the casting vote. He was very rarely wrong.

Last of the team was Andrew Welsh who, along with Malcolm Slesser in February, had smashed a huge Conservative majority to win South Angus. I was one of the few who had met him, partly because he was a constituency neighbour of mine and partly because he had consulted me previously when I was National Secretary. Andrew, a teacher, was at home with both education and local government. He was one of life's enthusiasts with the extra virtues of being reliable and hard working. No task would be beyond him.

If I said that this was the most talented Group in the Commons, this would have been an exaggeration. As I found out, there were many outstanding performers there, although there was also a lot of dross, too. Nevertheless, many media observers were sure that there was a great deal of talent and energy in the SNP 'First Eleven'. They questioned rather whether the SNP had the discipline and common interest to survive the tensions and stresses of life at Westminster and whether the Group would fall prey to votes along 'left' and 'right' issues. For the time being, the Government had a slim majority and the pressure of holding the balance of power as in the case of the parliament from March to October 1974, had eased.

On the other side of the equation, the SNP occupied a pivotal position in Scotland. We had sustained and exceeded the advances made in February 1974. In addition to the 11 MPs, there were also 42 second places and 32% of the vote – the Labour and Tory Parties were desperate. If the Government lost its majority, there could be a third general election and the prospect of wholesale losses of seats. There were problems enough facing the British government over the economy and the country's poor financial position, without the worry that Scotland with all its oil could secede from the UK. Outside parliament, the SNP was a major force, rapidly expanding its organisational base. There was expectation that a new era had begun – that Scotland could become independent. At the very least, it was assumed that the government had no choice but to deliver a directly elected Scottish Assembly and much of the debate was along the lines of how extensive would be its powers and how would it be financed. For the time being, the SNP had destroyed the notion that the Union was safe. The debate now followed a nationalist agenda.

Chapter 10

The Battle at Westminster

The advent of a large parliamentary group altered the balance of power within the Party. By dint of their victories, the MPs were not isolated within the Party at large. Their victories had won them respect and influence. Their constituencies had large memberships and numerous branches so that they could command considerable delegate voting power at Council and Conference. The MPs, too, were not necessarily united on policy matters and frequently took decisions by narrow votes. But from October 1974 onwards, the Party had to come to terms with a parliamentary group not elected by the Party as a whole and to accept, sometimes very unwillingly, that the Group had to work in a context where it did not choose the agenda. In the Commons, often at very short notice that did not allow for consultation, it had to vote tactically on policy issues. On some of these questions, there would be no SNP policy or where there was, it could not be easily adapted. The SNP's policy and decision making structures were far too ponderous and slow. By the time the monthly National Executive, the quarterly National Council or Annual Conference had come to a view, the issue would long have been settled to the political advantage or disadvantage of the SNP.

The starting point of the MPs was the October 1974 Manifesto. With the title, 'Scotland's Future', it was described as an introduction to a practical programme of social justice for the people of Scotland. The preface read:

> 'This booklet sets out the case for self-government with a parliament of real power, worthy of the people of Scotland. It illustrates some of the exciting possibilities in choosing the full responsibilities of Scottish nationhood; it shows how the wealth of the oil and gas fields of the Scottish coast, added to other natural resources and assets offers opportunities for greatly improved living standards to the people of Scotland – when they have a *Scottish Government*.
> Only then can they make Scotland a place of which they can be really proud, a place
> - where there is full employment and where wealth is distributed fairly to give everybody a decent house and good opportunities for education and employment and contentment
> - where individuals and communities are protected from exploitation - where compassionate sharing

motivates the social services
- which lets us take our share of international
responsibilities in the councils of the world.

The Scotland which we seek will be created only by
electing a Scottish Parliament, and by no other means.
To win support for this proposal and to make it
effective we must first elect MPs of the only party
which is committed to a Scottish parliament and full
self-government – the Scottish National Party.'

The Manifesto then gave an explicit description of the programme as
'social democratic'.[1] This was the first time the Party had used this term to
describe its policy and in doing so adopted a declared moderate left of
centre stance. It was pretty safe to do so. Social democracy had a multitude
of meanings in those days. Most of them applied to politics in mainland
Europe and the term had little resonance in the UK. Nevertheless, the
political Rubicon had been crossed. Billy Wolfe, who wrote the Manifesto,
acted with the support of the office-bearers who approved and amended
the text or passed it by acquiescence.

The Manifesto was based on the body of policy that had been developed
during the sixties. The Party gave a pledge to diffuse political power and to
'reverse the harmful effects of the centralising forces which have been at
work in government and industry and finance, controlling Scotland from
outside it'.[2] There was a detailed discussion of the democratic road to self-
government with a description of our constitutional proposals. In relation to
landownership, there were provisions for control of land that left it possible
for non-resident companies to own or lease their premises and non-citizen
individuals to own their houses. Land use was to be regulated by a Land Use
Commission with elected bodies at community level.

At international level, the SNP maintained its opposition to British entry
to the Common Market and was opposed in principle to the centralised
thinking inherent in the Treaty of Rome. It reserved the right to a Scottish
Government to hold a referendum on Scottish membership of Europe.[3] For
defence, the SNP was in favour of collective action by Western Europe and
there was no reference to NATO. The SNP declared that it did not wish
Scotland to have nuclear weapons or bases on Scottish soil or in Scottish
territorial waters.

The Manifesto had a substantial section on energy and envisaged setting
up a Scottish Coal Board to take over from the NCB in Scotland, to establish
an Oil Investment Corporation and a National Oil Company.[4] There were
avant garde proposals for energy capture from wind and wave power and

no opposition to civil nuclear power. Indeed, at this stage, the Party favoured international research into nuclear and other forms of energy and was pledged to continue work at Dounreay and Chapelcross 'atomic' plants.

With regard to industry, there was to be an Industrial Development Corporation. The party did not object to nationalisation so long as it was on a Scottish basis and was non-centralising. If anything, the policy had tinges of syndicalism with its demands for workers councils and election of workers' directors. The industrial proposals accepted the need for equal pay and a national minimum wage. There was a diatribe against centralised control from London and Brussels.

Later, the SNP displayed its new 'social democratic' credentials with substantial sections on welfare and the war on poverty. With new figures from the UK National Children's Bureau showing one child in ten to be 'socially disadvantaged' compared with one in sixteen in the UK as a whole, there was a powerful new compulsion for action.

Agriculture, fishing and forestry were all marked for expansion, while there were proposals for education, housing, the arts and broadcasting. Throughout the Manifesto, the key themes were social justice, development and decentralisation, all of which were linked to the winning of self-government.

Consequent to the election, the MPs re-jigged the spokesmen on 14 October with this result:

Energy and Oil	Gordon Wilson
Employment	Douglas Henderson
Scottish Assembly	George Reid
Finance and Industry	Douglas Crawford
Education and Social Services	Margaret Bain
Local Government and Transport	Iain MacCormick
Agriculture and Fisheries	Hamish Watt
Housing	Andrew Welsh
Health	George Thompson

The National Executive Committee met on 18 October 1974 and immediately dismissed by 11 votes to 3 a request from the MPs (10 votes to 1 against) that the Party should nominate representatives for peerages. It also made the recommendation that no SNP member should accept nomination.[5] More importantly, it received a request for funds for the employment of an office manager to run the Group at Westminster and one or two part-time secretaries, and the purchase of equipment. Although Margaret Bain, Douglas Henderson, George Reid, George Thompson, Hamish Watt, Andrew Welsh and I had been appointed as members of the

NEC by the Group, there was anxiety regarding the need of the Party to be kept in touch with what was happening in London and for full consultation on issues such as the Common Market. By December, further requests were made to the MPs for weekly or more frequent reports, although the financing of staff was held up by the announcement that the Group might be offered £9,700 from parliamentary funds for research and administration.[6] The Party was expanding rapidly (58 new branches recognised in December), but so was its staff and although immediate finance was given for the office manager, the Party tried unsuccessfully to claim part of the parliamentary allowance to cross-subsidise its Research Department that was giving much needed back up to the MPs.

At the London end, the position was just as critical since time rarely allowed regular contact with HQ in Edinburgh. On October 30, 1974, the Group appointed Andrew Welsh to phone HQ daily and to be the conduit. Douglas Crawford was to liaise with the Press Office for a two-way supply of press releases. It was also recommended that the Party Chairman should visit the Group for important business and this commenced on 12 November at a meeting with Gwynfor Evans MP, leader of the Plaid Cymru Group (composed of himself, Dafydd Wigley and Dafydd Elis Thomas), who proposed a united group. This would have knock on effects on party political broadcast entitlements since we would move to a potentially less advantageous UK basis and it was eventually agreed to invite a Plaid representative to join Group meetings to discuss the Business of the House. Both Donald Stewart and Gwynfor Evans were to make joint representations to the broadcasters with regard to media time. When Margaret Bain, at the December meeting of the NEC, raised the question of the MPs spending more time in Scotland, the general feeling was that this should not be done to the detriment of their activities in the Westminster Parliament.[7]

The first major task of the MPs was to respond to the new Queen's Speech and for the new members to make their maiden speeches. After Donald Stewart had spoken on the need for oil revenues to fund the SDA, controls over oil extraction, transport and welfare and social matters, he was followed by George Thompson on problems of young people and local matters. On the next day (30 October), Douglas Crawford covered the Scottish economy, including the strength of Scotland's balance of payments and on the day following, Andrew Welsh focussed attention on the advances made by the SNP and the need for action to deal with child poverty. Margaret Bain kept her powder dry for a major speech on the Social Security (Amendment) Bill.

This time there was no prospect of a Government defeat. After a speech by George Reid explaining we were against further centralisation, the Group voted for an official opposition amendment against more British nationalisation that was defeated by 310 votes to 296. Our amendment on oil was not selected, and the Group abstained on the motion to approve the Government proposals. The main Government motion was carried by 319 votes to 268.

Almost immediately, the SNP received its baptism of fire. In the second reading of the Offshore Petroleum Development (Scotland) Bill, it ran into a barrage of sustained and scathing criticism regarding almost every aspect of our oil policy, with much of the attack coming from John Smith, a junior energy minister. The Tories were not far behind. Although we battled to the end and emerged safely, if verbally battered and bruised, the scale of the attack had not been anticipated and our failure to anticipate it was a sign of naivety. It was a significant part of our learning curve. Nothing daunted, I framed a large number of amendments and in the ensuing exchanges on the floor of the House, during the Committee Stage, all was constructive with some of our amendments being accepted. On others, we divided the House although, when the Group reviewed the proceedings, I complained that too much of the drafting had been done by me; and other MPs felt that they should have had a battle plan, indicating which amendments would be pressed.[8] We were still in the early stages of learning, made obvious by SNP MPs going into different lobbies on a defence motion and facing both ways on the Local Government (Scotland) Bill where there was a split in the Group. And as the autumn session drew to a close, I found myself a member of the Oil Taxation Bill Committee.

This Bill was an eye-opener. I missed a few December sessions due to illness and resumed membership when the Commons re-assembled in January. Apart from the on-going fight with the Unionist Parties over oil, new adversaries had appeared on the scene fighting both Scotland and London to secure the maximum benefits from the resource. These were the major oil companies, both international and domestic. As Donald Bain reported after the October election, there were pressures we found difficulty in resisting.[9]

> 'Current research preoccupations are with oil and the Common Market. The need to remain up to date with our oil research is illustrated by the sheer financial muscle of the latest oil company campaign to convince the UK populace, and more especially, their politicians that the oil industry is in the North Sea for purely philanthropic reasons. Even if I were to devote my efforts exclusively to this area of research the manpower reserves, media access and financial resources of the oil company campaign are such that

to date we have been able to do little more than riding the punches coming our way. In this phase of the struggle we are faced with much more powerful, ruthless and intellectually well equipped opponents than we have had to face in our last skirmishes with British Governments and other political parties. Fortunately, we do seem to be making some progress with obtaining assistance from individuals engaged in petroleum research within industry, finance and the academic world (always remembering that some offers of assistance must be viewed with caution) and I hope to make maximum use of such help in the coming months. Specifically, I hope to prepare a booklet of 'accumulated wisdom' comprising short summaries by different experts of different aspects of the oil industry (e.g. production costs, future price trends etc) plus statistics.'

Through the means of the Oil Taxation Bill, the Government were endeavouring to put in place Petroleum Revenue Tax (PRT) to fill the vacuum left by the outgoing Conservative administration which had been savaged by a Report of the Public Accounts Committee earlier in the year for its negligence in failing to bring in a new taxation regime so that the British state could take some benefit from the development of the northern oil and gas fields in the North Sea.

Not having been on a Standing Committee before, I was surprised there were no prior briefings from the Ministry of Energy. Instead, as we ploughed slowly through the legislation line by line, I had to rely on the speeches made by Government Ministers. As I discovered later in non-oil legislation, this was standard as Committees normally had an inbuilt majority and the Government backbenchers were there only to vote, hopefully not to speak and certainly never to think! But oil legislation was different. As soon as the preliminaries were over, I received a stream of briefing statements from the oil companies. These presented amendments in an easily digested form, containing the text of the suggested amendment, an explanation of its meaning and reasons why it should be adopted.

This bore out what Donald Bain had warned. The oil companies spared no cost in striving to adapt the Bill to give them the maximum return on their investment. Sometimes, the efforts were so blatant as to cause derision – at least to me as the sole independent member of the Committee to whom the oil companies unwisely forwarded the documents believing that I was a member of the opposition, whereas on the tax issue I was more radical than the Government. For example, BP produced amendments claiming that the taxation scheme should be altered to encourage the companies to develop marginal fields. All very well, except their interest was to reduce taxation on the Forties Field, then the biggest oil reservoir discovered. The oil companies must have been delighted when the Conservative Opposition adopted many of their suggestions and pretended they were their own.

This was the first time high intensity American style lobbying techniques employed for Congress had been used to sway parliamentary decisions. They were only mildly successful. The Government proposals had already gone too far to be accommodating and any non-justified amendments would have been defeated in Committee by the Government MPs and me. But this was not the main weapon in the oil company arsenal. The British Government was close to bankruptcy. The economy was in trouble following the bitter industrial disputes of 1972 and 1973, the abrupt hike in OPEC oil prices and rampant inflation. The Government needed to borrow money. These markets were dominated by the United States and private warnings were issued by the American banks that they would have to downgrade Britain's credit rating unless steps were taken to speed up production of oil, and bring in much needed foreign exchange.

There were indications that the American government was also sympathetic to this view, no doubt after lobbying by the oil companies. The British Government surrendered. The taxation section of the Bill was abruptly removed from the Committee which moved to discuss later technical sections to allow the Government to renegotiate more lenient taxation provisions at Washington. When the Committee reverted to the earlier sections, there were Government amendments diluting the proposed taxation structure – and even there, the oil companies maintained their pressure through a constant service of amendments.

When the Bill returned to the floor of the House for Report (the Stage at which further amendments could be considered), with the assistance of Donald Bain, I put down an amendment to increase the proposed rate of PRT from 45% to 75%. It was an eerie experience. The amendment was taken seriously by Edmund Dell, the Treasury Minister in charge of the Bill. For once I had on site support as Donald sat in the rear gallery and was available like a civil servant to give advice.

From the outset, the Group was aware that there was no room for excessive individualism. The viciousness of the attacks, especially where there was inadvertent confusion in voting (always portrayed as splits), meant that the potential electoral implications could be expensive. So, in January 1975, the Group decided that members should not vote spontaneously where the Division was unexpected, that no information on discussions or decisions of Group Meetings should be released without the authority of the Group and that no member should be permitted to sign motions without the consent of a majority of the Group.[10] Some of these motions would be anodyne; others had the potential to be politically damaging. This was not as draconian as it sounded since at that meeting George Reid was given permission to sign a Motion relating to the Shrewsbury Pickets. The intent was to keep cohesion within the Group in the face of external attack and so that each of us should be aware of what the others were doing as it was not always possible for members on Committees or on the benches waiting to speak or to attend Group Meetings. The decision was ineffective since a week later, there was an argument on the way a decision to vote on Capital Gains Tax had been altered; so the rules were changed again to require a two thirds majority to call another meeting to review a decision and that all such meetings should take place in private. Yet the topic rose once more on 19 February 1975, when it was reported that there had been a split in voting between the Second Reading and Committee Stages of the Local Government (Scotland) Bill. As the Minutes recount[11]:

> 'After a lengthy and detailed discussion, it was decided that the group should have a show of hands to determine the voting decision. The minority was to have the right to abstain. Results: Three votes for the Opposition. Seven votes for the Government.'

Other disputes arose over the closed shop in the Trade Union and Labour Relations Bill in October 1975. While a final decision was postponed to obtain the views of George Reid, it was agreed to vote for an amendment excluding editors of newspapers from compulsory membership of a trade union, but if there was no amendment, the Group, with Donald Stewart dissenting and being given the right to abstain, agreed to support the principle of the 'closed shop'. At a subsequent meeting, the Group resolved to vote with the Government on all the main stages.

By now the SNP MPs had been pitch-forked right into social and economic legislation for which they had no cover either from the Manifesto or detailed policy. We were competing on the territory of the Labour and Conservative Parties. It was their battlefield – not ours. Whereas the Government had control of legislation, the Tories as principal opposition party were able to promote motions and amendments that defined their position. No such right was open to the SNP, Plaid Cymru or the Liberals to explain why we were voting for some proposition or other we had not sponsored – decisions that could be misconstrued or reverberate at home – and where abstention of the Group was not an option. The best we could do was to put down amendments which might or might not be taken and to hold press conferences in major cases. This was true particularly in relation to the Industry Bill setting up the Scottish Development Agency where Douglas Crawford lodged 280 amendments, mainly to equip the SDA with substantial powers not offered by the Government. He was also dealing with the Finance Bill, in itself a major task.

Socially, the Group also benefited from the incessant attacks as it brought us together for meals or drinks. It was recognised that the weight on the Chief Whip was too heavy and Hamish Watt was elected Deputy Chief Whip to strengthen Group administration. Additionally, the MPs recognised they had a duty to the Party at home. There was a discussion as to how best to spend time in the House and by mid January 1975 it was agreed, with immediate effect, that at least one member of the Group should spend the greater part of the week in Scotland to assist the Party in propaganda activities. A start was made by proposing that Douglas Crawford should meet the Chrysler shop stewards in Paisley. MPs were asked to provide Conveners for the National Assembly and George Reid agreed to chair broadcasting, Hamish Watt fisheries, Douglas Crawford finance and industry and Margaret Bain education, all of which meant a considerable workload. As a testimony of the Party's appreciation, the Group learnt that there were seven resolutions for the Conference saying that no MP should be able to stand for election to the NEC! With MPs having five appointed members and the prospect of standing for Party office, the resolutions were not unreasonable, but they gave a hint that there was some unrest at the influence the MPs enjoyed.

The problem was that the success of the Party in October 1974 was so great that too much was expected of the MPs. Battling away in the obscurity of the Westminster Committee Corridor on matters of detail did not bring much reward politically. Equally, failure to do the work would have led to adverse criticism of the Party and undermined the chances of those who wished to be elected at the next election – and that was in addition to the prospects for the MPs in their own re-election.

The MPs were not satisfied that they were making sufficient strategic impact and earmarked part of the Easter recess week-end to meet at Cambridge University to review all their activities. Just beforehand, Robert McIntyre visited the Group from the NEC. While congratulating us for our hard work, he spoke of the problems of communicating this work back to the people of Scotland. He contrasted the need to deal with special situations such as the EEC, Scottish Aviation, local government or the health boards as opposed to the self-government issue and the requirement to give Scotland a political and philosophical lead.

It was agreed that communication was the principal, practical priority and with the money designed to assist all the Opposition Parties with administrative and research support at last coming through, it was possible to engage Agnes Samuel as office manager in April 1975 and to recruit up to two researchers. The summer business passed in a rush with many late night sessions. I had been scheduled to speak at Oxford University and was replaced by Iain MacCormick to take over the more onerous, and less exciting, task of the Petroleum and Submarine Pipelines Bill, the last of the Government's major oil bills. This Bill had the support of the SNP at Second Reading and I was appointed to the Standing Committee which met intensively during the hot, sticky days of the London summer. The Committee met morning, afternoon and night. Apart from the hard work, it featured an innocent error on my part. While enjoying a pint on the terracing before the evening session with John Smith, the junior minister and others, John was complaining that the Tories were dragging out the proceedings. Incautiously, I told him that he was far too abrasive. Treating their amendments with contempt put their backs up. Alas, when we returned for the late night session, John Smith started lavishing flattery in large dollops. The Tories lapped it up. Having their amendment praised made it easier for them to accept its rejection. Sadly, I had helped project the career of a man who was to become Leader of the Labour Party – definitely not what I had intended!

As the summer session ended, Duncan MacLaren and Helen Finnie had been appointed as researchers and a weekly publication 'Contact' was in production for a trial run. We had succeeded also in having Winifred Ewing appointed as a member of the British delegation to the European parliament, in preference to a Liberal nominee, establishing a link that was to pay dividends in years to come. There was still a problem in getting the exposure in the Scottish media that the Party wanted. It was increasingly clear that the SNP faced a major difficulty in its membership of Scottish Standing Committees (these being the committees with a varying membership that handled the committee stages of Scottish Bills). We were rationed to one member, with the remaining members drawn from the Labour, Conservative and Liberal Parties). In this, we were also treated the same way as the Liberals, with the difference that while no one paid the slightest attention to the Liberal MPs, we were under constant sniping. Having two MPs would have made all the difference and this was particularly evident when we later obtained our first opportunity to choose the subject of debate in the Scottish Grand Committee. Douglas Crawford led off to a barrage of criticism, including the trivial one of the length of his speech. This time, I had the opportunity to sum up and dismiss those few criticisms that were worthy of attention.

By the end of the session and with a division record of 74.6%, the new Group had established a pattern of voting in circumstances where the Government had a majority.

Analysis for 1974/75

SNP Votes

with government	37.7%
with opposition	49%
with others only	10.9%
free vote	2.3%

The session for 1975/76 opened with the Queen's Speech. For once this was not the dominating issue as the White Paper on Devolution was due to be published at the end of November. It could not be ignored so the Group put forward amendments on devolution, oil and industry with major speeches scheduled to be made by Donald Stewart on devolution, Douglas Crawford on industry and George Reid on the delays in advancing legislation for the Scottish Assembly. Despite protests by Douglas Henderson and Douglas Crawford on points of order at the preference given to the Liberals whose amendment had been endorsed by fewer MPs, an amendment professing no confidence in the Government was not selected and the Group voted against the Speech as a whole as unanimously agreed in advance. And while other members of the Group spoke on the White Paper on Devolution and took part in a series of Press Conferences in Scotland and London, I became involved in the nightmare of the Aircraft & Shipbuilding Industries Bill, a highly controversial nationalising measure.

In March 1976, Hamish Watt succeeded Douglas Henderson as Chief Whip. Douglas had worked wonders since the February 1974 Election. Margaret Bain and Andrew Welsh were elected as his assistants. We also won a concession from the Committee of Selection that the SNP would be guaranteed membership of every Scottish Committee. In other ways, too, the growing influence of the SNP at Westminster was noted. The SNP was allotted a Supply Day jointly with Plaid Cymru where each party could choose the subject of a half day debate on the floor of the House. The SNP took the Scottish economy as its topic. Donald Stewart led the debate with a general attack on the mismanagement of the Scottish economy and the failure of economic policy. Douglas Crawford summed up amidst a barrage of insults from Scottish Labour MPs that he was a Tory and a racist, so much so that the Speaker had to intervene to curb 'unparliamentary' expressions and then Douglas got his own back by describing them as acting like Uriah Heep in their approaches to London!

Iain MacCormick had also won a place in the Ballot for Private Members' Bills. He chose divorce law reform and, with the help of the Scottish Office, steered the Bill into law. The Bill represented a major change in the grounds for which divorce could be obtained and was based on Scottish Law Commission proposals. It was a substantial achievement, being the first piece of legislation piloted by an SNP Member. In debate, George Reid questioned whether it went far enough, so that Iain learned that, on non-party political bills, you could not always expect 100% support from your parliamentary friends!

All this was set against the financial crisis where the SNP joined Labour rebels to defeat the government on public expenditure cuts and cause jitters about an early election. The SNP – and a Times leader - were sanguine regarding the outcome. The Times wrote[12]:

> 'The position of the two most important minor parties has changed since the last election in a way damaging to Labour: the Scottish Nationalists are stronger and the Liberals are weaker. The Scottish National Party would certainly be expected to take a number of Labour seats in Scotland, possibly fifteen.
>
> The most likely result of an early election would be that there would be no overall majority; the Scottish Nationalists might well hold the balance against any combination of other parties, except for a coalition of the two major parties. There is no obvious reason to expect this prospect to change in favour of the Labour Party. The new leader whoever he is, will therefore suffer from the very important constraint that he cannot go to the country at an early date without the probable loss of office, and must look forward to the probability of a hung parliament resulting from whenever he chooses to go to the country.'

Already, Donald Stewart was the longest serving of the parliamentary leaders with Conservative Edward Heath having been earlier replaced by Margaret Thatcher, Liberal Jeremy Thorpe by David Steel and Prime Minister Harold Wilson by James Callaghan. And the Government's lead was fragile.

By the end of the 1975/76 session, the SNP had participated in 285 divisions, 66% of the total.

Analysis for 1975/76

SNP votes

with government	35.4%
with opposition	45.6%
with others only	7.7%
free vote	11.3%

Prior to the opening of the 1976/77 session of Parliament, George Reid went out on a limb. Speaking at Oxford University on 12 November 1976[13], he said that Margaret Thatcher could not count on the SNP 'automatically' to vote the Government down. 'We are in nobody's pocket, and certainly not hers. In the present delicate stage of Westminster politics, our votes will be determined by one factor only: whether they will benefit the people of Scotland or not.' He then explained, while warning of the danger of Margaret Thatcher, why he would thole another year of Labour Government:

> 'First, because I believe the Tories would make an even greater mess of the economic situation, and bring head on confrontation with the trade unions.
> And second, because the SNP should want to get the Labour Government fixed firmly on the hook. Whether they get their Devolution Bill through or not is irrelevant to the needs of Scotland. But at least it is a start to the transfer of power north of the border. If they succeed, half a loaf is better than no loaf at all. If they fail, their Manifesto promises will seem to be utterly meaningless and they will be wiped out in their Scottish seats.

The main promise for Scotland in the Queen's Speech was the production of a devolution bill. As usual, the Commons was to be choked with legislation or, as Donald Stewart put it, 'But we find that the Westminster sausage machine is prepared to grind on as in the past.' He welcomed the devolution bill while regretting the Assembly's lack of powers. The devolution bill could be 'the catalyst to effect real social and economic change in Scotland', but not if the terms were as outlined in the White Paper. Pointing out that the King's Speech of 1945 had promised home rule, that Labour had been in power for 14 years since then and that almost 10 years had elapsed since the setting up of the Commission on the Constitution, he observed with wry humour:

'If that is the time that it takes between consultation and getting a Bill before the House, no wonder the dry rot has set in and this place is falling to bits.'

He closed by calling on the Tory Party to spell out its policy on devolution – as well he might since the Conservatives had been playing for time since the election of Margaret Thatcher as Party leader. Douglas Crawford the following day had to deny press reports in reaction to George Reid's speech that we were split; we were, he said, like the Party at home, in wishing an early General Election which will pave the way towards a sovereign Scotland.

For the next few weeks the Group was at full stretch on a rota with speakers and bench duty as the Scotland & Wales Bill passed its second reading and moved into interminable committee sessions on the floor of the House while both Labour and Tory members endeavoured to talk it out. During this period, MPs also spent time on lobbying duties, as there was intense international interest in the SNP and the processes of devolution. There had been a response from 27 Embassies to a briefing paper George Reid had distributed. Iain MacCormick and Hamish Watt met five ambassadors. Douglas Crawford lunched with Bank of England officials. George Reid met the Bulgarian Ambassador and I met Norwegian Ministers and the Libyan Ambassador. This latter meeting was in the Libyan Embassy and as I arrived at the door, I could sense the clicking of the cameras by the British security services. Libya, of course, had been accused of shipping arms to the IRA. Plaid Cymru officials had already caused embarrassment to their Party by visiting Libya and getting the gift of an electric typewriter and a rather derisory deal for Welsh sheep farmers. The meeting with the Ambassador took the form of a very courteous chat over coffee when I explained why devolution was being debated in the Commons. When I was asked if there were any needs, I quickly said 'no'. If Libya had not been a 'pariah' state, then I would have asked for introductions to OAPEC (the Organisation of Arab Petroleum Exporting States). But certainly not from Libya – the political price would have been too expensive!

In January 1977, Iain MacCormick replaced Andrew Welsh as Deputy Chief Whip and with the departure of Duncan MacLaren to be the SNP Press Officer in Edinburgh, Graeme Purves was appointed a researcher. George Reid was chosen to serve as a minority party representative to the Council of Europe (after conclusion of negotiations by Hamish Watt with Plaid Cymru and the Ulster Unionists over substitutes). There was a lull following the failure of the devolution guillotine motion and the Group had to deal with bread and butter issues like the Finance Bill, debates in the Scottish Grand Committee, the Coal Bill and others. Margaret Bain guided the Group through the Price Commission Bill, on which the MPs abstained at Third Reading.

George Thompson tested Harry Ewing, the Minister with amendments in the Committee Stage of the Marriage (Scotland) Bill. In June 1977, Agnes Samuel left to take on the job of National Organising Secretary with the Party.

In the spring, the Queen received Addresses in Westminster Hall – the ancient part of Westminster where William Wallace had stood trial - from both Houses of Parliament to celebrate her Silver Jubilee of coming to the throne. In her speech, she made a direct attack on the nationalist movement when she stated that she had been crowned Queen of the United Kingdom. At the time, we believed that the speech had been written for her by 10 Downing Street as is usually the case. There are now indications that the first draft from the Palace contained the damaging reference, corroborated by her unusual decision to take the Household Cavalry on parade with her through Glasgow several months later. Of course it might have been from innocence – but this is a virtue not normally ascribed to the Palace or Downing Street.

The British establishment was in a panic and it would not be surprising if a conscious decision was taken to play the Orange card. Perhaps the greater strength of the loyalist movement in and around Glasgow was the reason why this city was chosen rather than Edinburgh, the Scottish capital, for manifestation of the majesty of the British Sovereign. Immediately on hearing the reference in the Speech, I was aware of its importance. The Queen was intervening in domestic politics on behalf of the unionist cause. It was a radical, if not desperate, step for the monarchy had long been politically neutral and it was clearly aimed towards buttressing opposition to the SNP – and not just in Orange circles. It was calculated to cause those loyal to the Queen throughout Scotland and not sure of the SNP to stop and take stock. Whether the comment originated with the Queen or the Prime Minister is of passing historical interest. It certainly buttresses the view that in 1977, the British state was in a panic at the prospect of Scotland with its vast oil wealth leaving the Union.

My first inclination was to play possum and let the attack pass over unnoticed in the hope that the statement would have no impact. Donald Stewart saw it differently – to him it was a matter of principle - and before I could discuss it with him, he had launched a verbal counter-attack on the Queen by publicly warning her that her rule was based on consent of the Scottish people. Winnie Ewing was strongly of the same mind.

I agreed wholeheartedly with the constitutional basis of his case, but in this instance would have preferred it not said, as the Scottish press gave it a splash the following day. I thought it had no continuing impact; my wife, Edith who viewed things from a different perspective thought otherwise. She noticed a neighbour running up the union flag on her washing line opposite our house, and believed it was a tipping point for unionists. She was probably right. When the main aim of a political party is attacked by a supposedly neutral monarch, it is significant. From small ripples, waves can develop and it was the first serious check the SNP had received. It was also a reminder, if we ever needed one, that the British state was not taking the challenge lying down.

Over 7 to 14 June 1977, Douglas Crawford made a visit to the US, funded by the New York and Canadian Associations of the SNP. In the crowded schedule, he had lunch at the UN with the Norwegian, Swedish and Iceland Ambassadors, had dinner with senior bank and oil company executives, meetings at Congress, the State Department, privately at branches of the IMF and the World Bank in Washington, lunch at the Canadian Parliament in Ottawa and held several press conferences.

Later in the month, I went on an energy related visit to the United States, funded by the German Marshall Fund, established by the German Government in the US to honour the memory of American General Marshall who had masterminded the recovery of Germany and Western Europe after the war. The delegation consisted of British, German and Norwegian members of parliament and there were some heavy discussion sessions and visits to Congress. Each of us was twinned with an American congressman and we were expected to leave Washington with our congressman to visit his district. I was linked with Paul Tsongas from Massachusetts who was on the liberal wing of the Democratic Party. He represented a District that took in the up-market areas of Concord and Lexington, the birth places of the American Revolution – highly suitable for a nationalist like me – and Lowell and Lawrence, two cotton mill towns whose industries were on the rocks rather like the jute trade in Dundee. In Washington, we were given the honours. The Senate adjourned to meet us. Paul who was minority chairman of a Department of the Interior Energy Sub-committee wanted us to participate with his committee in interviewing the Governor of North Dakota who was to give evidence on exploitation of the huge coal reserves in his state. Paul's Republican colleague agreed. The Clerks were consulted and said there was no precedent. The joint chairmen decided to make a precedent and allowed us to take part after the Congressmen had finished, all with the blessing of the Governor who no doubt scented a good political story. It was a contrast to what would have happened in the moribund, stuffy Commons, bogged down as it was by the weight of superfluous history. There is no way it would have suspended proceedings for a Head of State, let alone a bunch of foreign parliamentarians!

After Washington, we travelled to Boston and stayed in Paul's house – a rather austere experience since his wife remained in Washington to look after a new baby. We visited the historical sites of the revolution and had many engagements. Three events struck home. The Democratic Party organised a breakfast reception and since there were many of Irish extraction, I was surrounded by people protesting gently but volubly about British troops in Ulster. As a nationalist, I had no imperial hang-ups and more remarkably found myself explaining that the troops had been sent to Northern Ireland to defend the catholic population from the loyalist mobs! The second took in a joint project with the Russians to develop nuclear fusion as a source of energy – something still not yet achieved- and a breakfast meeting at the Massachusetts Institute of Technology (MIT) where the scientists, even then, warned that the environmental problems of acid rain from the burning of fossil fuels were nothing compared to the future menace of carbon dioxide that is now central to the issue of global warming.

I took advantage of the visit to have the British Embassy arrange a private visit to Dayton, Ohio to meet senior executives of NCR which had factories in Dundee employing thousands. The corporation was in melt down and there were fears of closure. Conveniently, the company jet was in Washington and as it was due to go empty to Dayton, I was offered a lift on condition I made my own way back. At Dayton, I became aware of the industrial devastation caused by the company's reliance on outdated mechanical technologies. No promises were given and I was told while redundancies would take place, there was scope for a new electronic/mechanical product under development in Dundee. This turned out to be one of the first models of cash dispensers of which the Dundee plant became a world leader in production. On my return to Dundee, I addressed a mass meeting of over a hundred Shop Stewards and told them plainly of what I had learned. In due course, there were huge job losses when the cash till range ended and the City entered an age of rapid industrial decline, but NCR grew again on the back of the auto-teller.

There was supposed to be a return visit with the Europeans playing host, but that never took place. Paul had dinner with me in the House of Commons when he was over on other business. By then, he had ousted a Republican Senator and was junior senator for Massachusetts for a short while before contracting leukaemia. He came back to be a presidential candidate, won Maine in the primaries and retired from the contest. He died a few years later. He was a radical thinker and could have been an influential figure in American politics if his health had allowed it.

The session petered out to a close, enlivened by a searing attack by Douglas Henderson in an important employment debate which, with the aid of their new Liberal allies, the Government won by 312 votes to 282. The year had been dominated by the debates on the Scotland and Wales Bill, the treachery of the Liberals who had helped defeat the guillotine motion on the Bill which had died as a result and the establishment of the Lib/Lab pact that had seen the Government in March, with Liberal support, beat off a Motion of Confidence by 322 votes to 298.

Speaking in the Debate, Donald Stewart said that although he did not doubt the good faith of the Government in trying to put the Bill through, although their motives were different from those of the SNP, they had been frustrated by some members of their own party – 'If the no confidence vote succeeds', he said, 'the hon. Members who voted against the Government on the guillotine, will have dug their own Government's grave.'

Analysis for 1976/77

SNP Votes

with Government	37.0%
with Conservatives	43.0%
with others	10.9%
free vote	9.1%

Again, in the next session for 1977/78, devolution in the forms of separate Scotland and Wales Bills stalked the Commons. The SNP MPs had this additional burden on top of their normal heavy workload. Just six days after the tenth anniversary of her famous victory in Hamilton, Winnie Ewing made the opening speech for the SNP in the Queen's Speech debate, held that year in early November 1977. Brushing aside feeble objections from the Deputy Speaker that her speech should be on industry and commerce, she attacked the record of the Labour and Liberal Parties on the failure of the first Bill and on the timing of the Scotland Bill where she accused the Prime Minister of playing for time. After dealing with Scottish industry, she closed with a declaration of the total adherence of the SNP to the democratically expressed will of the Scottish people.

> 'The national movement will not go away. If the people of Scotland are satisfied with a mini-parliament, that is what they will have. Although we shall go on protesting that they want more, if the Scottish people do not want more we shall not win elections after that. It is a simple matter of democracy.'

George Thompson gave a constructive and humane contribution to the debate on crime and detention. He stressed his strong belief in the need to preserve family life of a prisoner in order that he might return home to a stable home environment upon release. He dwelt on social factors such as multiple deprivation, poor housing and employment as the causes of crime. Donald Stewart summed up on the final day of the debate on the Address.

He pointed out that when Labour had come to power on the slogan 'Back to Work with Labour', unemployment had been 4.1% whereas it now stood at 8.5%. Youth unemployment was especially worrying as in Scotland, 13.3% of teenagers were jobless, compared with 9% for the UK as a whole. He set out priorities for action and concluded:

> 'It is becoming increasingly clear that Scotland's economic, industrial and employment problems will not be solved by outdated and unsuccessful UK policies. What is really needed is the opportunity to use Scotland's wealth in natural resources for a radical new approach to our problems. We are determined that this wealth shall be used to remedy the scars that have been allowed to fester owing to the casual approach of Governments in this place. The next election will show that my Party is the only one that can offer the strength of commitment to foster hope and confidence in Scotland.'

The SNP put down an amendment criticising the failure of the Leader of the Opposition to develop a policy on devolution. As usual, this was not selected for voting – no nationalist amendment was! On the broader question of the economy, the Group supported a Conservative amendment regretting that the Speech contained no proposals for creating long term business confidence essential to reducing unemployment. With Liberal support, the Government had this rejected by 299 votes to 272.

By now Margaret Bain was entrenched as spokesman on shipbuilding and in December, she supported the Government on its proposals to give a subsidy to win a Polish shipbuilding contract. With the aid of the SNP, a Tory motion of censure was easily beaten off. This was followed in February 1978 with the Shipbuilding (Redundancy Payments) Bill, following problems with Swan Hunter – so obviously, nationalisation was not working! In addition to his responsibilities on the Scotland Bill, George Reid had extra work dealing with the electoral system for the European elections under the Direct Elections Bill. As the year progressed, there were debates on steel and fishing. I served on the Community Service by Offenders (Scotland) Bill. George Thompson pursued a crusade against Windscale and nuclear dumping while Douglas Crawford undertook the onerous task of amending his fourth Finance Bill, always a huge job. Hamish Watt, relieved of his duties as Chief Whip, was in a jaunty and active mood. Winnie Ewing concentrated on the European Parliament.

In June 1978, the Government elected to turn a motion of censure on the Chancellor of the Exchequer into a vote of confidence sure in the knowledge that they had the Liberals by the tail. Donald Stewart slammed the Government's policies on Scotland. He attacked the Government for its failure in economic performance, the misuse of the oil resources, the failure of the Government to set up a Scottish Oil Fund, while draining the oil revenues to the Treasury, the scandal of social deprivation and unemployment which had risen from 93,000 in 1974 to 196,000. With the SNP joining the Conservatives and the Ulster Unionists to vote in favour of a censure motion on Denis Healey, the Chancellor of the Exchequer, and with the Liberals and Plaid Cymru abstaining, the Government scraped home by 287 votes to 282.

This was followed on 22 June 1978, by a rare SNP Supply Day where we had framed the following motion:

> 'That this House condemns Her Majesty's Government for its mismanagement of Scotland's oil resources and its refusal to establish an Oil Development Fund for Scotland to be used for restructuring the Scottish economy, encouraging industrial growth and reducing unemployment.'

My speech required careful consideration and research. True, the glory days of the oil campaign were over and the UK Government steadfastly refused to make any concessions to Scotland. Still, my colleagues had chosen the topic over others and we needed every bit of impact we could. I covered all the ground – the failure to maximise jobs from oil related work, the refusal of the Offshore Supplies Office to release figures showing the number of jobs and percentage of work that went to Scottish firms, low taxation, ineffective participation agreements and reckless depletion with no downstream development.

The attack was pursued by Margaret Bain, who concentrated on unemployment, emigration and poverty, saying:

> 'Too much of the burden of the last 150 years of Scotland's history rests on the shoulders of young Scots today. It is disturbing to find that they react with a sense of hopelessness and despair. Today's young Scots are tomorrow's future, and they need investment to change that future from one of despondency to one of hope.'

And adding:

> 'There is no long term Government policy to guarantee a future for West of Scotland for industries such as Singers and shipbuilding.'

Douglas Henderson summed up the debate by alluding to the central problem of tackling Scotland's industrial structure and unemployment. In his own area of Grampian, the Government had cut the local authority grant for oil related development. He warned:

> 'This debate shows the division between those of us who believe that Scotland's resources are the property and right of the people of Scotland and those who believe that they should be controlled from London. There is a polarisation in Scottish society between those who believe fundamentally that the resources and problems of Scotland can be tackled only by Scots responsible to the Scottish electorate and those who believe that Scotland's resources and problems are better managed from London.'

The motion, which was supported by Plaid Cymru and Jim Sillars' Scottish Labour Party was defeated by 131 votes to 14 – so much for the interest the Commons was taking in Scottish Affairs.

It was a heavy week for Margaret Bain who spoke on the Select Committee Report on Violence in the Family and for Iain MacCormick who spoke on the Royal Navy as defence spokesman and made a debut speech as Housing Spokesman, having taken over from Andrew Welsh, now Chief Whip. The SNP voted with the Government.

The session ended with Scottish Grand Committee Debates involving Douglas Henderson, Douglas Crawford, George Thompson, Andrew Welsh, Iain MacCormick and me on such opposition subjects as industry, employment, agriculture, forestry, nuclear energy and housing. The SNP topic was 'The Land of Scotland' in which Donald Stewart, Hamish Watt and Andrew Welsh were nominated to speak. These Scottish Grand Committee debates occurred at the end of the session when most MPs were tired and disgruntled. These were meaningless, mean-minded, incestuous debates given only passing cover in the press. They showed Scotland at its most parochial.

This is, of course, only a taster of the work done. Apart from speeches, the MPs were tied to Westminster by three line whips and speaking duties on the Scotland Bill and voting with Plaid Cymru on the Wales Bill.

Analysis for 1977/78

SNP votes

with Government	63.2%
with Conservatives	17.3%
with others only	11.7%
free vote	7.9%

Chapter 11
Fault Lines

The new session in 1975 sidetracked me into a debate that would take me out of involvement in SNP politics, in Parliament and Edinburgh alike. It started innocuously enough. I had a constituency interest in shipbuilding with the Robb Caledon yard that employed around 1000 men. It had a good reputation for designing complex merchant vessels and a bad one for industrial relations. I had also visited Scottish Aviation in Prestwick and had obtained the assistance of Donald Stewart who had written to the Prime Minister seeking aid for that company. In agreeing to take part in the Aircraft and Shipbuilding Industries Bill designed to nationalise these key industries, I found myself in a parliamentary marathon in a very contentious area.

The SNP lodged a reasoned amendment expressing concern about centralisation and discouragement of industrial decision making within Scotland. As usual, this was not selected for voting so there was no alternative to voting against at Second Reading. When speaking on the Bill on 2 December 1975, I recognised that there were problems with the world economy for shipbuilding and echoed the call by Prof. Kenneth Alexander, Chairman of Govan Shipbuilders for either a subsidy to British shipowners to buy British or to construct ships in advance to meet future demand. I warned that nationalisation was not a guarantee of full employment and would not ensure good management. Scottish Aviation, being a small unit, would like small shipbuilders, be rationalised out of existence. I concluded, having quoted support by the Scottish Council Development and Industry for decentralisation of industrial decision making, with a warning that the Bill removed the opportunity for smaller yards to find their own markets.

The decision of the Group to oppose nationalisation of shipbuilding in Scotland on a British basis was an assertion of long standing policy of the Scottish National Party that there should be the maximum amount of decentralisation and decision making within Scotland. There was no opposition to nationalisation *per se* although it had a poor record of investment and job retention. As with oil and gas, electricity, rail and coal, a policy reaffirmed by a Conference Resolution of 1975[1], we wanted nationalisation to be organised on a Scottish basis and we would have accepted a Scottish Shipbuilding Board without any trouble and indeed, our reasoned amendment set this out clearly.

But we had difficulty in getting this message over. The Trade Union movement wanted nationalisation, so our line on decentralisation was swamped by mobilised opposition from the unions, aided and abetted by Labour whose majority was beginning to dwindle. Soon after the vote, workers at Scottish Aviation passed a vote of no confidence in the SNP –

notwithstanding the efforts that Donald Stewart and I were making on their behalf following my recent visit. This prompted the Group to ask George Thompson to go Prestwick to explain matters. From the point of view of the workforces, their anger and worries were understandable. This was the seventies when nationalisation was still part of the Labour Party programme. The trade unions were extremely powerful with many under Communist leadership at yard level. So, even if the order books in Scotland were reasonably strong, shipbuilding had always been a cyclical industry, swinging from strength to weakness and if it survived, back again; and when in weakness, men's jobs were at stake. With the slowdown of the world economy, it was reckoned that forward orders for both ships and planes would dry up.

None of this impinged on the Party at home at the time although in coming years, some Party members on the left attributed the Party's decline to our votes on the Bill. The SNP was doing well in local elections and the issue of the Scottish Assembly and the deficiencies of the Government's devolution proposals were holding centre stage. The Government was also in the middle of a financial crisis with cuts in public expenditure. The Party was maintaining its profile by running industrial campaigns, such as on steel and factories facing closure. The records show that there was no worry expressed by Margo MacDonald as Senior Vice Chairman and Tom McAlpine, Director of Industrial Campaigns about the shipbuilding vote. Industrial Campaigns found it difficult to find an expert who would write a booklet on shipbuilding policy although one was eventually produced long after the nationalisation controversy. Having said that, one would have to be blind not to recognise that there was heavy pressure from the trade union side that should be addressed and we arranged meetings with Shipbuilding Shop Stewards and the STUC, and on 29 July 1976 – after the votes - Steve Butler, the Industrial Officer advised the NEC in his monthly report:

> 'Without doubt, the major topic over the last two months on the industrial front has been the Shipbuilding and Aircraft Nationalisation Bill, and its stormy passage through the Commons. I attended the two meetings our Parliamentary Delegation had with the Joint Shop Stewards Committee and later the STUC. Both these meetings had one similar topic – Nationalisation of Shipbuilding. The meeting with the Stewards was a very constructive one and should be viewed in the longer term implications of both job security in Shipbuilding, and the effect upon similar workforces in other industries and their attitude to our Party.'

Before the third reading, we produced a special leaflet for shipyards at short notice, and it was distributed at all the yards in Clydeside and Dundee. This was part of a larger campaign to impress upon the workforce the need for a Scottish structure. In retrospect, under attacks from Labour, more effort should have been devoted by the Party to explain why the SNP had opposed the Bill. With MPs from the central belt or the city of Aberdeen which had the Hall Russell shipyard, we would have had the entry to the shipyards that I had in Dundee. Margaret Bain's constituency of East Dunbartonshire was close to the Clyde industry and included shipbuilding technical staff and supervisors, but not so many of the hourly paid workers.

In a perfect political world, the SNP should have kept a low profile over the Bill and reserved its stance for the phases that were dealt with on the floor of the House such as the Second Reading, Report, Third Reading, Guillotine and Lords Amendments. These are usually less contentious, but this Bill was the exception. Almost every stage was charged with controversy. But we had no choice as we had no representation on the Committee of Selection which at that period kept us out of Scottish Committees at times and pushed us on to UK Committees when we did not volunteer. And apart from the Committee stage, the crucial votes involved the whole House of Commons and these could not have been evaded.

On my part, having found myself appointed to the Bill Committee, something I could not refuse without adverse comment, nationally and locally, I had to make the best of it. I took steps to explain the position to the workforce. It was an intimidating experience and I did it twice before the General Election. With a substantial working class membership, Dundee SNP had members in the boat yard. They put out posters for the first lunch time meeting and I turned up with my long range loudspeaking equipment. To my consternation, it failed to work and I ended up encircled by 400 angry shipbuilders. I was perfectly safe - though it did not seem so to begin with. The meeting was run by Harry McLevy, the Convener of Shop Stewards whose affiliation was then to the Communist Party. Harry invited me to speak. I told them that, having spoken to Ministers, I knew that the industry would be rationalised and that as a yard with the worst capital investment in the UK, the Caledon would be marked for closure despite having a good design section. I emphasised my aim was to keep marketing and design in Scotland so that they in Dundee would be masters of their own destiny. I probably did not fully convince them at either meeting, but the fact that I was not scared to come and meet them face to face, paid dividends when several years later, an election meeting at the yard saw many of the men wearing SNP 'stickie' badges.

The Committee ran morning and afternoon for months and with 58 sessions became one of the longest Committees ever to consider legislation.

During the sessions, Richard Wainwright, a Liberal and I struck up a working relationship where we would support most of each other's amendments. On one occasion, delayed by a telephone call, I was three minutes late and believed myself safe since there were several amendments before mine. As I entered the room I heard Richard speaking to an SNP amendment. The Tories, seeing I was absent, had sneakily dropped some of their own. Within a minute I had consulted my notes and taken over from a relieved Richard Wainwright who had not had time to prepare a speech on industrial democracy, but had the initiative and the ability to fill the gap.

The Bill eventually returned to the House on 27 May 1976 in the same centralised form under which control was to be taken away from Scotland. Both Donald Stewart and I spoke amidst criticism from the Minister. Donald had the satisfaction of putting down David Lambie, Labour MP for Central Ayrshire who had suggested that Scottish Aviation would be better off as part of a Scottish unit within British Aerospace by pointing out that he had voted against an SNP amendment calling for the creation of a Scottish division.[2] The SNP voted against the government in the two divisions that followed. The first was a draw (303 each) and the second was won by the Government by 304 votes to 303. The Speaker had to adjourn the House due to 'scenes of great disorder'. The Labour MPs had sung the Red Flag. Michael Heseltine, the Tory spokesman on Industry seized the Mace and swung it about him, living up to his name of 'Tarzan' and there were at least three fist fights.

Occasionally, political fortune smiles! I had taken the sleeper to Glasgow and was the first MP at the Party Conference in Motherwell where I launched into an attack on Westminster and piously claimed these scenes of disorder would never take place in a more civilised Scottish Parliament. The UK media were there in strength and my remarks were carried on all bulletins until the evening. Obviously, a case of the early MP getting the worm and even more obviously, a source of disappointment to colleagues who had travelled by air and arrived later! Despite being a very close and disciplined group, we were still highly competitive. Since I had done the work, it was a just reward.

Debate on the Bill resumed on 20 July. The Government sought a guillotine without which the Bill would have run out of time. We took the view that its long passage was causing problems for the industry and abstained on the guillotine motion which effectively kept the Bill alive. On the ensuing amendments, we voted for exclusion of mobile drilling rigs, for fairness in competition for the remaining private sector, for fairer compensation, in support of Plaid Cymru, to stop the nationalisation of ship repairing and with the government to enable the shipbuilders to have a wider range of activities. With much agitation in the Group where opinions were divided and on the basis of a narrow majority, we had earlier attempted to negotiate with the Government to have last minute concessions on decentralisation. Margaret Bain and I had a meeting with the Minister of State, Gerald Kaufman. Unfortunately, the Government came back with a worthless formula pretending to look after the interests of Scotland and Wales and we were forced to vote against the measure at Third Reading. Worse, Hamish Watt as Chief Whip had received a large number of telegrams from the trade unions, and without consultation, three MPs insensitive to the needs of the Party in the industrialised central belt were seen by the Labour MPs and the Press, tearing up the messages – an act of sublime political folly.

Margaret Bain took over responsibility for Lords Amendments on 22 November 1976 almost a year after the Bill had started its course and dealt with them until the legislation passed in February 1977. In due course of time, British Shipbuilders, comfortably ensconced in Newcastle, wiped out most of the Scottish shipbuilding industry. I have dealt with this legislation in detail. Not only did it tie me up from December 1975 to July 1976 with over 140 hours in Committee and more time on the floor of the Commons, it reduced the amount of time I could spare for involvement in the affairs of the Party and the Parliamentary Group at a pivotal time. In fact, by the time it ended I felt isolated from both. The vote against nationalisation has been interpreted as part of an ideological war between the Group and the NEC. Nothing could be further from the truth. Although the Group was voting in terms of the SNP policy of decentralisation and trying to keep power of decision making within Scotland, there was a split amongst the MPs where decisions were taken on a knife-edge majority. It is a testimony to Group loyalty that the dissenters voted with the majority and in seeking negotiations with the Government, the MPs were aware of the political implications and were ready to compromise, provided that the Government gave some concession on decentralisation in return. By contrast, no complaint was raised at National Council or NEC until the September 1976 meeting of the NEC when Tom McAlpine, Director of Industrial Campaigns merely asked for a simplified explanation of the votes for use by canvassers and others at branch level. The plain fact is that the SNP was still riding high and the eyes of the Party were fixed on devolution which was the issue that dominated the parliament.

This did not prevent personality disputes flaring up and these were aggravated by the Party effectively having three leaderships, one in London, the NEC and Margo MacDonald. Margo, as Senior Vice Chairman was chairman of the Strategy and Tactics Committee, which MPs rarely could attend, especially when meetings were held mid-week. It frequently met with no representative of the Group present. Margo was working to an agenda with the primary aim of the SNP attracting Labour voters. In a memorandum to me of 8 January 1976 (misdated as 1975), she confirmed this, but in the setting that our industrial devolution policies should present them 'as the best and fairest way of ensuring a fair deal for ordinary Scottish people/workers and their families'.[3] That was acceptable so far as it went. The problem was that the Group knew that she was in constant touch with the media and had ample confirmation later when the NEC authorised a refund of telephone expenses of up to £125 a quarter - an astronomical sum for those days - and believed rightly or wrongly that she wished to present the Party as 'socialist'.[4]

So when a report appeared in the Scotsman on 1 April 1976 purportedly claiming 'since the bulk of support for the party, both within and without, was now of an essentially left wing nature, they must now be considered a Socialist party, slightly left of centre', it was widely believed. The early edition of the Scotsman was the one that was read at Westminster and the Tories put down an Early Day Motion, quoting Margo's remarks and notified the Press who contacted the Group for comment. Unfortunately, Billy Wolfe had refused to comment on Margo MacDonald's 'socialist' claim and it was left to Donald Stewart to issue a strong rebuttal.   A minority of the Group, including me, were happy with the 'social democratic' tag that had appeared in the Manifesto – indeed I had agreed its use - but 'socialist' had not been authorised by the Party and at a time when the Tories were recovering, use of the word was gratuitously damaging. The episode was messy. Margo denied having made the statement and objected to her word not having been accepted. The Chairman had managed to get the story cut out of the second edition and phoned Winifred Ewing to explain. This message did not get through and there were problems with the MPs contacting HQ and HQ contacting the Group and Margo MacDonald. In my letter on behalf of the MPs to the Chairman on 8 April 1976, I pointed out that Margo had said on an earlier occasion, after an STUC meeting, that the SNP was part of the Labour movement. While the incident was a storm in a tea cup, it did stick in the minds of the press that there were ideological differences between the MPs and the Party leadership.

It exposed in a revealing manner that there were problems over communications and lack of mutual respect. Even so, two and half years after election of the seven MPs, NEC Minutes were not supplied to those MPs who were not serving on the NEC and by and large, the MPs did not follow what was happening on policy development in the National Assembly. Some MPs did serve as Policy Committee Conveners and their knowledge was specific to their responsibilities. Others had no contact with policy making at sub-assembly level. During the parliamentary recess, it proved possible to hold a joint meeting on 4 September 1976 of the MPs and the National Executive.[5] It was called to discuss communication and reciprocal consultation, tactics and general attitudes to the devolution Bill, contact between the policy committees and the Group, general strategy and a review of the position for a General Election. The meeting was cathartic rather than productive; but it did air complaints and led to better communication – for a while.   Minutes and policy papers were to be provided with an enhanced role given to parliamentary researchers. It was also decided that no impression should be given that we were committed to or satisfied with devolution and that amendments should be made to increase the powers of the Assembly. We should also proclaim as loudly as possible the benefits of independence.

A year later, another row blew up.   It began innocuously at the end of the Conference in May 1977 when Douglas Crawford was alleged to have disclosed a conversation with the Queen. The old problem of communication cropped up. The Party Chairman was contacted by the Press and turned to me for advice as he frequently did and then issued a rebuke in the Press. His fear was the story would grow unless checked. At the National Council in June, a criticism of the Chairman's approach was made by Margaret Bain.[6] He explained that he was unable to contact Douglas Crawford and on hearing that the leak to the Press had not come from Douglas, had given him an apology. Both he and Douglas Crawford had agreed that was the end of the matter. Then I received Group minutes for 23 and 29 June (which I had been unable to attend and virtually erupted with anger).[7] The minute for 29 June read:

> Mrs Ewing asked that it be put on the record that she 'deplored the disloyalty' shown by Mr Wilson towards Mr Crawford on the question or retraction of the statement issued by Mr Wolfe on the subject of Mr Crawford's conversation with the Queen.'

No one had dissented and, from earlier comments, it was apparent that colleagues did not share my view that my primary loyalty was to the Scottish National Party and not to the parliamentary group. Why Winnie had raised it at this stage, I do not know. Winnie Ewing was always protective of Douglas because of his abilities and his loyalty to her. I can only assume she had been away in Europe and acted on a slow fuse out of outrage over the way Douglas had been criticised. On my return to Parliament on 4 July 1977, I wrote to Donald Stewart as Leader of the Group, objecting to the minute and asserted 'my primary loyalty to the Scottish National Party as a whole as the collective instrument by which self-government will be achieved.' I added:

'In that connection I regard myself free to give such advice to any member or office-bearer of the Party or indeed to take whatever action within the rules of the Party I consider desirable as being in the best interests of the Party, unfettered by any special parliamentary group privilege.'

Against a lack of sympathy for my views amongst the Group, the question of resignation became uppermost. I asked Donald to raise again the question by a motion of confidence. He persuaded me against resignation and lodged a motion. Only two members of the Group appeared on 6 July and the meeting was inquorate. I then stepped down as Deputy Leader and refused to comment further.

The outcome was a wave of bad publicity directed at the Group and a number of quotes in the Press from 'Party officials' made matters worse. Margo MacDonald had phoned me with her support and I had a shrewd idea from her tone and comments that she (as well as others) had a hand in the anti-MP briefings. Comments along the lines of that from 'a leading official', - 'The parliamentary group is simply a wing of the party. Its job is to implement policy, not formulate it' - were close to insulting, and intended to be so. As ever, the source of the quotes could not be identified. The bad news could have run and run if the issue had been picked up by the National Executive and National Council. Nobody wanted this and several weeks later, having been nominated by Douglas Crawford, I was quietly re-elected Deputy Leader. None of us emerges from this contretemps with any credit. Thankfully, by shock therapy, if nothing else, the incident brought us together. There was a top level meeting in London between Donald Stewart, Billy Wolfe, Robert McIntyre and the Group on 20 July 1977 from which recommendations were made to the Executive. Amongst other matters, it was agreed to form a joint working group of MPs and NEC members to establish 'clear lines of communication, consultation and responsibility in order to achieve better co-ordination and co-operation.'[8] There was also to be increased liaison between the NEC through its representatives, the Chairman and the President, Robert McIntyre and the MPs through Andrew Welsh and Margaret Bain. Later the Chairman and I drafted a procedural document called the Protocols setting out intra-party rules for managing disagreements. It was amended by the Executive before approval. The MPs procrastinated, wishing instead to discuss strategy. The Protocols were overtaken by the General Election.

All this paled into insignificance against the advances the Party made in 1977. The failure of the Scotland and Wales Bill added to our polling support. Local government by-elections were being won, and in May 1977, the SNP had a landslide victory in the local elections, with 110 gains, 11 losses and won control of Clackmannanshire, Falkirk and East Kilbride. The average vote (overall) was 24% and 38.4% if one only took into account the seats contested. In Dundee, for instance, by a political decision at my urging, no seats were fought. Some thought this was an error as it gave no incentives to our activists, but in the 1979 election those areas that had local government representation fared worse than those which had a lower council profile.

In organisational terms, 1977 saw the peak. There had been a worrying slowdown in 1976, as if the Party were drawing breath. In my own constituency, during the summer recess, I set out to do some canvassing and was concerned by the lack of response from members compared with the enthusiasm of 1974. I was unaware of any political or personal reason and had to assume it was mid-term apathy amongst activists. By the next year, the SNP was responding better though on a fluctuating basis. There were working SNP Associations in the USA and Canada, and although they sponsored visits by MPs and office-bearers, they were not a source of income. A major weakness was that there was no major strategic reserve to meet the costs of the 1978 Regional elections, the Devolution referendum, the European Parliament election scheduled for 1979, the elections to the proposed Scottish Assembly and the Westminster General Election. The Party was dependent on membership dues and branch levies. The outgoings on the HQ office were massive. A large legacy forming the Neill Trust helped with Westminster elections from 1978 onwards.

Apart from local elections when the Party was at its peak, there had been no parliamentary by-elections that would have given us unstoppable momentum and concentrated the minds of the Unionists at Westminster over delivery of devolution. In the spring of 1978, the first challenge arrived with a by-election in Glasgow Garscadden. There was some doubt over the existing candidate, Keith Bovey. Keith was a solicitor and long time member of the SNP – and splendidly independent. He was also a pacifist, atheist and CND supporter. The pacifism was a problem since Yarrow's Naval Shipyard was in the constituency. If the opposition exploited this, as the Tories did on receipt of a letter from Keith setting out his views that Margo MacDonald still calls the 'suicide' letter, it would put the campaign on the back foot. The SNP had won three District seats the previous year and hopes were high. A look at the 1974 figures should have dispelled premature optimism as we had trailed Labour by 7600 votes (a gap of 20%), especially since polling ratings had begun to drift downwards since December. The campaign had a large Glasgow input; in fact it was mainly a Glasgow production rather than a national by-election, leading subsequently to the view that HQ must take control of future elections. Labour put forward one of their best candidates, Donald Dewar who had formerly been MP for Aberdeen South. In the event,

Labour lost 5.5% of its vote while the SNP gained only 1.7% and Labour cruised home.

Glasgow Garscadden By-election Result (April 1978)

Labour	45.4%
SNP	32.9%
Conservative	18.6%
Others	3.1%

Given the circumstances, it was not a bad vote, but expectations had been too high. The SNP had been bullish from the start when there was boasting that we could win with a 5,000 majority, and the impression was given that we were defending the seat rather than facing an uphill battle to win it. When we did not win, the media hailed the result as if we had lost Garscadden to Labour and our credibility suffered.

In an article in the Scotsman on 24 April 1978, John P Mackintosh, Labour MP for Berwick & East Lothian, in a very fair assessment, pointed out that 'the drive behind the SNP is a mixture of disappointment about the economic record of Britain and a desire for local democracy' and that the SNP MPs had difficulty in many debates in finding a distinctively Scottish aspect. Looking at the issues in Garscadden, he wrote, using a Market and Opinion Research International (Mori) survey conducted through the election and Scotland generally:

> 'The quality of the candidates though much remarked on, made no discernable difference and despite the abortion issue, the Catholic vote was preponderantly Labour. Indeed the Labour candidate was held to be the one best able 'to do something' about abortion.
> The poll concentrates attention rightly on the deeper issues. The most significant finding was that the important matters disturbing voters were unemployment, prices, vandalism, housing and taxation in that order. To this has to be added the view voters took of which party was better able to handle these problems and 20% of SNP voters thought that Labour was best on the key issue of unemployment.'

On just about every other index such as prices, housing and education, Labour was in the ascendant. It was only on the issues of the Assembly and North Sea Oil that Labour voters favoured the SNP by 24% to 21%. John

Mackintosh also observed that the polling figures indicated the Government's proposals for a Scottish Assembly had undermined the SNP's support in the areas of Scottish problems and Scottish government. In a further detailed analysis I received from a senior party member, it was pointed out that if the Assembly is seen as a credible proposition, it looks as if we shall have temporarily lost the running on the devolution-independence issue. On prices and unemployment it was unlikely that we could convince the voters that we could do better than Labour or Conservative merely by producing clever technical background papers or equally clever debating points in television arguments.

From both these comments, it was evident that the SNP was in trouble. No longer did we have a clear proposition to put to the electorate. Labour had trumped us on devolution. We had long since stopped campaigning on oil, a distinctively Scottish issue on which we had won massive support in 1974. The MORI survey also drew attention to unemployment where the voters preferred Labour's policies.

No time was available to the SNP to review its position, and given the entrenched opinions of the majority of the Executive members that we should campaign on industrial and devolution issues, it was unlikely there would have been a different strategy. Instead we faced other immediate challenges, the first being the May Regional Elections where our vote fell. It was not a disaster, despite being depicted as such by the media. Robert Crawford, the Research Officer analysed the position in these terms[9]:

> 'In the main it reinforces the trend that has been evident for several months now – a noted slippage in the industrial seats with Strathclyde and Central doing particularly badly.'

By now the Party was shell-shocked. As in 1970, the SNP had had a great deal of optimism. All its activity had been predicated on the creation of a Scottish Assembly. Candidates had been chosen. Reams of policies had been produced. Even during the Garscadden By-election, the Executive was considering papers on 'dual mandate'. It could be argued that it had taken its eye off the ball. Yet this was harsh. There had been a change at Westminster. In the spring of 1977, Labour had entered into a governmental pact with the Liberal Party. No longer was the SNP perceived to have clout. The Government had a majority and the SNP ceased to be 'interesting' to the media and had been side-lined. As the spotlight was dimmed, so, too, did the flow of publicity and the perceived relevance of the SNP diminished in line with its support in the opinion polls, one of the reasons for the poor result in Garscadden.

In June, on the heels of the Regional Elections, came a by-election in Hamilton. The NEC selected Margo MacDonald, the winner at Govan in 1973 and one of the SNP's most high profile office-bearers and threw its weight behind the campaign. This appeared to combine the best of both worlds since Hamilton itself had been the place where Winnie Ewing had first thrust the SNP on to the British political scene with her break-through victory eleven years earlier. Obviously, a key player in the election would have been Winifred Ewing. Yet Margo MacDonald was quoted as not wishing her involved in the campaign, apart from addressing a meeting at the end. Margo has confirmed that this was on the advice of the local campaign committee that wished a fresh start unconnected with the loss of the seat ten years before. Douglas Henderson and Douglas Crawford intimated to the same meeting of the Parliamentary Group on 19 April 1978 that they, too, had been discouraged from participation.[10] Busy as I was, I, also, would have been glad to have been elsewhere since I ended up with sun stroke after a long day's campaigning – a rare achievement in the Scottish spring!

Isobel Lindsay said that the result was little to do with the campaign or candidate[11]

> 'It was the wider national trend. A few doorstep comments I recall that capture the Scottish cringe – 'I wouldn't vote for Margo – she just talks like people round here' and the usual range of 'our oil isn't worth that much', 'who's going to buy our oil' etc.'

Hamilton By-election Result (May 1978)

Labour	51%
SNP	33.4%
Conservative	13.1%
Liberal	2.5%

The outcome was a third blow to the SNP's solar plexus, leaving the Party with complete demoralisation. And just to prove that when things go wrong, decisions that would have otherwise proved acceptable can blow up in the face very easily. In the summer, John Mackintosh died suddenly, leaving a vacancy for Berwick and East Lothian. This was another blow. Not only did the SNP not want another by-election at this time. We certainly did not want it in our worst performing constituency - 71 out of 71 - in 1974. Also, John Mackintosh was a good man who believed in devolution and would have led the fight from the Labour side in the referendum. The existing SNP candidate was deemed inexperienced and not suitable for the extraordinary rigours of a by-election. The Constituency Association proved loyal to its candidate. The candidate declared himself loyal to the 'grass roots' and refused to accept the requirement in his candidacy papers that an intervening by-election might require him to stand aside. The end result was a damaging dispute well publicised in the Press. Isobel Lindsay agreed under pressure to become the candidate and the situation became even more messy when it was leaked that she was pregnant. Rosemary Hall who had been Constituency Association secretary nobly agreed to be election agent. The result was disastrous.

As Isobel ruefully commented later[12]:

> 'Under the best of circumstances we were not going to do very well in the seat but it would have been better than a lost deposit.'

Berwick & East Lothian By-election Result (October 1978)

Conservative	47.4%
Labour	40%
SNP	8.9%
Liberal	3.7%

The run of poor elections, combined with pressures of leading a divided party over devolution strategy and difficulties with his own business had sapped the will of Billy Wolfe. He and I had exchanged a series of letters regarding the Party and had a long chat in November over dinner at the House of Commons. We both agreed that the SNP was in a very difficult position. He and I frequently disagreed over strategy and yet had always been friends. After receiving a further letter from Billy, I came to the conclusion that it was time I shouldered more responsibility and suggested that we meet. Billy was shrewd enough to guess what was coming and arranged a private lunch at his mother-in-law's flat in Edinburgh. When I broached the question of standing for the Chair, his relief was evident. He had been National Chairman for 10 years and had steered the SNP through a number of crises, from the collapse of the Party in 1969/70 to the current problems. He had also been closely identified with the victories of 1974 while suffering the personal disappointment of not winning West Lothian in either contest. During the seventies, he had encountered particular difficulties over the splintering of leadership. Not being an MP had not made his life easier. It posed problems over communication with the MPs who had frequently to make voting decisions at short notice to which he was not a party. In Donald Stewart, leader of the Parliamentary Group, there was another leadership figure. It was not in the character of Donald to seek power within the Party, but he was Parliamentary Leader and had to defend the Group within the SNP and in public. It was also true that he and Billy Wolfe did not have much in common.

This was not Billy Wolfe's only problem. He headed the Executive Committee which was also split, with traditionalists who supported the MPs on many issues, a group on the left such as Tom McAlpine, Willie McRae and Isobel Lindsay who were his main supporters and his Deputy, Margo MacDonald. During the 1974/79 period, Margo was the main public figure of the SNP in Scotland, always on the news bulletins and in the political columns of the newspapers. Billy Wolfe was not. He had his own business to run and peace to keep within the SNP. His decision to fight the obviously politically barren Edinburgh North by-election in 1973 was a gamble unlikely to add to his political credibility. No doubt also there was some deep frustration at not being elected in 1974. If so, he was not alone. Many of the problems of the Party stemmed from envy within the leadership as much as from policy.

His contribution to the growth and development of the Party was massive. He joined before it grew in the early sixties, fought the by-election in West Lothian in 1962 with a remarkable performance, became Policy Vice Chairman and then Senior Vice Chairman, focussed new attention on social and economic research, wrote the seminal pamphlet 'SNP and You' which reworked the Party's philosophy and placed greater emphasis on social caring. Some people did not like this new direction and he lost support, as bearers of new ideas tend to do. He was also responsible for introducing professional design to leaflets and the emergence of the SNP's iconic symbol. In many ways, his role during the sixties was more influential than when he became Chairman. His weakness as Chairman lay in not imposing order on the competing personalities and factions. As time went on, as many middle class people do, he toyed more and more with socialism as a 'quick fix' to persuade the industrial classes and trade unionists to support the SNP. In this, we were apart. As the holder of an industrial seat in a city heavily split along left/right and class divisions, I put more stress on campaigning on nationalist and Scottish issues that I deemed more unifying and productive. But then, we did not always agree!

What Billy Wolfe and I did support was the need for collective leadership, however difficult this might be to achieve. The SNP constitution did not have provision for a single, pre-eminent leader. Prior to 1963, primary responsibility was shared by the President and the Chairman. It was only in 1963, that the precedence of the office of Chairman was established. The other political parties with their roots in parliament gave power to the Parliamentary Leader. In the SNP, the Chairman was elected by the delegates at Conference annually and was directly responsible to the Party. His main task was to chair the Conference, National Council and the National Executive Committee. The Chairman was guardian of the Party Constitution and in the Executive Committee was first amongst equals. And while this role gave the Chairman considerable initiative and influence, he had to work with the other office-bearers who were elected to executive office in their own right. It was not an infrequent occurrence for the Chairman, any Chairman, to be out-voted. The role of Party Leader did not exist in the SNP nor was there any requirement that the Chairman be an MP.

At the time of Billy Wolfe's announcement of his intention to step down, the main challenges of the forthcoming referendum and Assembly and European elections were known and not likely to affect the Conference that would elect the new Leader. The statement was seen by the media as an indication that the SNP would have new ideas and this was welcome, given the on-going speculation that the Party was programmed for disaster. I announced my candidacy and accumulated a large number of nominations.

Chapter 12
The Growing Divide

The last session of the 1974/1979 parliament opened with a bang and ended with cataclysm. In the middle, there was a parliamentary soft centre where most of the action took place off-stage and away from Westminster. In the run up to the opening session of the parliament, the MPs and the National Executive had both been exercised by the prospect of a General Election. In the early summer of 1978, the Liberals had cancelled the Lib/Lab pact with the government under which they had agreed in the spring of 1977 to vote with the Government provided they had prior consultation over legislation. They were not in coalition and, presumably, had a right of veto by refusing to vote for anything repugnant to them. This had given the Government a majority and the ability to continue in office. It had done nothing beneficial to the Liberals' standing with the voters and, sensing that the Callaghan administration might call an early election in the autumn, they pulled out of the pact to create a *cordon sanitaire* between them and Labour.

In the meantime, unemployment had risen to uncomfortable levels and the economy, although improved from the bankruptcy levels of 1975 and 1976, was still in poor order. Price inflation was also high. So, voting with the Government had its dangers! Voting against them raised problems over delivery of the devolution mandate and the referendum. In the event, the Prime Minister, after keeping everyone in suspense, announced facetiously at the TUC Conference in September 1978, that he was not going to the country. This did nothing for his reputation. All the parties had spent large sums getting ready for a General Election. The SNP had allocated a spend of £12,000 on poster sites, most of which was not reclaimable. Donald Stewart as a privy counsellor was entitled to prior information on a hyper-secret basis. He told the story of how he had received a telephone call from No.10 asking if he would speak to the Prime Minister on a confidential privy counsellor basis. He agreed and shortly after received a call in which Jim Callaghan said; 'Donald, I just wish to let you know that I shall be announcing later today that I shall not be going to the Palace to call an election'. Later, when walking through the streets of Stornoway, people kept asking him if he was ready for the election. He could only respond that he was, while reflecting that there was no point in having a secret unless you could tell someone.

In the SNP, the decision not to have an election immediately provoked the question of what we should do over the Queen's Speech and any further vote of confidence. There was a long lead time between the announcement of a non-election and the opening of parliament for the new session as it was customary for the Commons to meet in October to wrap up legislation by dealing with Lords' amendments so, as well as there being time for careful consideration of how the Group would vote, there was also a prospect for lobbying and internal splits to be exposed to a watchful media.

Initially, the Party was unanimous that the Government had betrayed Scotland over the economy and oil. In preparation for the expected election, seconded by Margo MacDonald, I moved a resolution, agreed unanimously, at the meeting of National Council on 2 September 1978, condemning the record of Labour and calling for a Scottish Parliament with full economic powers and investment of oil revenues.[1] Earlier, Party Chairman William Wolfe had set out five main issues – oil revenues, rebuilding of education, increased pensions, abolition of bridge tolls and improvement of roads.[2] The independent parliament, he envisaged, would be able to use our national resources to reduce unemployment.

Immediately beforehand, Donald Stewart as Leader of the Parliamentary Group moved a resolution again instancing the need to use resources and called upon the Scottish people to 'assert their belief in democracy by undertaking their responsibilities to themselves and the world as a nation, not as second class citizens in an exploited province'.[3] There was not a word about devolution, other than from the Report by Chief Whip, Andrew Welsh which noted the passage of the Scotland Bill into law. The Chairman clarified 'unequivocally' that the Party had at no time favoured a pact with the Labour Government or any other party.[4] But this was a story that had been running, rolled out by Margo MacDonald in the summer, in reports in the Guardian on 20 July 1978 and The Scotsman on 21 July 1978. The Guardian reported that the National Executive of the Party led by Margo MacDonald, Neil MacCormick, Isobel Lindsay and Stephen Maxwell had agreed two weeks before that an accommodation with the Government over devolution could have 'tactical advantages'. The following day, the Scotsman reported that the Parliamentary Group had decided to take no action on a letter from Jim Sillars, now the SLP MP for South Ayrshire, suggesting that they should work to sustain a Labour Government to help devolution. Feeling that they were being manipulated, the MPs publicly rejected any prospect of a pact with Labour.

Margo MacDonald who had been riding high for the previous four years had suffered a reverse within the SNP as a consequence of the poor result in Hamilton. During the summer, she had changed from being a strong supporter of independence to a proponent of propping up the Labour Government. It is a moot point whether or not this was due to her assessment that the Party had fallen so much that we needed to get something out of Westminster or whether the SNP should be more clearly seen on the left of the spectrum or both. But on 6 September 1978, she broached these views to a two day meeting of parliamentary candidates. Almost immediately, her support amongst many of the candidates plunged, suggesting that they thought she was putting independence on the back burner.

Yet, it would be wrong to say that the issue of devolution had disappeared as an issue within the SNP. The Act may have been on the Statute Book. And as will be seen, there was still a need to achieve 40% of the total vote on the electoral roll in a referendum. As far back as 5 July 1978, before the Bill passed into law, there had been a meeting in London between the National Chairman and President, Robert McIntyre and the members of parliament when, it was agreed amongst other matters[5]:

> '1.   that the Group would continue to give support to the Scotland Bill where possible and to secure its passage. Mr Wolfe said it was the unanimous view of the NEC, and, he believed, the view of the over-whelming majority of the Party, that the Scotland Bill should be enacted for the benefit of Scotland, and that the Parliamentary Group should be prepared to vote with the Government if circumstances arose in which the Bill might have been lost.
> 2.   Mr Wolfe said it was the unanimous view of the NEC that the Group should endeavour to ensure that the Party was not put on the defensive over any issue related to the Bill which would enable the Labour Party to claim with apparent justification in the eyes of the electorate, that the SNP had not been prepared to ensure the passage of the Bill.'

Billy Wolfe found the meeting very unpleasant. Douglas Crawford had launched a fierce attack on him as Party Chairman for his failure to control Margo MacDonald's manipulation of the press over the issue of pacts with Labour. To Billy's surprise, Robert McIntyre, his fellow representative from the NEC, backed up the Group. I have recently spoken with Billy Wolfe (2008) on the issue. He told me it was the worst meeting he had ever attended and he had felt very low. I was not surprised by Robert's views. Winnie, Robert and Douglas may not have been a 'gang of three', but they most certainly were mutually protective! At the meeting, I stated that the leaks about possible pacts had gone too far and gave my support to the Chairman who was caught in the middle. I took Billy off to a meal in the Commons cafeteria. Despite the abysmal quality of the food, he wrote later to thank me for rescuing him.

Yet the MPs were faced with conflicting demands from the Executive which was disunited on strategy. Earlier, on 30 June, the National Executive asked the MPs to vote for the guillotine in support of devolution (which they did) and to insist that the Government commit itself to setting up an Oil Fund for industrial development, leaving the MPs with two clear, but not necessarily compatible, imperatives.[6] As the autumn progressed and with the General Election postponed, the battle between the NEC and the Group re-ignited – this time over the tactics for the Queen's Speech. On 13 October 1978, Andrew Welsh reported to the NEC that the Queen's Speech would be published on 1 November with the first vote in the Commons due on 6 November.[7] The NEC requested a joint meeting with the MPs. The Chairman tested opinion in the Executive by asking the following questions:

'1.   How would you vote on a Conservative amendment to the Queen's Speech of confidence in the Government's economic policy, record on unemployment etc?
Vote   10 against the Government
                6 for the Government
                5 abstentions
2.   Would you prefer the Assembly referendum to be before the General Election?
Vote   13 yes
                 4 no'

There was a majority on the Executive for voting against the Government on the issue of its running of the economy. The question of the holding of the referendum was an interesting one. What would happen if Parliament were dissolved? I had taken the step of obtaining advice from the Home and Parliamentary Affairs Research Division of the House of Commons Library. Section 68 of the Act dealt with the situation where Parliament was dissolved <u>before</u> a referendum was held. Any order setting a date would fall with dissolution. There was no bar to a fresh order being promoted and there would be at least a three months gap before the referendum could be held.

Speculation in the media was feverish to a degree that led Douglas Henderson to observe that the political journalists were displaying a degree of anxiety and stress to a much greater extent than the politicians. Of course, no one could take a decision until the terms of the Queen's Speech were known and what opposition amendments had been tabled and selected for debate and division. On 1 November 1978, the Speech was published. It contained the following passages which would be the key.

'My Government's economic policies will continue to be directed to overcoming the evils of inflation and unemployment, the two most serious social problems facing the nation today and sustaining the growth in output which is now under way...
Building on the stronger domestic economy and using the benefits of North Sea oil further to improve long term recovery, they will vigorously pursue their policies designed to promote the success of industry and to increase productivity.'

With inflation running at a high level and much public dissatisfaction with the surge in food prices and rising unemployment in Scotland, support for continuing these Government policies did not have much attraction. There was some increased financial support of a modest nature for the Scottish Development Agency and no sign that the Government was going to concede the Scottish oil fund that the SNP demanded as a minimum.

The Speech confirmed that the referendum would be held on 1 March 1979 - a good year behind schedule. Prime Minister James Callaghan in his speech made a brief reference to Scotland:

'As regards Scotland and Wales, we shall, of course, make progress with the devolution Acts that require us to hold a referendum before these Acts commence in each country. The House knows only too well that unless 40% of persons entitled to (vote) vote 'YES', the Government must introduce an Order to repeal the Acts. The condition laid down in the Acts is 'entitled to vote' and not those voting. Therefore it seems to the Government essential that we should ensure the fairest possible test of public opinion by holding a referendum on the most up-to-date register of electors available.'

And, adding the remark that I found particularly irritating:

'So many things are going well for Britain through the advantages of North Sea oil.'

In his response, Donald Stewart for the SNP commented, after a sustained criticism of the running of the Scottish economy, including unemployment of 7.9% against the comparable figure for the UK of 6%:

'The SNP makes no distinction between the Unionist Labour and Tory Parties here. They have all failed Scotland in the past. The sad record is there for all to see. My hon. Friends and I came to this House with two objectives. The first was to assist in the beginnings of a Scottish Parliament. As Mr Neal Ascherson said in The Scotsman,

'Labour provided the Bill, but the SNP gave the orders.'

That objective has now been achieved. An Assembly for Scotland is now in the bag. The Scotland Act requires the Labour and Conservative Parties to hold a referendum, and both are pledged to hold it in March. The second objective was to bring maximum pressure to bear on the Government of the day to expand the Scottish economy. The Government have totally failed to do that. Our objective must be to give a lead, as we gave a lead before, and to force this Parliament to return to Scotland the oil revenues which have been filched away. The Government took a deliberate decision not to set up an oil fund. Just as the weight of public opinion drove them to an Assembly, so it is only a matter of time before the weight of public opinion in Scotland forces them to adopt an oil fund.
As before, the SNP is the only vehicle by which justice will be made available to Scotland. In tonight's Division we shall be voting to begin exerting pressure on United Kingdom Governments to establish a Scottish oil fund and give Scotland true economic justice at last.'

Responding to an intervention from Denis Canavan, Labour MP for West Stirlingshire, he quoted the terms of the SNP amendment that had, as usual, not been selected by the Speaker for voting:

'Our amendment regrets that the Gracious Speech contains no proposals to reduce unemployment in Scotland and fails to implement the main recommendations of the Scottish Office Report ... that only the investment of oil revenues within Scotland can bring about any long term structural improvement in the Scottish economy.'

A leading article in the Scotsman of 15 October 1978 had earlier put the SNP dilemma in these terms:

> 'Its date (the referendum) will be announced in the Queen's Speech, as part of the Premier's effort to bring the SNP into the lobbies behind him in confidence votes. But Mr Callaghan, while making more firm his commitment on the referendum, leaves his own attitude to it very much in the air.
>
> He refers to the 'historic' decision to be taken over devolution but stops short of endorsing the 'Yes' vote. This is somewhat of a Trojan horse for the SNP. If they are persuaded on the strength of a promised date to support Mr Callaghan, if they emerge during the referendum campaign as the Party of the Assembly, then are isolated as the party of failure should the 'Noes' prevail, and are left with their aims of independence sullied and muddled (sic). A 'Yes' vote is possible only if the Labour machine in Scotland is mobilised behind it, (with) the old atavistic Labour loyalties. Here the Prime Minister is in difficulties because the Party in Scotland are not universally cordial about devolution.'

The language was opaque; the analysis of the dilemma correct. The article suggested that the SNP should support the Government beyond the referendum date on terms that required the Prime Minister to sponsor the Assembly with the authority of his Government and the warmth of an unequivocal commitment. This was exactly what the Prime Minister could not do. There was deep seated hostility in the Parliamentary Labour Party to the whole concept of devolution and hatred of the SNP. The Scotland and Wales Bill had been killed by Labour wreckers. A referendum had been conceded during the parliamentary processing of the Scotland Bill - with a qualifying vote of 40% of the totality of Scottish voters on the electoral roll, alive or dead, resident or moved. There had been over four years of procrastination with the Government's efforts undermined constantly by members of the Parliamentary Labour Party who were out of control and coalesced with the Tories to butcher the Bills. In Scotland, the Labour Party viscerally hated the SNP and as soon as the SNP's support declined, even a supporter of devolution such as Denis Canavan asserted during the Queen's Speech debate:

> 'I am pleased to hear from reports that have come
> from Government circles that the Government have
> ruled out any possibilities of a pact with the
> nationalists. We do not need a pact with them. We
> have them over a barrel.'

On her part, speaking in the Queen's Speech Debate on 1 November, Margaret Bain denied that there had ever been any question of a pact between the SNP and the Labour Government, saying in response to Denis Canavan that the idea was more abhorrent to the SNP than it was for him. She pointed out that both the Labour and Tory Parties were unionists. She declared that the SNP stood for the establishment of a democratic independent government in Scotland and added:

> 'Devolution is the result of the people of Westminster
> responding to pressure from the people of Scotland.
> We have accepted we are getting an Assembly which
> has been granted grudgingly by Westminster. But it is
> merely a step in the right direction. We saw what
> happened to the Scotland and Wales Bill and then the
> Scotland Bill as they made their passage through this
> place and the other place (the House of Lords). We
> saw more and more powers taken away. But we are
> still prepared to accept the Assembly because it is the
> first internal constitutional change in Britain since 1707.
> At least that is something of which we can be proud
> because it is something that sets us on the road to self-
> government.'

On the same day, Andrew Welsh and I went to a studio for a video-conference to be faced with members of the National Executive Committee, banked in three rows like a hanging jury. We explained the current position to the NEC and heard their majority view that we should vote with the Government or abstain. We listened carefully and went over the parliamentary options, including the fact that we did not yet know the terms of any amendment that would be selected for voting.

Our response did not satisfy the Chairman. In an unprecedented move, William Wolfe issued a questionnaire to all Constituency Association Chairmen, for their views to <u>confirm</u> the view of the National Executive Committee in its general <u>advice</u> to the Parliamentary Group. *(my underlining)* The Chairmen were asked to phone around to get representative views. The questions were rambling and totally loaded. There was no consultation with the MPs over the wording of the questions or whether the questionnaire should go out! The questionnaire recorded that the NEC had voted 2 to 1 in favour of option 1 and for option 3 c. In the background comment, the choice was for integrity (option 1) as against 'the overwhelming acceptance by the Party in Annual Conferences of an Assembly as the first step to self government ever offered to the Scottish people, and expressed the view that the short term interests of the Party were less than the long term interests of the people of Scotland.' It was a clear, and clumsy, attempt to railroad the MPs into doing what the majority, but not all of the members of the NEC wanted, a kind of blackmail. With the questions summarised and the narratives removed by me, to make sense of the mess, the outcome of the opinion poll was:

For a General Election now, before a referendum on the basis that an Assembly is more likely to be established by the present Labour Government than another   6

We prefer not to have a General Election before the referendum   30

Then, if there is a vote of confidence on the Government's economic record that might lead to a December election

For voting against the Government whatever the consequences   12

For abstention   11

For voting for the Government to get a referendum in March   16

The danger of trying to decide issues before the detail was known became evident when, on 9 November, an amendment was tabled by the Conservatives to the effect that the policies set out in the Speech were totally inadequate to deal with the serious economic problems of the country, and that the Government had denied the British people the opportunity to elect a new administration capable of creating a lasting prosperity in which we can all share. The problem, then, for the Party was how could we fight a General Election, having voted for the economic policies of our Labour rivals, especially since the NEC itself had previously advocated a vote against the Government on economic issues. The Scotland Bill had also proceeded to the statute book and the referendum was promised by both the Labour and Conservative Parties. My colleagues took the views of the NEC into account, though not the *vox pop* survey, and there were differing views within the parliamentary group. There were also telegrams, letters and telephone calls from party organisations, members and candidates, by-passing Party HQ and mostly encouraging the MPs to make their own judgement. I took a realistic view of the tactical position. There was no way of reversing the slide in SNP support. The Party was going down the electoral 'tubes' fast and disaster loomed. The sooner the election came the better!

The Group decided to vote for the economic amendment, but not without serious discussion and division. George Reid broke loose and voted with the Government and Hamish Watt abstained. It is significant that these two, of all the MPs, had the shortest period of Party membership. Later, the NEC, on the casting vote of the chair, narrowly turned down a motion by Margo MacDonald seeking to interfere in Group disciplinary arrangements to the effect that the two errant MPs should not be disciplined – as good a way of causing continuing friction as any.[8] George Reid and Hamish Watt were publicly rebuked by the Group. The economic amendment was defeated by 312 votes to 300. There was to be no election.

In the flurry of events, I had accepted the commonly held view that this was purely a battle between the Parliamentary Group and the NEC over devolution. Having researched the position, I am convinced this is too simplistic. Apart from differences of opinion amongst the MPs – and there were - there was a muddle in Party strategy. The Party oscillated between devolution as against independence and devolution against economic issues. And in this long drawn out dispute, two separate political agendas collided. As a consequence of the poor by-elections, the Parliamentary Group had lost confidence in party management. Everyone had expected an autumn General Election and to that end, the MPs exerted their influence at a meeting on 5 July to ensure that there were changes. Douglas Crawford drew up an election plan that was broadly agreed, even though this sought to give more Press Conference slots to MPs and to ensure that Group leader, Donald Stewart was given equal exposure on TV election broadcasts to Party Chairman, Billy Wolfe. The NEC did not accept their proposal that, as the Senior Vice Chairman, Margo MacDonald was temporarily associated with defeat, her share of the limelight be dimmed to a shadow by a self-denying ordinance, but by 14 July 1978 an Election Working Party accepted that her television appearances would be restricted rather than excluded.

There was also a question of what role was being played by key staff in Party Headquarters, some of whom were involved later in the setting up of the socialist 79 Group that was to cause widespread and damaging disruption in the Party.   As far back as June and later in August, the NEC received research papers showing a significant drop in SNP support amongst skilled workers (C2) and a corresponding transfer of support to Labour. With the poor central belt by-elections, it would not have been surprising if it was thought that visible SNP association with the Labour Government could prove beneficial. Apart from being naive – changing direction in a political party takes almost as much time as a super-tanker turning, the eve of a General Election is the worst time to do so. Looking at the documentation again, I have come to the conclusion that the row over the Queen's Speech and urging of support for the Government – especially after the Bill became an Act was less to do with devolution and more over an intended strategic identification with Labour.

The Government moved into the 'winter of discontent' at war with the trade unions on wage restraint that diminished its credibility. In the meantime – and during the *furore* - the MPs had to deal with bread and butter business, such as speaking in the Queen's Speech debate itself where speeches were made on health, children's panels and other matters. Much of the Speech was given over to days on English education and two days on Rhodesia. Later in the month, the referendum orders were presented. It was clear that the dice were loaded. Apart from the high fence of the 40% based on the total numbers on the electoral roll, with insufficient discounts for the dead and dual residencies, there would be no Government finance or even a leaflet (unlike the European referendum). Additionally, there were to be no curbs on the spending of the powerful NO lobby.

On other matters, the MPs agreed to vote against the EMS on a vote on a Government Green Paper and generally to support the Government on many useful and humdrum Bills on banking, weights and measures, social security, the Pay Commission and others although we continued to vote against the Government on a financial censure motion in early December and on pay sanctions. Margaret Bain resigned as spokesman on social security matters and frightened us when she presented a paper showing that the brief covered social work, employment of disabled people, pensions, hypothermia, supplementary benefits, mobility allowance, disability income, one parent families, special pressure groups, widows and war widows, child benefit, welfare, poverty and deprivation! It is worthwhile spelling out what even one portfolio included. There were only eleven of us and we had been spread very thin as many of the duties extended well beyond the Commons with meetings with interest groups and factory and other visits when at home.

Analysis for 1978/79

SNP votes

with Government	46.7%
with Conservatives	20%
with others	18.3%
free vote	15%

The UK press had lost interest in the SNP at Westminster as we were deemed dead in the water following the disastrous by-election in Berwick and East Lothian and by now the action had moved back to Scotland for the referendum campaign. Apart from the political situation and a vote against the Government's expenditure plans, the MPs had the feeling they were marking time until the referendum result was known. In due course, the referendum led to a vote of confidence. The Government was defeated by one vote. The Parliament ended and a General Election proceeded.

What will be the epitaph of the SNP in the 1974-1979 Parliament? There is no doubt that the SNP punched above its weight and managed to deliver legislation on the Scottish Assembly. For most of the time, in 1974 and from 1977 to 1979, there was a minority government when SNP votes counted on a whole range of measures, many of them controversial and divisive. On all occasions, the SNP MPs followed the Manifesto and had to decide votes on matters not covered by the Manifesto in the light of SNP philosophy. Frequently, these decisions were taken at short notice, with little opportunity to consult office-bearer colleagues at home. Rarely were the MPs able to force votes on Scottish issues or set an agenda and when it called divisions, the Group would be trounced in massive defeats.

In this, the SNP was no different from the Liberal Party. The Liberals had been around for a very long time and they, too, were squeezed by the two party system, based on the Government and an Official Opposition. The SNP was in a more difficult position than the Liberals. The MPs had arrived at Westminster with high expectations. There was enormous public support at home. The novelty factor worked to our advantage and publicity levels were high. The SNP held the balance of power. By and large, after initial embarrassments, the MPs mastered the archaic procedures of the House of Commons. Their role in the Party as a whole was limited by time and distance, not helped by the problems of holding the balance of power and being tied to Westminster night after night as the devolution legislation was filibustered by an unholy alliance of Labour and Tory members, some from Scottish constituencies, and all doing their worst.

In the early to middle stages, up to 1977, there were few problems with the Party at home and certainly not from Party members or National Council delegates. All parts of the SNP worked to common advantage. As the Party failed electorally and politically, it was another story. No doubt, the Group could have done better - and would have done if there had been a by-election up to 1977 in a good constituency. A victory would have sustained the momentum and given the SNP more clout in the negotiations with Ministers over legislation and other matters. Remarkably, there were no Scottish by-elections between 1974 and 1978, a very long gap. When they came, it was too late. The SNP had run out of steam and devolution had run its course.

The MPs paid a personal price, apart from defeat. While bitter opposition and abuse had served to keep the Group united, eventually exhaustion, long hours, stress from making important decisions and being away from home all caught up with people. Because a General Election could have been called at any time, most accommodation arrangements were temporary. I was in hotel accommodation for five years. It was no surprise that there were health and social problems for some. There were other candidates in the Party who would have done as well, perhaps even better if they had been successful in the election lottery – and indeed, the SNP would have been better balanced if some – perhaps, not all - had been within the parliamentary tent. Fewer of the petty jealousies would have been encountered. The Magnificent Seven and Scotland's First Eleven occupied a pivotal role as parliamentary pioneers. Their perspective was a nationalist one. They were hardened by experience of Westminster obstructionism to a degree not shared by their Party colleagues in Scotland. It was from this standpoint that their tactics over devolution were dictated. Equally, the hostility of the 'British' majority in the Commons was entrenched and SNP leaders today would find it beneficial to study what happened as an indicator of the opposition and resources London will mobilise to stop Scotland from gaining independent statehood.

Chapter 13
Devolution – A *Danse Macabre*

Tension in the SNP between independence and gradualism has always existed. The Scottish National Party was formed in 1934 out of two distinct and disparate groups - the National Party of Scotland founded in 1928 and the Scottish Party formed shortly afterwards. Primacy between them was held on ideological grounds by the National Party of Scotland, which was radical in policy and in its support for independence. The Scottish Party, partly created out of a secession from the Cathcart Branch of the Unionist Party, had believed in home rule within the Empire and was more conservative in outlook. The National Party had an organisation and a membership, whereas the Scottish Party had a small membership and no organisation. It did, however, have a number of respected leadership figures and these filled most of the offices in the amalgamated SNP. The union of the two parties brought with it a fault line that was to bring division from time to time when gradualist policies collided with nationalism. This was seen particularly when a large section of the Party departed during the immediate post-war years to form the all-party Covenant Association which obtained around two million signatures to a petition for home rule. The Association eventually came to grief when the incoming Conservative Government in 1951 bluntly declared that only seats in Parliament counted.

The aim of the SNP from the formation of the National Party of Scotland was to win independence by fighting elections. It had been created out of desperation amongst home rulers. Over a long period of time, the self-government movement had relied on applying pressure to the existing political parties. Promises had been made and never kept. Between 1889 and 1979 at least 24 formal attempts were made in the Commons to recall the Scottish Parliament in one form or another. In the beginning, support was slim. It is also a matter of chagrin that a Scottish Home Rule Bill achieved a Second Reading in 1914, but with war imminent, debate was adjourned and not resumed. This Bill rode at the coat-tails of a similar Irish Bill and had reasonable prospects of enactment. In 1927, a definitive and far reaching Government of Scotland Bill was introduced by the Rev James Barr MP, assisted by Thomas Johnston MP, later a distinguished Secretary of State for Scotland and, like many another measure, was talked out in a filibuster. The nearest the movement came to progress was when a Scottish home rule promise featured in the Labour manifesto in 1945. This, too, was never implmented; on the contrary the Labour Government adopted policies that stripped power from Scotland.

The fifties were marked by division within the SNP and, with the Party's weakness, the vision of an independent Scottish Parliament receded from sight. Instead, Scotland was tied tightly to a Unionist framework in which parliamentary representation was divided equally by a centralising Labour Party and a stridently unionist Conservative Party. Only a stray Liberal, Jo Grimond in Orkney and Shetland, adhered to home rule and he was reduced to holding the jackets in the ongoing left/right parliamentary punch-up.

Left/right divisions, entrenched as they were in West Central Scotland by Orange and Green bigotry, were strong, allowing little choice for those who might vote differently. The Labour and Conservative Parties under an unionist umbrella were mutually supportive in opposition to a Scottish Parliament. As support for the SNP grew, the picture changed. The Party followed up its excellent performance in the Glasgow Pollok By-election (1967) with victory in Hamilton in the same year. The winning of a parliamentary by-election accompanied by a landslide performance in the local elections of 1967 threw Scottish members of parliament into panic, with their leaders not far behind.

The Conservatives broke first with Edward Heath as Leader of the Conservative Opposition making a major declaration at their Scottish Conference in Perth that the Tories were ready to consider a Scottish Assembly. Mr Heath then appointed Sir Alec Douglas Home MP to head a Review. Not to be outdone, Prime Minister Harold Wilson set up a Royal Commission on the Constitution under the Chairmanship of a trusty Yorkshire friend, Lord Crowther. Both leaders were playing for time, hoping that the sop, or rather the offer of a sop, would turn public opinion. Neither was serious. Lord Crowther believed that Scotland was a region like Yorkshire and, when taking evidence from the SNP, publicly questioned whether Scotland was a nation. When Edward Heath became Prime Minister, there was no follow-up to the Douglas Home Review – but by then the SNP had lost Hamilton and its support was low. Not even the winning of the Western Isles in 1970, the first seat gained in a General Election - and a major achievement - was enough to tilt the balance towards action.

As the SNP advanced in the early seventies, the climate changed for the better. The discovery of Scotland's oil in the North Sea made self-government more acceptable to the electorate. It was obvious that Scotland was economically viable. The good performances in Stirling Burghs (1971) and Dundee East (1973) enhanced the SNP's political standing. Meanwhile, just to show that cynicism does not always pay, the leadership of the Royal Commission on the Constitution, still meeting after four years, changed. Harold Wilson's appointee, Lord Crowther was gathered early to his ancestors and the chair of the Commission was taken by the independently minded Scottish judge, Lord Kilbrandon. On the eve of the Glasgow Govan and Edinburgh North By-elections (November 1973), the Commission reported.[1] It was divided; however, the majority sided with the proposal to establish a Scottish Assembly. It was enough to allow the SNP to edge through with a win in Glasgow Govan. This gave the Party two MPs for the first time and the momentum led to further victories in the February 1974 General Election when the Party romped home with seven seats and 22% of the vote. As the Government did not have a majority, it was obvious that there would soon be another election. Devolution - now the technical name for home rule - and the oil issue were to dominate the short parliament between February and October 1974. Instantly there was pressure on the Westminster parliament to establish a Scottish parliament.

The Kilbrandon Commission did what it was programmed to do. It dismissed independence or separation on political grounds.

> 'Para 497. The paramount reason for demanding or rejecting independence must always be political. For separation to succeed, it must command the general support of the people concerned. If it is not widely supported it is a complete non-starter; if it has that support then even the most serious economic obstacles will not be allowed to stand in its way. In our judgement the necessary political will for separation does not exist. The vast majority of people simply do not want it to happen. We believe that the national aspirations of the Scottish and Welsh peoples and their desire for better government are more likely to be satisfied within the United Kingdom than outside it.'

In Para. 539., federalism was dismissed (even allowing for the difficulties of placing England within a federal structure) mainly on the grounds that it was necessary for the undivided sovereignty of Parliament to be maintained. 'We believe', ran the Report, 'that only within the general ambit of one supreme elected authority, is it likely that there will emerge the degree of unity, co-operation and flexibility which common sense suggests is desirable.'

Leaving aside this definitive statement of where power would really lie, the Commission commented on devolution in Para. 1102:

> '... the general impression we have formed is that, while the people of Great Britain as a whole cannot be said to be seriously dissatisfied with their system of

government, they have less attachment to it than in the past and there are some substantial and persistent causes of discontent which may contain the seeds of more serious trouble. We think that devolution could do much to reduce the discontent. It would counter over-centralisation and, to a lesser extent, strengthen democracy. In so far as the discontent is not regional in character, but arises from unsatisfactory aspects of the relationship between government and people at large, devolution would probably be of limited value; and we comment on this at the end of Chapter 26 and again in Chapter 27.'

In the Report, eight out of the thirteen members of the Commission supported legislative devolution for Scotland.[2] The majority proposed the creation of Scottish and Welsh Assemblies (directly elected for a fixed term by the single transferable vote system of proportional representation and with one chamber). They were to be given powers to determine and implement policy on and to legislate on a range of subjects, with freedom to determine spending priorities. Westminster would have full sovereignty, including the right to veto legislation.

There were other models, with options of assemblies for five English regions, councils for Scotland and Wales and eight English regions that did not find favour. There was a powerful Minute of Dissent from two Commission members promoting executive devolution for Scotland and Wales and eight English regions. This was very well conceived and had the aim of applying proposals for administrative devolution uniformly throughout the United Kingdom. It did not support legislative powers. The incoming Labour government was attracted to this minority scheme and touted it around to see if it could displace the setting up of assemblies. In this, the Government was unsuccessful.

The long awaited response of the Government in the form of a Discussion Paper, 'Devolution within the United Kingdom: some alternatives for discussion' appeared in June 1974. It was a damp squib. As expected, it rejected separatism and federalism out of hand. It looked at the Kilbrandon options and underlined the problems. It made no attempt to outline Government policy. Off-stage, the Labour Party was concerned by opinion polls showing that Labour would take a tanking unless it made concessions. In this, it was egged on by two Scottish MPs, Jim Sillars and Harry Ewing who called for the devolution of economic powers. A major concern with Labour in London was the hostility of the Scottish Council of the Labour Party to any form of devolution. Patience ran out and the Scots Party was issued with a *fiat* to convene a Special Conference, and with assistance from the Unions, to change their stance – which they duly did. This freed up the Government to address the problem in preparation for the October 1974 election. Thus, in September, they issued a further White Paper, Cmnd. 5732, supposedly based on their consultations over the summer. In reality, the re-statement was a political requirement for Labour's Manifesto. They had to claw back Labour voters in Scotland if they hoped to consolidate a majority at the election. True to recurrent form, the White Paper repeated the Government's negative position towards anything material; and specifically, it confirmed its view that there was a need to sustain the economic and political unity of the United Kingdom – as good an expression of continuing centralisation as you could get.

Still, something was needed for the electoral show case and the White Paper conceded the need for directly elected assemblies for Scotland and Wales, with some of the powers, in Scotland, of the Scottish Office, domestic legislation and spending out of the Scottish block grant. There were to be no transfers of economic powers and as for oil, something over which the Westminster Government could make no concessions, given the bankrupt state of the national accounts, there was only flannel disguising that nothing was on offer to Scotland or the Scottish Assembly (para.35):

> 'The Government is determined that the community as a whole and the regions in need receive their full and fair share of the benefits resulting from the exploitation of these new energy resources. This must mean that maximum benefit goes to redress the regional imbalances in Scotland, Wales and England which have followed in the wake of the first Industrial Revolution.'

This formula bought off opposition in the North of England that was resolutely hostile to Scotland getting anything more than their region did. Its general vacuity allowed politicians in Scotland and Wales to trumpet that additional regional resources would be made available. It worked. The SNP made large gains from the Tories and failed to make further inroads on the Labour vote.

Despite agitation from the SNP and the media, the Government went into purdah and no further major proposals were made until a year had elapsed. The third paper in the series, Cmnd. 6348, 'Our Changing Democracy: devolution to Scotland and Wales' was published in November 1975. This time it contained a summary of detailed proposals for implementation in forthcoming legislation. Again, there was confirmation that on offer was a directly elected Scottish Assembly with a fixed term of four years, composed initially of two Assembly members for each Westminster seat. It would have power to legislate on local government, health, social services, education, housing, private and criminal law, physical planning, the environment and roads. It had details of executive structures and promised complete control over spending of the block grant. There would be borrowing powers and the right to impose a surcharge on rates. There was no provision for a referendum. Once again, as if the leopard could change its spots, complete sovereignty would remain with Westminster and the Secretary of State would control economic planning, regional policy, agriculture and fisheries and trade and industry.

The White Paper was more forthright, even pugnacious on oil, as the election was safely over (para. 97)

> 'The Government are well aware that the discovery of major oil fields under the North Sea has given rise to ideas of a quite different kind. There are some who argue that oil revenues should be controlled directly by those parts of the United Kingdom off whose shores the oil is found, whatever the effect elsewhere. Let there be no misunderstanding: such a proposal – whether their advocates recognise this or not – would mean the break-up of the United Kingdom. The Government believe that oil must be treated in the same way as other national resources (like the big coal deposits recently found in England and the natural gas off its shores) and the benefits brought into the national pool for distribution in accordance with relative needs. Any other course would destroy not only economic unity but also political unity. Those who wish to reserve to Scotland oil or other revenues arising there are in effect demanding a separate Scottish state. The circle cannot be squared: it is not possible for Scotland - or any other part of the United Kingdom – to enjoy rights which can only go with separatism yet not to have separation itself.'

A Government statement on 25 May 1976 and a supplementary White Paper, Cmnd. 6585, of August 1976 reconstituted some of the Government's pre-legislative thinking. Most of the previous announcements remained in place. However, the number of seats was increased to 150; the Assembly was to be given increased powers on pay and other housekeeping matters; the question of vires (the legal powers) was transferred from the Scottish

Secretary to the Judicial Committee of the House of Lords with relaxation of Westminster control over legislation and executive decisions.

A supplementary levy on rates was abandoned, conferment of sole responsibility for the Scottish Development Agency passed to the Assembly and Executive and wider legislative powers were to be granted to encompass Scottish domestic law, along with administrative control of the Courts and regulation of the legal and teaching professions.

All of this obviously had stretched over a considerable period during which the SNP had become even more suspicious of the delay – and the reasons for it. As far back as December 1974, Margo MacDonald in her circulated report to National Council as Senior Vice Chairman and Convener of the Strategy and Tactics Committee had warned of the danger of promises for a 'meaningful Assembly' being eased into support for an 'anti-meaningful Assembly', and prophetically hoping for a couple of good by-elections![3]

The basic assumption, despite the Government's procrastination, was that an Assembly of some type would materialise, although few believed that major economic powers would be devolved. The SNP was still riding high and in the immediate background was the expectation of an early General Election, should the Government collapse. Yet, the SNP was vague on priorities. In a report to the NEC on 14 May 1976[4], Margo MacDonald reported the unanimous view of the Strategy and Tactics Committee that we should not call the next election the 'independence election' even though we should be promoting independence at the expense of devolution – and this advice was passed to the Parliamentary Group at the behest of both the NEC and the Committee. The general view of the Executive when the Bill was published was to present publicised amendments strengthening the Government Bill rather than present an SNP Bill for comparison. Yet by September 1976, the Party was told that the Strategy Committee had unanimously agreed that between then and the next General Election, the Party should conduct a hard line campaign on the theme of independence![5] Ahead was the prospect of a referendum. Nowhere, in the Labour Manifesto, had there been any proposal for a referendum. Nor in the various White Papers had the Government conceded one. Yet, it was perfectly clear that devolution was deeply unpopular with Labour MPs. Not only was there a philosophical objection to any decentralist measure that could interfere with the socialist imperative of delivering economic and social change from the centre by control of government and industry, there was also regional opposition. Apart from deep seated objections within the ranks of Scottish Labour MPs, there was hostility within groups of Labour MPs from the north east and north west of England who feared that Scotland was being given special advantages through devolution – and the block of Northern MPs was numerous and influential within Labour circles – challenge them if you dared! So, in the media, emanating from Westminster came rumours of dissent and rebellion, linked to possibilities that the Government might consent to a referendum to lever support for the Bill.

John McAteer, the National Organiser had sensed the danger. We had been bested in the EEC referendum only a year and a half before. In a memorandum to the Executive dated 21 September 1976, following upon an earlier one of 13 February 1976 where he had warned of the need to prepare the Party psychologically, he advised[6]:

> 'Party activists at branch level certainly believe it (a referendum) is going to happen and are seeking expert guidance from the top. There is particular concern that virtual silence on the face of sustained, well-publicised support for a Referendum from influential sources has been interpreted by our opponents as a sign of fear on our part. Such an impression can only help to boost the morale of the opposition and make a Referendum even more likely.

> I therefore suggest that we should:

> 1.   take up an attacking public stance, welcoming the opportunity to put the issue of Independence to the Scottish people and expressing our determination to make London regret having re-course to such a patently dishonest delaying tactic;
> 2.   campaign vigorously for a set of rules for the conduct of the campaign which are at least as fair as the Representation of the People Act, especially in relation to expenses, access to the media and forming of the question(s);
> 3.   demand UN supervision of all aspects of the campaign;
> 4.   run an internal campaign aimed at giving the Party an appetite for a Referendum and a dispelling any fears left over from the EEC Referendum.'

In the NEC, there were split views on strategy and the matter was referred to the Strategy and Tactics Committee whose proposals were scheduled to be considered in the Spring Campaign. On the assumption that there would be an Assembly and an Assembly election, the Party concentrated its efforts on producing detailed policy statements on which the Manifesto would be based. Since devolution was not the sole pre-occupation, there was also consideration in a prolonged debate of the mandate for independence, The Democratic Road to Self Government.[7] A majority of SNP Westminster seats was the priority and a majority of Assembly seats would give a mandate to negotiate an extension of powers. There was a bizarre attempt by Iain MacCormick MP on behalf of Oban Branch to amend the proposals by heightening the requirements for the Westminster mandate to include a majority of voters in addition to seats. I opposed this amendment and it was defeated overwhelmingly.

Hitherto, George Reid had been the devolution spokesman and had, with the great help of researcher, Helen Finnie, drawn up analyses of the Government's proposals. Both Billy Wolfe and Donald Stewart believed that George needed additional support to deal with the imminent legislation. I was appointed joint Spokesman for Devolution in late November and was relieved of my responsibilities for aircraft and shipbuilding, home affairs and law reform, while retaining energy and oil.

At last, the Scotland and Wales Bill was published. Despite clear indications from the White Papers and Statements that it would have limited powers, it was greeted by the Scottish press with derision, especially in relation to the lack of powers to be given to the Assembly to tackle Scotland's deep rooted social and economic problems. It also met with hostility from unionist MPs of all persuasions. The Bill was given four days for debate in mid-December – a very considerable time for the Commons. Donald Stewart led for the SNP on 13 December 1976, declaring that although it was a mouse of a Bill, the SNP would seek to put 'some backbone and a few teeth into it' – although there was no hope of turning it into a lion. It was a first step and the SNP would work within its framework to widen its control. He rejected the need for a referendum.

He was followed by George Reid who expressed doubts at the passage of the Bill through its stages and into law with, 'No guillotine, no Bill; no referendum, no guillotine. In the case of Scotland, - 'no referendum, no Bill'. During his speech, George Reid had to deal with many hostile interventions which he did with great agility. He spelled out the history of the campaign for home rule over the years and confirmed the SNP would seek to strengthen the Assembly by giving it fiscal powers for responsibility and accountability in the raising and spending of money; access to oil revenues; and control over the outposts of central government. George Reid concluded with a quotation, for the benefit of Labour MPs, from James Barr accompanied by Tom Johnston and Jimmy Maxton (distinguished members of the Labour movement in Scotland) at the Wallace Monument on 27 August 1921 and asked Labour members to reflect upon it:

'Let nations learn a fundamental principle of government.
If you would make nations trustworthy, trust them. A
true democracy must yield to all other peoples the
claim it makes for itself. Contrary it is to all democracy
to hold a nation against its will.'

Later, much later, at 4.25 am, Margaret Bain responded to the question
of a referendum. She stated that it had been Party policy for some time; that
the SNP would oppose it if it were merely a delaying tactic; that a
referendum was part of the Scottish tradition as the people were sovereign;
and that it would serve as a useful precedent for the extension of the
powers. On the third day of debate, Andrew Welsh pointed out that the
Westminster governmental system had reached the end of the line with the
restricted opportunity to put oral questions to the Secretary of State only
once every four weeks and with the previous Grand Committee debate on
education having ceased six times because of the lack of a quorum. On the
final day (16 December 1976), barracked ineffectively by Neil Kinnock,
Douglas Henderson summed up. He stated that the 'basic weakness' of the
Bill was that Westminster would remain the Parliament of the United
Kingdom while becoming an English Assembly. He also attacked the
Conservatives for their failure to make a statement of their position on the
whole issue.

The Bill moved into Committee on 13 January 1977. As it was a
constitutional Bill it was taken on the floor of the House and without a
guillotine (a timetabling device to curtail debate), it was in danger of being
talked out in a filibuster. This was all the more so since the measure covered
Wales as well as Scotland and in Wales, opposition was greater. To give a
taste, the first amendment was to exclude Scotland, and, of course, the
debate would be repetitively restaged for Wales. The Opposition, having
voted against the Bill at Second Reading, hypocritically pretended thereafter
that it was acting constructively. It did not have to be pro-active when the
'dirty work' was being done by Labour MPs as well as by Tory backbenchers.
To those who have faith in the workings of the 'mother of democracies', a
reading of these endless and trivial Committee debates is a useful corrective!

There was no issue avoided that might be an impediment. There was, for
example, an amendment to exclude Orkney and Shetland, perceived by
opponents as one of the SNP's weak points, since many of the major oil
fields were to be found in the East Shetland Basin. It was also an attempt to
persuade Jo Grimond, MP for Orkney & Shetland and a supporter of home
rule in the Liberal tradition, to change posture and join the mischief. On this
occasion it was not successful. Then there was a debate on a Clause that the
Bill did not affect the unity of the United Kingdom or the supreme authority
of Parliament to make laws for the United Kingdom. I countered with an

amendment (19 January) that would provide for the devolution powers not to be subject to erosion save with the consent of the Assemblies. This was defeated by the Government steamroller by a vote of 14 for and 146 against.

Despite hostility from Deputy Speaker Sir Myer Galpern, a Glasgow Labour MP , who failed to call Group members to speak (as a result of which I led a charge of colleagues to the Opposition Front bench to argue points of order), the SNP persisted with support for constructive amendments: on proportional representation (defeated by 244 votes to 62); a Liberal amendment to term the Assemblies 'National' (defeated 156 votes to 24); a John P Mackintosh amendment for an independent official to perform the remaining functions otherwise left to the Secretary of State (defeated by 293 votes to 26) and so on. By now the debates of up to three days a week and late nights were as George Reid put it causing 'whey-faced' Labour members to stumble into the lobbies, not knowing what they were voting for. They were not alone. It was harder going for SNP MPs who had an active role and had to be aware of 'mine-trap' amendments.

Eventually the Government, in the face of lack of progress, conceded a referendum and on 15 February 1977, put down the necessary clauses and amendments, provoking almost two hours of points of order. By now the SNP was in a difficult position. We knew well enough that a referendum was at worst a wrecking move and at best, one that would delay implementation of devolution. The mandate given by Labour's October 1974 election manifesto was being surrendered in face of opposition, especially within the ranks of Government. No one believed the referendum had anything to do with democracy. Quite simply, the Government was desperate. The Bill was being talked out and in danger of being lost.

The jungle of amendments can be seen in the nonsensical exchange between Opposition spokesman, Frances Pym and rebel Labour MP, Tam Dalyell:

> 'Mr Pym: "we have tabled an amendment which is lettered k^6 –(kkkkkk) and another which is letters (iiiiii) or i^6 which we seek to include in substitution for the two existing appendices...'
>
> Mr Dalyell: I do not know whether it is a bias against me, but my amendment is lettered (zz).'

Faced with the loss of the Bill, the SNP felt it had no alternative but to give support to a referendum. To oppose it would have suggested weakness and encouraged the opposition to redouble its efforts. Apart from that, the referendum clause was bound to succeed, as in fact it did, by 231 votes to 24. The Party was still very confident. Its support was running at 31%, very much on par with the outcome of the October 1974 election. It was confident that the Scottish people would support the Assembly in a referendum and it had nothing to lose!

On 22 February 1977, the Government acted. It tabled a guillotine motion. This at least allowed the SNP to accuse the Government of failing to deliver its promises. The Group voted with the Government and in a vote that should have gone down in infamy, there was a widespread defection of Labour MPs and the Liberals who preferred to vote with the Tories rather than deliver devolution. The guillotine motion was defeated by 312 votes to 283. 21 Scottish MPs voted against, 48 for, with two abstentions.

The Government stopped progress on the Bill. Because of internal sabotage, it was dead in the water. The SNP rubbed it in by producing a draft abbreviated Bill that sought to allow the detail to be settled in Scotland on the basis that any proposals from Edinburgh would require an affirmative vote of both Houses of Parliament. Naturally, the SNP Bill was for publicity purposes only and even without this step, support for the SNP in a March poll rose to an unprecedented 36%. Shortly after, the SNP voted against the Government on a motion of confidence that was defeated with Liberal support. So also was a censure motion on 4 July. The Lib/Lab Pact had come into force and, with devolution off the agenda for the time being and the Government having a secure majority, the SNP lost visibility and its influence over Westminster business dwindled. So for the Group, it was back to legislation as just another minority Party.

The loss of momentum was felt equally strongly at home. Although the question of supporting the Government was made irrelevant by the Lib/Lab pact, it nonetheless cropped up from time to time as, for example in the Strategy Committee ('Tactics' had been dropped from the title) in May 1977 when it was agreed that we should support a devolution Bill as before (if a new one appeared), while not keeping the Labour Government in power artificially, nor should we accept any promises nor make any deals with the Government.[8] While at the Executive in August, Andrew Welsh advised that the MPs would challenge the Government to introduce a guillotine on the threat of a motion of confidence.[9] In reality, the Party was in limbo waiting to see what would emerge from Whitehall. The SNP was happy to ride the devolution and independence horses at the same time. There was no sign of any dispute within the Party or between the MPs and the leadership. As for the bulk of the Party membership, they looked for a lead.

There was also a great deal of hyperbole about alleged splits within the Party on the issue. Isobel Lindsay thought that much of this was imagination and commented[10]:

> 'The gradualism/anti-gradualism tensions ran throughout the decade. This was never a dispute

about ultimate objectives but about strategy. (Also like all disputes it had a distinct element of positioning for personal power and of personality clash). Should the SNP support or engage with any process that fell short of independence? The 'engagement with gradualism' approach became the predominant one throughout the 70s but never without controversy. The adoption by Labour in 1974 with Liberal support of an elected Scottish Assembly and the election of SNP MPs who would have to vote in one way or another and whose votes could be decisive, meant there was no viable alternative that the Scottish public would understand other than to give this critical support.   There were three positions:

1)   Those against any compromise on principle because anything short of independence would be no better than the status-quo and would undermine support for full autonomy and for the SNP.

2)   Those who accepted the potential gains from a Scottish Assembly but thought a non-cooperation approach would win more concessions.

3)   Those (I include myself) who thought it unlikely that the Scots would choose to go to independence in one stage and who saw an Assembly as a way of building confidence and momentum.'

On the Westminster front, in May 1977, an invitation was received from Michael Foot MP (who, as Lord President of the Council was in charge of devolution) offering a second round of consultative meetings on devolution. The MPs felt they were being used and asked me to obtain a note of the agenda. This turned out to be 'Devolution – possible next steps'. I was asked to respond by reminding Mr Foot that it was for the Government to make progress since the Bill had been torpedoed by Labour Government supporters in collaboration with Conservative and Liberal MPs. I drew his attention to the SNP's short draft Bill, designed to break the parliamentary log-jam and offered a meeting to discuss this solution. Needless to say, the offer drew a blank response. The Press were advised.

Play resumed in November when Parliament re-assembled for the new session. The defeated Scotland and Wales Bill had fallen and was replaced with separate Bills for Scotland and Wales. This simplified matters considerably and avoided both the mish-mash of a conglomerate Bill and tangential contributions (at least from a Scottish standpoint) from Welsh MPs. Not that this reduced the work load since it had been agreed between Plaid Cymru and the SNP that each party would support the other in votes without participating in their debates. Because of the Lib/Lab pact, the Government had a majority and with SNP and Plaid Cymru support, was sure to win a timetabling motion.

The Bill had its Second Reading on 14 November 1977. During the debate, I approached the arguments from a different angle. I told the House of Commons that the Scots objected to 'the smug assumption that this House is the norm of good government and economic management.' On being quizzed by Teddy Taylor MP (Cons. Cathcart) as to how the Bill could improve the economic situation, I asserted that the Assembly could improve the quality of government, effectively monitor administration through a better committee system, press the UK government on oil revenues and other natural resources and accrue greater powers. I also quoted a Strathclyde University analysis showing that Scottish MPs had participated to a decreasing extent in UK standing committees. I closed with the inducement that we would accept an amendment to reduce the involvement of Scottish MPs in English business and vote to support the creation of an English parliament. This last was a handsome offer that could not be disregarded and the Bill got its Second Reading by the margin of 307 votes to 263!

More important than this was the outcome of the guillotine motion on 16 November, only two days later. George Reid led for the SNP, promising full support and saying, 'If there is no guillotine, there will be no devolution. Only through a guillotine can the promises that were freely made to the people of Scotland be enacted.' Interestingly, in the course of his speech, he revealed that at a meeting between the SNP and the STUC two days before James Milne, the Secretary of the STUC, had given it as his opinion that the Bill was not the end of the road and he had wanted revenue raising and full industrial powers with separate links between the Assembly and the EEC. The guillotine motion was carried by 313 votes to 287.

With the advent of timetabling, it was not only the time wasting activities of the anti-devolutionists that were curtailed. The requirement to complete each sequence of the Bill within a restricted time-frame meant also that the SNP was similarly thwarted. By now, tedium had set in. The first Bill had seen deployed all the arguments for and against and even the opponents had not the same enthusiasm. They had a further ploy in mind.

Before the House at the same time was the Committee Stage of the European Direct Elections Bill that distracted the opponents, and since George Reid covered the debates when Winnie Ewing was at the European Parliament, it took up some of our time, too. Amendments to the Scotland

Bill were prepared by George Reid, Douglas Crawford and me. Basically, they set out to increase the powers of the Assembly in such fields as finance, industry and the economy, energy and broadcasting. The devolution amendments were presented by a range of the SNP members and debated over two days on 17 and 18 January 1978. In all cases, the amendments were thrashed to a greater or lesser degree, depending on whether they attracted support from the Liberals, Plaid Cymru, the SLP and occasional strays. The Tories set out to entrench Westminster sovereignty and had egg over their faces when they successfully forced a vote where, with SNP support, they knocked out the preliminary Clause 1, which declared that the provisions of the Bill 'do not affect the unity of the United Kingdom or the supreme authority of Parliament to make laws for the United Kingdom'. The Government was not happy! Much of the remaining time was spent resisting hostile Opposition amendments during which the Tories refused to explain their conduct and their overall attitude to devolution. Their reply was that the Bill was a bad Bill and they were trying to improve it. Nobody was deceived!

Everyone knew that the main attack was reserved for the referendum. The assault came from Labour dissidents. On 25 January 1978, Bruce Douglas Mann, MP tabled amendment (No. 586):

> 'If it appears to the Secretary of State for Scotland that less than one third of the persons entitled to vote on the referendum has voted 'Yes' in reply to the question posed in the Appendix to Schedule 17 of this Act, he shall lay before Parliament a Draft of an Order in Council for the repeal of this Act.

With this, the Chairman selected an amendment by George Cunningham MP, supported by Robin Cook MP

> – 'If less than 40% of the total electorate vote or if any overall majority voting 'Yes' is less than two thirds of all votes cast, the Secretary of State shall deem the legislation to be null and void, such decision to be laid before Parliament by Draft Order in Council.'

The 40% was to be based on the total vote on the electoral roll not on those who actually voted, thus turning the screw. Without much surprise, the increased qualification carried. These amendments were designed to wreck devolution by setting up impossibly high standards. Unlike the previous referendum on Europe in 1975, where a majority of those voting was the criterion for success, the Assembly referendum outcome was to be based on the total electorate, whether voters participated or not. In parliamentary elections, it was rare to get turnout over 80% - there were always abstentions or people might have moved or be dead. This gave rise to the incongruous situation, where the dead had a vote – a negative one! It was patently unfair. From the outset, the YES vote had a handicap of 20%, that is, people who did not vote or could not vote were deemed to have voted 'NO'. Of those with two addresses and two entries on the voters' roll, if their vote was 'YES', the unused second vote cancelled the first with an automatic 'NO'. If the original 33% was set as the standard, it was very high. 40% was crippling and intended to be so.

Also, just in case Scotland might still escape this attack from within – both Bruce Douglas Mann and George Cunningham were Scots representing English constituencies, - Jo Grimond, the MP for Orkney & Shetland tabled an amendment for an 'opt out' for his constituency if there was a local majority against. This was hugely popular with English MPs since Westminster MPs rashly assumed that oil in the East Shetland basin would remain under London's control. There were two votes with the Cunningham amendment being preferred by 168 votes to 142. The SNP amendment had not been selected – surprise, surprise! Douglas Henderson and Hamish Watt refused to leave the voting lobby and had a heated argument with the Government and Opposition whips. They held up the vote until the deputy Speaker sent in the Serjeant at Arms, clutching his sword, happily sheathed. To add salt to the legislative wounds, the Orkney and Shetland opt out went through by 204 votes to 118.

I had been selected to put the SNP case and made the following remarks:

> 'My reaction to these amendments is one of anger, because the Committee is endeavouring to prevent the Scots from achieving self-determination.'

And later:

> 'Initially the referendum was unnecessary. It is now becoming an instrument by which the anti-devolutionists are seeking to change the plans. I am perfectly sure the vote and the turn out will be quite satisfactory from our point of view, but we are not prepared to accept the rules of the game being changed as we go along.'

I was putting a brave, and not very credible, face to it. The Bill had been castrated. The game was a 'bogey'. Perhaps the greatest wound was the sapping of confidence as people realised the extent of the handicap that had been imposed. It wiped out the last of the 1974 momentum which had not been refreshed by good by-election results. The worst was we could not admit the problem publicly for fear of causing more damage to morale. We also had to see the Bill through its further stages.

The Committee stage ground to a halt shortly afterwards and the final stages, Report – an abbreviated committee stage on the floor of the Chamber dealing with second thought amendments – and Third Reading. Denis Canavan MP (West Stirlingshire) moved an amendment on 15 February to remove the 40% hurdle, but this was defeated by 298 votes to 243, so the die was cast, made all the more so as the House passed an amendment from Tam Dalyell MP (West Lothian) to provide for a delay of at least three months between a General Election and the holding of a referendum. It was evident that the Government had lost control of its own back benchers.

The SNP leadership was in doubt as to what to do. The Party had invested so much in the creation of a Scottish Assembly and now 'the toy' had been thrown out of the pram. A special meeting of the Executive and the Group was convened for 20 February 1978 in Glasgow to review strategy in the light of events.[11] This included voting on the Third Reading as several MPs felt that we had reached the stage where we should face the reality that it was impossible to win the referendum and that the Party should take the initiative by ditching devolution completely to avoid going down with the ship. Against this, a by-election was pending in Glasgow Garscadden and people would not understand why we had changed our position. The meeting decided in favour of the Bill by a margin of 15 to 1 and the MPs then voted for it unanimously. Margaret Bain said frequently afterwards that she wished she had voted against.

Speaking in the Third Reading debate on 22 February 1978, Donald Stewart said the Bill had begun life as a measure designed to bestow a minimal degree of decision-making to Scotland and had been severely mutilated in Committee. He described the referendum process as 'blatantly anti-democratic ballot rigging'. He analysed the voting on the Scotland Bill thus:

- taxation powers – 40% of Scottish MPs **for** and 90% of those **against** were non-Scottish.
- 33% referendum hurdle – 53% Scottish MPs **against** and 94% of those **for** were non-Scottish.
- 40% referendum hurdle -- 48% of Scottish MPs **against** and 93% of those **for** were non-Scottish
- Orkney & Shetland opt out – 40% of Scottish MPs were **against** and 90% of those **for** were non-Scottish.

Because of the guillotine, the Commons failed to consider 60 of the Bill's 83 clauses. The Bill was given its Third Reading by 297 votes to 257 and passed to the House of Lords to undergo fresh scrutiny. What is interesting in Donald Stewart's analysis is not the role played by non-Scottish MPs – that is not surprising in a unitary parliament, but the degree of opposition amongst Scottish MPs to devolution. These included a significant number of Labour MPs who defied their Party and the Labour manifesto commitment.

The Lords devoted 47 days between March and July 1978 to scrutiny and made 239 changes, of which 170 were agreed by the Commons. The Orkney/Shetland opt out was removed on the promise of an enquiry to look at their needs and status and provision of a veto by the Secretary of State against Assembly decisions. The Lords introduced a delaying power for 14 days reconsideration of any decision affecting England carried on the votes of Scottish MPs. It also deleted powers over gaming, abortion and forestry and these were retained to Westminster.

The Bill limped back from the Lords on 4 July to be met by a further guillotine. Some of the Lords' amendments were constructive – for example, an amendment introducing proportional representation which the SNP supported, although it was defeated on a free vote by 363 votes to 155 and another on taxation. Most of the other amendments were exercises in 'nihilism and emasculation' according to George Reid. After hearings on 4 and 6 July, messages of dissent were sent to the Lords as part of the discussions between the two Houses of Parliament and later in the month, the Bill became an Act.

Chapter 14

Referendum and the Aftermath

Before the Queen's Speech, the Government fixed the Referendum date for 1 March 1979 and shortly thereafter published the regulations for the conduct of the referendum. As expected, there was to be virtually no Government involvement or funding. Instead, when moving adoption of the regulations, Bruce Millan, the Secretary of State for Scotland concentrated on dealing with the absurdities – unfair absurdities, at that – arising out of Parliament's insisting on 40% of the 'persons entitled to vote' rather than the normal standard of 'those voting'. He proposed discounts and acknowledged that there were still problems from deaths, those under 18 with no vote, prisoners on the electoral roll with no right to cast a vote and those with dual registrations such as students. Bruce Millan was correct to say that the Government had advised against the 40% hurdle and even wiser not to describe how little the Government had tried to whip its supporters into line to oppose it.

In my response, I concentrated on the huge barrier of turnout. In October 1974, turnout was 73.9% and in the European referendum only 61.7% for which there was no discount under the regulations. With every non-vote being treated as a 'No' vote, it was vital for the 'YES' campaign to get the vote out.

With 1 March 1979 being the referendum date, exactly 5 years had passed since the Government had come into power. They had played for time and had left it too late to get their full devolution plans through. Other events such as the 'Winter of Discontent' had so poisoned the reputation of the Callaghan administration as to make it impossible for the Government to use their prestige to influence the people to give the Assembly their full backing.

Even before the setting of the 40% limit, there had been limited moves within Westminster to seek a common purpose. In early December 1977, at the request of Donald Stewart, I represented the SNP at a meeting with John Mackintosh and Jim Sillars. John Mackintosh, MP for Berwick and East Lothian had been one of my history lecturers at Edinburgh University. Unlike most of his Labour colleagues, John Mackintosh had long been enthusiastic about home rule and in the ensuing debates on the Scotland Bill, he was to be active in moving amendments to give the Assembly more strength. He was well respected in the media and academia. Jim Sillars had been elected Labour MP for South Ayrshire in the by-election of 1969 and then re-elected in 1970 and 1974. Beforehand, he had been a trenchant enemy of the SNP and had been a co-author of a memorably colourful diatribe, 'Don't Butcher Scotland's Future'. Between the 1974 elections, faced with internal Labour opposition in Scotland to the whole concept of an elected Scottish Assembly, along with his friend Harry Ewing, he had successfully persuaded Labour to feature the promise of economic powers for the Scottish Assembly in their Scottish manifesto for October 1974. Then, as the Government dragged its heels, he had become increasingly disillusioned, and, in 1976, along with John Robertson, Labour MP for Paisley had defected from Labour to form a new party, the Scottish Labour Party (SLP). The SLP had enjoyed some initial support from the media and was in process of being destroyed by warring Trotskyite and Marxist members. Nevertheless, we recognised his ability and his strong adherence to a Scottish parliament, while regretting that he had not given the SNP a boost by crossing the floor.

None of us at the meeting was under any illusions as to the difficulty of winning the referendum. We were tried and tested political professionals. We had seen how business and financial interests had won the day in the European referendum only three years before. We anticipated that many of the same interests, mobilised by a revitalised Conservative Party hostile to democratic advance in Scotland, would be well organised and well funded.

The 'YES' camp could not rely on much help from the Government and both Jim Sillars and John Mackintosh expected outright opposition from many Labour sources, including the trade unions. For this reason, Jim Sillars suggested an umbrella organisation heavily dominated by the SNP. I was of the view that the SNP might wish to fight its own campaign and reserved our position. We then went on to discuss areas of co-operation. The discussion centred around the following, as set out in a memorandum to the NEC on 7 December 1977.

> '1.   There would be a need for an umbrella organisation to administer the allocation of TV time as in the case of the EEC referendum.
>
> 2.   There was a need to attract the support of non-committed influence leaders as one of the main tactics of Scotland is British would be to subvert Scottish confidence by using establishment names.
>
> 3.   There was a case for a common poster and car and lapel 'stickies' on the theme 'Yes for Scotland'. It was hoped that the SNP with its design expertise would give the lead. More arguably there was a case for a limited common leaflet. I made it clear that the SNP would have its own leaflets for national and constituency distribution.

4.   I was non-committal about common meetings although this was advocated strongly. I understand that, other than for exceptional occasions, joint platforms would not be welcome for SNP activists.
5.   In reducing observable SNP involvement in the joint campaign, I suggested that Lord Kilbrandon be invited to be President, that there be parliamentary vice-presidents (one of whom would be SNP) and that Ludovic Kennedy be invited to be Director. Since the proposals were speculative there was no discussion of functional organisation. It was assumed that funding would be by appeal.'

I asked John Mackintosh to consider promoting an amendment to the referendum clause of the Scotland Bill to place cash limits on press advertising during the campaign since this would remove the unfair advantage which the 'NO' campaign would have. Implicit in the memorandum were two assumptions – that the YES campaign would need the SNP organisation to deliver and that it would be better for devolution if the YES campaign were seen to be separate from the independence standpoint of the SNP, as a close link would serve only to incite the all party unionist grouping 'Scotland is British' to wage an anti-separatist war. They would do this anyway and there was no point in giving them new sources of ammunition.

The MPs decided they wished to discuss this memo with Margo MacDonald and Billy Wolfe early in the New Year. By 13 January, 1978, there was a division of opinion.¹ The MPs voted narrowly in an advisory capacity against involvement in an umbrella group while the NEC voted for by 22 votes to 2, although envisaging that the SNP's distinctive case for a YES vote would be developed. The matter was left to further discussion at National Council and I was permitted to pursue external discussions which, given the difference of opinion, was not possible. The NEC agreed also the twin aims of a 'Yes for Scotland' campaign:

1.   To represent the 'Yes for Scotland' side of the Referendum Campaign in co-operation with the broadcasting authorities in their administration of the broadcasting of the allocation of TV and radio time.
2.   To provide a non-party organisation producing 'Yes for Scotland' publicity material for use by all those who are in favour of a 'YES' vote in the Referendum.

The MPs and the NEC met in Glasgow on 20 February 1978 to discuss strategy arising from the Scotland Bill. By then, there were pre-occupations with more immediate matters than the Bill since there was to be a critical by-election in Garscadden. At the March National Council, Margo MacDonald and I put forward a resolution that members of the Party should be free to support the non-party Kilbrandon Committee that had been established to promote the 'Yes for Scotland' campaign.[2]

The following year, the SNP participated in the umbrella organisation and also ran its own campaign. The Labour and trade union movements sat on their hands and refused to support even the nominal efforts of their Government. Prime Minister Callaghan came north. The visit was not a success. After the Winter of Discontent when he had outraged the trade unions on wage restraint and the general population which had suffered from the inconveniences of the ensuing strikes, he was 'damaged political goods', left with little authority from his office of Prime Minister. There was no co-operation with the SNP, other than through a small number of works meetings.

The SNP referendum campaign was organised by Margo MacDonald and Stephen Maxwell and promoted a respectable national effort compared with the Labour campaign. This was not difficult since their effort was nominal! On the ground, the SNP campaigns were patchy. Those who wanted devolution campaigned hard; others who favoured independence went through the motions or did nothing. By contrast, 'Scotland is British' made the running. It had unlimited funds. The press had turned from being favourable to being lukewarm or, especially in the case of the Express, actively hostile. The threat to the Union from separatism was played up. With large scale donations from business, it mounted substantial advertising programmes that the pro-devolution lobby could not match. Even so on 1 March 1979, Scots voters provided a simple majority of 51.6% (or 32.9% of the eligible vote – very close to the original hurdle of 33%).

It was, however, well under the 40% standard and as I watched Donald Dewar representing Labour on television at the Strathclyde Count visibly crumble to defeatism, I knew that the will was not there to resist the arbitrary limit of 40% and defeat the compulsory draft Order for repeal. The referendum was not binding. It was advisory. If the Government was unwilling to make the issue a vote of confidence to coerce the Labour hostiles into line, we could still do it. But if Donald Dewar's collapse was mirrored in London, the Assembly was truly lost.

Little time was given to the SNP to consider its position. The Referendum result announced on 2 March, was followed by a meeting of the National Council on 3 March.[3] The debate was led by Party Chairman, William Wolfe who said that following the close result of the Referendum, he expected a period of political turmoil. Despite the weakness of the Labour Government's campaign, the result was a victory for the people who had faith and confidence in Scotland. He felt that the Government was morally obliged to set up an Assembly and convince Parliament to accept the result. The SNP should now make a fresh and unequivocal call for self-government, for never was there a greater need for Scottish control over Scottish affairs.

There were hurried discussions before the meeting, leading to the presentation of an emergency resolution setting out the Party's stance. Seconded by Professor Neil MacCormick, I moved the following resolution:

> 'The Scottish National Party declares its satisfaction that a majority of the Scottish electors has voted in favour of Scottish Home Rule in the first ever democratic vote on the issue, pledges itself to use all its efforts to secure that the decision of the majority is respected and demands that the Government honours its Manifesto commitment to establish the Assembly and recommends to its Members of Parliament that, if Parliament rejects the Scottish majority decision, they seek an early General Election on this issue.'

The resolution passed by acclamation with no dissent. It was, of course, an exercise in damage limitation and followed an earlier decision of the Executive to fight the next Westminster Election on devolution. Nonetheless, it reflected the genuine anger of all sections of the Party, gradualist and nationalist alike, over the manipulation of the referendum. There was desperation to make some gain to compensate for the loss of the SNP's political standing. The only weapon left was to use the 'nuclear' option of threatening the Government with an election if it refused to concede the Assembly.

It is a moot point whether the same attitude would have been taken if there had been more time for consideration. I do not think there would have been a change. With polling support under 20%, and falling, the Party was aware that it faced a loss of many of its MPs and post-election influence. And what else could we have resolved that would not have been construed as weakness when approaching the coming Election? There was also another binding consideration. It has always been a prime concept of Scottish constitutional law that sovereignty is vested in the people, not Parliament as was the case in England. In this referendum, the people had spoken and many in the SNP regarded it as their duty to implement the decision of the people – regardless of the political consequences.

Looking at the issue later, Isobel Lindsay ventured[4]:

'I was one of those who supported the decision to back a no confidence vote. I calculated (obviously wrongly) that when the Government thought they would lose the confidence vote and realised they would not win any subsequent election, they would make a substantial concession on the Scotland Act given that there had been a majority in favour. I recall that Michael Foot said in a later book that they had gambled on the SNP abstaining when it came to the crunch.'

From this point, the battle moved back to the Commons. The Group discussed the National Council resolution and went over the position in great detail, before reaching a view on the tactics to be followed. It was recognised that the ball lay in the court of the Government. The Group would ask for a Supply Day for 29 March while Donald Stewart would seek a meeting with the Prime Minister. To soften up the Government, it was envisaged that the topic for the SNP Supply Day could be a vote of confidence. The MPs did not want the issue to drift and were aware that the Party office-bearers, after a meeting with Andrew Welsh and me, had authorised a series of advertisements in the evening papers, the Daily Record, the Courier and the Press & Journal at a cost of £2,800. There was also to be a party political broadcast, a press conference, a photo-call with the eleven MPs outside the Assembly Building on the Calton Hill in Edinburgh, and a national rally, all with the view to crystallise within the public mind the fact that a majority of the electorate had supported the Assembly and that the Government ought to deliver.

All of these steps were necessary as the Government had retreated into silence after March 1. Eventually, the Prime Minister made a statement on 22 March 1979, in which he advised that the Repeal Orders for Scotland and Wales were to be presented by the respective Secretaries of State in terms of the statutes and that these would be debated and the issue decided. He acknowledged that, unlike the case in Wales, there had been a majority vote in Scotland and that this could not be ignored. He offered a short intermediate stage to allow bilateral discussions with the parties to see what modifications to the Act might be acceptable and agreed to listen to any other proposals that might emerge.

Reacting, Donald Stewart reminded him that there had been a clear commitment in the Labour manifesto with no referendum or 40 per cents and criticised the delay of three weeks during which the proffered talks could have taken place. George Reid went further:

'By refusing today to give a clear guarantee that the vote on the Scotland Act will be on a three line Whip, does not the Prime Minister confirm what the House already knows – that there is a Scots majority for the Assembly, an English majority against the Assembly and enough members of his own party who would rather see the Leader of the Opposition in Downing Street than honour the clear manifesto commitment to the Scots people?

If it is clear to the Prime Minister by tonight that there are no takers for his bilateral talks, will he have a vote next week anyway?'

The key to it all was whether the Government would budge. It would not be easy for the Government to do so. It had been battered by the industrial disputes during the winter. It had abdicated its duty of government and had lost ground to the Conservatives under the dynamic – and ruthless – leadership of Margaret Thatcher. The loss of the referendums in both Scotland and Wales had further damaged its prestige. Labour was split from head to toe over devolution, and if it had not been for SNP pressure, the Bill would have been sidelined a long time before. The last thing the Labour Party wanted was to split on the eve of an election or to fight one over Scottish devolution. The English would not have understood!

The SNP held back lodging its motion of confidence for as long as it could, while putting out hints that this could happen if there was no progress. Andrew Welsh and George Reid were invited to a meeting with Michael Foot, who was still in charge of devolution to see if the Government would commit to a vote countermanding the Repeal Order on a three line whip that would be treated as a vote of confidence. They presented a copy of the motion of no confidence on the devolution issue, signed by every SNP MP. Andrew Welsh said that Michael Foot blanched and undertook to take it to Cabinet. On the following day he phoned to say that the Cabinet could not agree to our demands. On hearing the news, the Group authorised Andrew to lodge the no confidence motion.

It seemed the Government thought it would win and did nothing too serious to secure a majority. Plaid Cymru, with three MPs and the reluctant support of their Leader, Gwynfor Evans was bought off with a Bill, suddenly and coincidentally, brought forward to give compensation to slate quarrymen in north Wales, suffering from pneumoconiosis. Gwynfor Evans declared that there would be a political price to pay for this deal. He was right. He lost Carmarthen. The Ulster Unionists were ignored. Frank Maguire, the Republican MP for Fermanagh and Tyrone was offered some 'goodies', rumoured to be IRA releases from internment, to allow him to break his usual policy of abstention and vote for the Government. And for the SNP - nothing, save offers of talks about talks! Donald Stewart had his meeting with the Prime Minister and put forward the request of the SNP that the Government defeat the Order for repeal that the Act forced them to bring before Parliament, treating it as an issue of confidence that could provoke an early election. In his book, 'A Scot at Westminster', Donald recounted:

> 'I had a meeting with him in his office on the evening prior to the censure debate which ended the life of the government. Nobody else was present and we had a friendly talk in which he appeared relaxed and even fatalistic as I made clear the intention of the SNP to vote against the government unless the Scotland Bill was submitted on a vote of confidence basis. He made no effort of begging us to call off. Presumably he had realized that it would not be possible to dragoon the rabid anti-devolutionists in the Labour Party into supporting their own government's legislation. And he may have sensed that the die was cast.'

No bribes like oil revenues for the SDA or 'face-savers' like aids to quarrymen were offered! In a perceptive article in the Spectator (31 March 1979), Ferdinand Mount commented:

> 'The government did not have to fall. The votes were there for the taking. When all the sums are done, it is hard to avoid the feeling that Mr Callaghan had simply lost the will to carry on. Survival - even if for a matter of weeks – was still worth something to Labour's election chances. The significant thing is this time the government exerted itself so little and so late to improve those chances by dealing seriously with the minor parties who hold the balance and who, except for the Ulster Unionists, have nothing to gain from an early election… Right up to the last few days, the government seem to have lost the instinctive greed for power which keeps politicians going in off-peak moments. … Their negotiations with the minor parties were, it seems, frigid and sporadic. Labour Ministers seemed to have no idea how to approach the Scottish Nationalists. Nor had anyone much idea about what form the proffered all-party talks were to take nor what might plausibly be expected to emerge from them.'

It is interesting to speculate what would have happened if the Government had come up with an industrial package rather than action on devolution, say, the setting up of an Industrial Development Fund from oil revenues. This would have put the SNP MPs on the spot. With the Party at home running a desperate devolution campaign, back-tracking by the MPs with 'pork-barrel' spoils, could have been construed as an effort to save their seats at the expense of home rule! In the event, no such question was posed. Under the heading of 'Government Betrayal of Scotland', the fateful motion of no confidence signed by all 11 MPs was lodged.

> 'That this House condemns Her Majesty's Government for its failure to implement the Yes vote in the Scottish Assembly referendum and declares that it has no confidence in a Government that has failed to honour its manifesto commitment to the Scottish people, without which they would not have been elected.'

The gauntlet was cast. The Government did not move. The Official Opposition, circling like sharks, put down a simple motion of no confidence. In the absence of firm proposals for the setting up of the Scottish Assembly, the SNP MPs were still united in their decision to vote against the Government. The issue had come to a head.

In all my experience of Westminster, the vote of confidence debate on 28 March 1979 was the finest I had heard. James Callaghan was on great form. His jibe against the minority parties - not just the SNP - that this was the first time in recorded history that turkeys had been known to vote for an early Christmas was not original, but clearly effective. He jeered at the Conservatives for their deals with the Liberals and saved his excoriating criticism for David Steel and his Liberal band. Of course, the debate was only marginally over devolution. It concentrated, naturally enough for the English MPs, on unemployment and inflation. In his attack on the Government on devolution and also on their general record, Donald Stewart began:

> 'The Scottish National Party tabled a motion of no confidence in the Government because of the Government's refusal to honour their manifesto commitment to the Scottish people.'

And later:

> 'As the Prime Minister said yesterday devolution has been a question in Scotland for at least 10 years. Yet,

although every political party on the Scottish scene
went into the last election committed to an Assembly
all that happened after the election was there were
more talks and more White Papers. We then had the
first Scotland and Wales Bill, which was killed off. After
that we had the Scotland Bill and the 40% provision
was inserted. Now that the campaign in favour was
successful, Westminster wants to kill the Scotland Act.'

After dealing with prices, inflation and the economy, Donald closed with
the following:

> 'I end by returning to the question of Scottish government.
> I say to the Government and the Conservatives that
> the Scottish desire for self-government is thriving.
> Resentment is growing over the apparent wish of the
> majority here to frustrate that desire and to make
> divisions in Scotland. There can be no excuse of a bad
> Act, no all-party talks as a further exercise of futility and
> no propaganda that tries to turn a majority vote into a
> minority.
> These do not take a trick any longer. It is a pity that
> more Labour MPs do not back their own party policy
> and legislation, and that the Government may have to
> pay the price.'

And the debate wound up with a brilliant tour de force by Michael Foot,
Lord President of the Council, when he left the House spell-bound. It was
not so much the content as the way in which he played with words and the
opposition parties. Nevertheless, in scenes of high drama with false alarms
as to the way the vote had gone, the motion of no confidence scraped home
by 311 votes to 310.

Behind the scenes, and disclosed much later on a BBC Radio Four
programme, tales were told by Walter Harrison, the Depute Chief Whip of
how he had refused an offer by his Opposition counterpart, Bernard (Jack)
Weatherall) (later Speaker of the House) to abstain on a point of Whips'
honour since the Opposition had not kept to the usual conventions of
counting seriously ill MPs in their absence. Both actions were taken without
the knowledge of their superiors. I was also told in a background briefing by
a programme researcher how an SNP MP panicked and tried to vote both
ways, but was too late. Either event would have eliminated the majority. The
real reason was more prosaic. Frank Maguire, the independent from

Fermanagh had been told of an accusatory speech by Gerry Fitt of the SDLP which had persuaded him to abstain. Thus, the vote the Government had thought safe was not available. So on such a small miscalculation, the Labour Government fell.

Immediately after the vote, the Prime Minister made a statement declaring that an election would be called after essential business had been tidied up. The Government had been brought down essentially, but not exclusively, on its devolution policy. It had taken ten years from the setting up of the Kilbrandon Commission until the demise of the Government in 1979 – the longest slow burning fuse in history.

For the SNP, the less said about the election the better. The Party had been expecting an election for five years although in the light of recent events it had receded from its consciousness. It had spent inordinate amounts of time and energy preparing policy for the Assembly elections. The Manifesto for the General Election had been prepared in August 1978, when even then the press were estimating that the SNP would be reduced to five MPs. The polling performance had slumped following progress on the Scotland Bill from 27% in March 1978 to 21% in October, and to 17% in April 1979.

In January 1979, the various Party committees presumably not in touch with events were still diligently discussing the Assembly Manifesto and standing orders for the Assembly, as well as planning the devolution referendum and EEC election. I thought there was a more immediate danger and had sent a paper to the Electoral Planning Committee, at its request, warning of a Spring General Election and the likelihood that any election campaign could be prejudiced by the referendum and exhaustion of interest amongst the public in constitutional solutions. I argued that if 'YES' prevailed, then the electorate would assume the battle won and give the credit to Labour. If the result were 'NO', then this would damage the SNP more than the Government, since the Assembly was peripheral to the left/right battle and the UK. Wrongly, I also predicted that if Westminster rejected devolution through non-attainment of the 40% hurdle, there would be a tactical advantage for the SNP.

I recommended that the SNP concentrate on putting over an economic message based on Scotland being held back by London while subsidising it, evidence that more oil jobs from the North Sea were being created in the United States than in Scotland, the need for economic powers through self-government and attacks on Labour failures on oil policy. The political message would be Five Years of Labour Betrayal. I should have saved my breath. Colin Bell and Willie McRae moved rejection and the paper was hit into the long grass by being remitted to the Electoral Planning Committee by 7 votes to 6, on the Chairman's casting vote[5]. If I remember correctly, only

Stephen Maxwell amongst the major office-bearers gave support. So, I left them to it and concentrated on Westminster matters.

In the election, I did my share of media appearances. Charter flights brought Donald Stewart, Winnie Ewing and Hamish Watt to the central belt with good publicity. There was another problem – no leader figure on tour. Donald was constrained by distance and Billy Wolfe limited by his published decision to stand down as Chairman. Inside the HQ Campaign team, there were difficulties in co-ordination and direction.

After so many set-backs, the SNP was treated as finished. With the failure of devolution, it had no credible standing. The Referendum had burnt out the Scottish dimension. British ideas were in the forefront. Things were made worse by a lack-lustre first press conference and confusion over an addendum to the Manifesto. The British broadcasting media and press were uninterested. We were yesterday's news. The consequent absence of coverage on UK news programmes that we had enjoyed in 1974, did us real damage. To be honest, the electorate in Scotland were of the same view. They were not interested. Duncan MacLaren, the Press Officer said, 'I can only add that I doubt very much if our results would have differed given the circumstances and the swing of the vote against us', and from Helen Davidson, Deputy Director of the Campaign Team, 'Without public sympathy and a national swing it was impossible to win'. The end result was a savage drop in our support to 17.24% and a reduction in the number of seats to two, the Western Isles and Dundee East.

Back in Dundee, I had loyally followed the electoral strategy – somewhat difficult since the Party had failed to set clear themes. I was up against a superb Labour candidate, the charismatic Jimmy Reid who had led the Upper Clyde Shipbuilders work-in just a few years earlier. He had the enthusiastic support of the trade union movement, particularly the AUEW (the engineering union) which then dominated in Dundee. Exasperatingly, he had been awarded a medallion for services to Scotland by Wendy Wood, leader of the Scottish Patriots. He brandished this 'gong', as my agent Dave Keddie described it, at every opportunity. It was by no means certain that my large majority would withstand the pressure and I was conscious that a survey in the spring had predicted the loss of the constituency. Ten days into the campaign, I came to the conclusion that the SNP strategy of fighting the campaign on the need to achieve devolution and Labour's 'broken promises' was not working. My campaigning as usual was based on loudspeaking throughout the constituency from the city centre to the peripheral estates. I shifted themes. I abandoned devolution and adopted these three priorities: independence; Scotland's oil; and food prices. I was re-elected on a reduced majority of 2,519.

In Dundee East and the Western Isles, we lost votes to Labour, and in Clackmannan and East Stirling, and Dunbartonshire East to both Labour and Conservative. In Banff, the Labour vote increased due to the absence of a Liberal, whereas Argyll was lost by a swing to the Liberals. In Aberdeen East, South Angus, Clackmannan and Perth and East Perthshire, the electorate had risen respectively by 7,000, 6,000, 4,600 and 5,000 votes on the roll. In Moray & Nairn, we won the civilian parts of the constituency, but lost due to a huge turn-out of the RAF vote. In Galloway, the electorate also increased while the SNP vote went up. So there was a multitude of reasons why my hope of five seats was reduced to two. The end result was we had no credibility left and this was to have grave consequences for the future. As to the pattern in all seats, Robert Crawford, the Research Officer said:

> 'There is no evidence that we can find that there is any correlation between level of effort among PPCs, the size of constituency organisation or the money spent and the final vote. The SNP in this election were the victims of history. An election occurred when we were at our weakest for many years. The reality is that there is not a great deal we can do to roll back a swing – except perhaps recognise where we are most vulnerable electorally.'

Less charitably, and no doubt with my eye on the future contest for the post of Chairman, I wrote to the Executive:

> 'The poor result is a direct result of indecisive collective direction of the Party which has wandered in only two years from full-blooded independence to obsession with devolution. The NEC must bear responsibility for the dismantling of the oil campaign with its phase out as a priority issue and its further rejection of the Electoral Planning Committee recommendation that we use economic material during the referendum in preparation for an early General Election.
> Any Party, which does not know where it is going, and is disunited on strategy stands little chance of obtaining support from the public.'

We were indeed both the victors and victims of history – and time, too. Many mistakes were made at Party and Parliamentary level during the seventies. Yet, despite concerted opposition, we held public support until the second Bill on devolution. Instead of being given credit for this, it seems in the eye of the public that we had served our purpose and were redundant. We had sustained the cause of self-government from 1973 to 1978 which is a long time in politics. The Lib/Lab pact may not have helped the Liberals. It certainly removed the SNP from the high profile that came with holding the balance of power in a 'hung' parliament. The 40% hurdle did considerable psychological damage to the friable confidence of the Scottish people as well as to that of SNP activists. We also had no control over the political agenda and the mood of the nation became defeatist in the run up to and after the Referendum. The plain judgement must also be that Scotland was, when it counted, a unionist country. The inheritance of two hundred and fifty years of union with England was dominant, if breached for a short while. Neither Scotland nor its political establishment was ready for change.

Chapter 15

A Plague of Jacobites and Jacobins

On 15 September 1979, my political luck ran out. I was elected Chairman of the Scottish National Party. It was not the inheritance I had hoped for. When I first put forward my name, the SNP with eleven MPs and a large number of Councillors was a major force in Scottish politics. True, our poll ratings had dropped drastically compared with the 32%, we had won in the October 1974 General Election, but ahead of us was the referendum where our strategists thought we would win if a Scottish Assembly was approved and where in the unlikely prospect of a defeat, Labour would take the blame. All eyes were on the referendum and final touches were being put to the policy platform on which the Assembly elections would be fought.

The bare YES majority and the failure of Labour to deliver did not produce a fighting response from the Scottish people. The gamble of coercing Labour to deliver devolution had failed. The Government were defeated and the SNP crashed to disaster in the ensuing Westminster General Election of 3rd May 1979 when the Party lost 9 of its MPs and saw its vote drop to 17.2%. It was also locked in a prospective leadership battle. An early respite was given in June 1979 when Winnie Ewing, with the incredible energy and commitment that had won Hamilton and Moray and Nairn, took the Highlands and Islands Constituency in the European Assembly Election with 33.9%. Overall, the SNP gained 19.4%, up on the General Election. So we still had representation in both Europe and Westminster. Nevertheless, the Party was in desperate straits, facing estimated annual deficits of £31,500 for 1979 and 1980.[1] Membership had dropped over the preceding years and Headquarters was running with high staff levels. The NEC presided over redundancies for the Assistant Research Officer, Depute Press Officer, Industrial Officer, the National Organising Secretary and a telephonist/machinist. Even so, the savings would still lead to estimated net losses of £11,000 for each year.

This was depressing; but the Party was inured to disaster and it was hoped that recovery would ensue as had happened in the past. The financial crisis disguised the political problems. Throughout all levels of activist membership, there was bitterness. We had come so close to success and had been left with nothing. Little was expected from Westminster – indeed the worth of contesting parliamentary seats was under question by many activists - and there was no surprise when the incoming Conservative Government voted to repeal the Scotland Act. Some of this anger was vented against the Scottish people for their defeatism. The reaction went deep. Given the level of manipulation in the Referendum, some members lost faith in democracy. This anger turned – against the former Parliamentary Group, against the office-bearers and Executive, against the devolutionists, against purported right and left wing deviationism. Of course, there should have been room for civilised discussion. In her report to Conference as Senior Vice Chairman, Margo MacDonald set out her analysis:

> 'Our first mistake was that we did not join the great debate on economic strategy in a way which linked Independence to better, and fairer, economic and industrial policies (e.g our spokesmen made only sporadic and tentative forays into wage policy and industrial relations, yet these were the two topics which dominated politics in the last two years of the previous government). It was not enough to have voters believe that the SNP thought that Independence would solve these huge political problems. We required to say how Independence would help to solve them.
> Because as a party we lost ground to the unionists on the economic and industrial policy front, it was that bit more difficult to make the constitutional policy relevant. We might have re-established the relevance of the constitutional question if we had thrown ourselves wholeheartedly into the Assembly Referendum. We did not and I believe this was a huge mistake.'

I easily agreed with her first assertion and indeed had tried to persuade the Party to fight the 1979 election on economic issues. Her views on devolution were another matter and her remarks on this amongst others must have contributed to her downfall in internal elections for office in the Party. Her views also presaged strength sapping internal debates on the constitutional question and how to make the SNP appeal to Labour voters in Scotland. The divisions and internal agonies all had their roots firmly pre-1979, but it was the electoral failure that brought them to the fore and enabled them to dominate this period. Nevertheless, factionalism had already started and the ingredients were there for the vicious civil war over the next four years that was to bring the SNP to the brink of a major schism. On many occasions, I was in despair, as the SNP began to rip apart. It was a matter of profound regret that this happened at a time when Scotland faced the onslaught of the Thatcher Government and needed a strong, determined and united SNP. The SNP let Scotland down through its obsession with navel gazing.

The main faction emerged on the left. This was the Interim Committee for Political Discussion (or more commonly the '79 Group) formed on 31 May 1979, with Andrew Currie, Margo MacDonald, Stephen Maxwell, Roger Mullin and Robert Crawford amongst its members.[2] With other membership, it was evident that a left wing cell had been operating for some time at Headquarters. In a letter of 27 June, the Party Chairman had observed that with formal membership and annual subscription, the ICPD as an 'organised dissident faction' within the Party would weaken rather than give the Party new strength. Again on 9 July he took the view that the Party would not adopt the marxist-oriented ideology of the '79 Group'. He favoured the SNP adopting a moderate left of centre stand and felt that failure to take this route would be more serious than the loss of members of the 79 Group. By 23 July, Billy Wolfe was exercised by newspaper reports of the Group's July meeting and wrote as Chairman of the Party to Andrew Currie, Margo MacDonald and Steve Butler whom he believed to be its three co-chairmen in the following terms:

> 'I write to make sure that you are aware of Rule 116 of the Party's Constitution. As I do not know all the facts about the 79 Group, I cannot interpret the Party's Constitution in relation to it. However, I advise you to consider carefully the details of that Rule and its possible implications for the 79 Group in particular and for the Party as a whole.'

Since Donald Stewart had forecast the danger of the 79 Group provoking the formation of a counter-balancing right wing group, the Chairman viewed such a body as also likely to fall foul of the provision of the Constitution relating to involvement with another political party. In the meantime, claims were made - and denied - that the 79 Group had access to membership records at Headquarters. There were reports, too, that Headquarters' facilities had been used to produce a stencil for 79 Group literature.[3] And so, in the run up to Conference in Dundee, tension grew. Conference itself was in a reactive mood. It deplored the formation of unofficial groups with left or right policies[4], reaffirmed independence as the Party's campaigning issue in elections, rejecting devolution, assemblies and 'meaningful' talks[5] and committed itself towards withdrawal from the Common Market.[6]

The elections for office-bearers showed that the Party had turned its back on those who had supported devolution by electing nationalist candidates. When the results were announced, Douglas Henderson who had been elected Senior Vice Chairman, turned to me and in an aside remarked that the selection of office-bearers was too one-sided. I agreed! By March 1980, some of the indicators had improved with membership card sales above the level of the previous year, recruitment of younger members and more branches paying their dues.[7] Overall, the finances remained in deficit and there were gaps in the organisation. In Glasgow, for example, 7 out of 12 of the Constituency Associations had been reduced to single Constituency Branches.[8] Lack of credibility of the Party remained the greatest problem.

There were few changes at the 1980 Conference in Rothesay. Billy Wolfe replaced Robert McIntyre as Party President and Margo MacDonald and Isobel Lindsay were both re-elected to the NEC at the ensuing National Council. Iain Murray had earlier replaced Chrissie MacWhirter as National Secretary. In terms of policy, there were no surprises and Conference passed two lengthy policy resolutions on Community Enterprises and Shipbuilding. On the face of it, the Party was settling down, but both Edith and I noticed that there were undercurrents of hostility. I also welcomed Jim Sillars to Conference as a new party member. Jim had been a Labour MP and had headed a short-lived Scottish Labour Party that had been torn apart by factional in-fighting!

The SNP had, however, taken a thrashing at the District Council elections when the Party lost many of the Councillors elected at the peak of its support in 1977. Even so, it gained 24% of the vote, 7 % above that of the General Election and had advanced in Tayside and Grampian. The SNP had also done very well in a by-election in Glasgow Central where its candidate Gil Paterson led the fight.

Glasgow Central By-election Result (June 1980)

Labour	60.8%
SNP	26.3%
Scottish Conservative & Unionist	8.7%
Others	4.2%

But the storm clouds were gathering. I returned from holiday in August to find a full scale public row had broken out between Douglas Henderson, Senior Vice Chairman and NEC member, Willie McRae. I was not amused. The subject of the row was a press conference on nuclear dumping sites. Willie McRae who was excitable at any time had blown his top in the press and Douglas Henderson had allowed himself to be drawn into a verbal fracas. The authority of the leadership was diminished at a time when we were going to need every ounce to deal with the approaching crisis.

At the meeting of the NEC on 8 August 1980, the Committee heard complaints about the behaviour of another splinter group, Siol nan Gaidheal

(SNG) at and after the annual Bannockburn Rally in June. This body, purportedly 'cultural', had paraded in tartan with broadswords and dirks. It had its own flag party and drum corps. It insisted on joining the SNP at demonstrations. Whereas the 79 Group was mainly a middle class body, SNG recruited largely from SNP members living in working class housing areas. The NEC was sufficiently concerned to appoint an investigating committee and a month later passed a resolution to the effect that only the national flag, Party banners and placards relating to unemployment be carried during a major demonstration in Glasgow planned for October.[9] Following an adverse report from the Committee of Enquiry, the October meeting of the NEC, amid a welter of amendments, proposed a resolution that membership of SNG was no longer compatible with that of the SNP.[10] This resolution had to be heard by the National Council in Arbroath on 6 December 1980. There were also three other resolutions on that agenda – two for groups and one against the 79 Group.

In my Chairman's Report to that Council, I warned the Party of the consequences:

> 'The SNP can also learn a lesson from what is happening to the Labour Party. Some have recommended that the SNP should follow Labour's practice of having wings and factions. The events of September and October for Labour show how disunity can lead to bitterness and internal strife.'

This advice was ignored. Amid a torrid, emotional atmosphere, the NEC Resolution banning SNG moved by Prof. Neil MacCormick and seconded by Jim Fairlie was defeated by an overwhelming majority and another resolution giving conditional approval of groups was passed similarly. The anti-79 Group resolution from Tayport Branch was also heavily defeated.[11] It was noticeable from the speakers and votes that the left wing 79 Group gave support to the SNG which many SNP members regarded as protofascist. This left/right alliance was to tie the hands of the Party centre. In the meantime, SNG's militant behaviour continued to draw bad publicity, while organised 79 Group activity spread to the branches to obtain their support for a slate of candidates for the 1981 internal elections.

While the SNP was distracted by internal squabbles over ideology, the Tory Government under Prime Minister Margaret Thatcher was resolving an economic crisis at the cost of Scottish de-industrialisation. The move by Labour to the left under Michael Foot did not give rise to political success and Labour was infiltrated by the Trotskyite Militant Tendency. The troubles in the SNP mirrored those in the British Labour Party – save that the SNP disputes were arguably more bitter. The leftward moving Labour Party under Michael Foot had led to influential former Labour ministers, such as David Owen, Roy Jenkins, Shirley Williams and Bill Rodgers forming the Council for Social Democracy and eventually creating the Social Democratic Party. These developments did not leave much room in the political spectrum for the Scottish National Party. People living in the central belt had a deep loyalty to Labour, regardless of its splits and betrayals. With the moderate left of centre now occupied by the SDP, the SNP's social democratic stance was easily drowned out; we – I included - were convinced that the phenomenon would not spread to Scotland. We were wrong. In a preponderantly British political system, it is impossible to insulate Scotland from major British trends. Our view that they would not put down roots in Scotland was correct although they were still able to do us serious damage over the next few years.

Efforts were made to secure agreement on strategy – but with a large section of the Party organising a 'putsch', this was going to be difficult! There was a special NEC meeting on 29 June 1980 that reached some consensus on campaigning while facing both ways on wider strategy and another on 14 February 1981 where the major conclusion was to raise national consciousness and make Scotland relevant to the big international issues. Political techniques were looked at in detail.[12] A memorandum from the National Organiser to the Chairman dated 8 April 1981, showed that membership which had risen from 14,087 in 1979 to 14,972 in 1980 dropped sharply in comparative card sales to 12,617 for 1981, as good a sign as any that the political health of the SNP had worsened.

The 1981 Conference in Aberdeen in May brought matters to a head. The 79 Group had launched a major campaign at branch and constituency level to dominate the Agenda and ensure their slate of candidates was elected. The delegates were also in a militant mood carrying a resolution on direct action on industrial issues as part of a Scottish Resistance,[13] and another calling on SNP MPs to operate in Scotland and obey Party direction (while partly neutered by amendment) was carried by 223 votes to 211.[14] Another resolution supported armed neutrality,[15] while one more steered the SNP into complete opposition to Common Market membership.[16] All in all it was a magnificent exercise of cussedness and isolationism. Against the floodtide, there was little I could do.

In my speech to Conference, I put in a despairing word in favour of multilateral defence. I also dealt with the economy, accusing the Labour Party of steadying the hand that wielded the Thatcher axe. This was the first of many assertions that the Scottish Labour MPs were not defending Scotland. The 1981 Conference heard a rousing speech by Jim Sillars, calling for Scottish resistance and civil disobedience. With magnificent rhetoric, he finished on a crescendo that it was only when the cell doors slammed shut that the Scottish resistance would win. Stirring stuff, indeed! I had no real objection to civil disobedience in the right circumstances (indeed I had cut my political teeth on the illegal Radio Free Scotland two decades earlier). This time, I knew the Scottish people had no stomach for a fight. Yet the leadership had been lumbered with the policy of civil disobedience and the Party would expect action. The resolution was, of course, a 79 Group ploy intended to undermine the leadership, if nothing was done, so in closing the Conference, I nominated Jim Sillars, newly elected as Vice Chairman for Policy, as the person in charge and transferred the 'black spot' to him.

The Conference was, however, a triumph for the 79 Group as they had many supporters elected. Andrew Currie was elected EVC Organisation to join Jim Sillars on the NEC. Alex Salmond also made his first appearance on the NEC. Billy Wolfe who had jumped ship from having been an opponent to a supporter of groups, was narrowly elected Party President in a contest against Donald Stewart MP. Very definitely, the balance of power in the Party had swung to the organised 79 Group. Although they had tasted power and professed to be representative of the left in the Party, this was not so. Tom McAlpine and Isobel Lindsay, leaders of the left in the 1960s and 1970s did not join.

In her memorandum, Isobel commented[17]:

> 'The 79 Group saga (you must still have the grey hairs) was born out of deep frustration of the referendum and electoral failure but as usual there was also an element of positioning for power within the party. My own view, as someone on the Left, was that their analysis was wrong. I didn't think there was evidence that the main reason for electoral failure was because the SNP's policies/image was insufficiently left just as I didn't think it was because we had compromised by supporting devolution. There is a proportion of the electorate who are tribal in their party affiliation but the others look on the parties instrumentally – who is likely to bring the kind of changes they want. The SNP was the driving force that had resulted in the Scottish Assembly proposals and the failure to get change was (unfairly) linked to the SNP. Another important flaw in the 79 Group analysis was that they had a vision of working-class Scotland as traditional (male) workers just at a time when major changes in employment patterns had taken place and was likely to accelerate. It was a very dated view of Scotland.

The reason why I didn't support the 79 Group was that I felt one of the SNP's strengths in comparison to my experience in the Labour Party was the absence of organised factions and this led to much more open thinking and debate rather than people coming to discussion with a pre-determined group position. The formation of a counter grouping is inevitable when you get this 'party within a party' and it then develops its own dynamic and becomes even more difficult to pull back.'

Another socialist, Jim Fairlie, had strong views[18]:

'I had little quarrel with the 79 Group arguing about policy because there was little in the current SNP policy with which they could quarrel. I was also on very good terms with people like Stephen Maxwell and Andrew Currie ... my attitude to the 79 Group began to change when I was invited to attend one of their meetings. As I had a pretty good relationship with many of them, there was little personal animosity to me but their attitude to the leadership of the party in general was scathing. The meeting was conducted fairly enough and I was never abused or under any great pressure, the bulk of the criticism being centred on others in the leadership, including yourself. What appeared in the press the next day bore little or no relationship to what actually happened and I remember your telephoning me to commiserate with the alleged treatment I had received. It was made obvious to me at that meeting that the Group was not interested in simply getting changes, they wanted control of the party and were not fussy how they did it.
Before the NC in Arbroath I went to great lengths to persuade the 79 Group they were under no threat but that we had to get rid of the SNG. I promised them my full backing if they went along with the NEC and got rid of SNG ... The atmosphere in the hall was intimidating to some although I did not feel in the least intimidated. However, when I saw the 79 group voting to keep SNG in the party all my sympathy for them disappeared. From then on I was just as determined to stop them as I was to get rid of SNG.'

The civil war within the Party raged at all levels. Both SNG and the 79 Group were active within the Branches and Constituency Associations, including my own. The '79 Group's strategy was to take control at local level as a precursor to assuming overall command. It was divisive and led to bitterness and frustration amongst those excluded. One young nationalist wrote to me a year later:

> 'I too, Mr Wilson, am a left winger, but I do not put that desire above the cause of Scottish independence. I also do not take too kindly to the idea put about by the 79 Group that their young members were the ones with true talent in the party. I found, especially in the Edinburgh area, that if you weren't a member of that particular clique then what you had to say wasn't of any particular worth.'

Another member commented:

> 'I joined in May 1979 and became conscious of the deep internal trouble in the Party later in 1979 as I began to attend National Council. Internal groups came to the surface in 1980 with Siol nan Gaidheal. There was never a National Council without there being trouble and internal tension of some sort. Elections were ferocious battle grounds and ultimately the issue came to a head in the 1982 Conference. It became clear to me that – not for the first time – that the Party was in a position where internal tension could lead to its destruction and things were very volatile in 1981 and 1982 with effectively quite open challenges to the Party leadership and also severe disagreement between the Party leadership and some of the direction of party decision making. I certainly felt there was a genuine opportunity for authority within the Party to collapse at that time.'

For the next two years, my strategy was to keep a divided party from schism (to which the Party had been prone in the past). This meant that as Chairman of National Council and the National Executive Committee, I attempted to persuade the warring factions to work in harness and get the organisation moving again. I knew the SNP was unlikely to return to political health until the various people concerned and their factions tumbled to the political benefits from working together. I was the conductor of a very discordant band hoping it would learn to play in tune. When the time was ripe, I wanted to introduce policy reforms to make the SNP electable once more. Meantime, I had to postpone any hope of achieving political success. The survival of the Party was my goal and this would lead to unpopularity with the nationalists who wanted complete expulsion of the factionalists and the factionalists who wanted control 'by hook or by crook'.

The first clash of views came with a debate over the topic of the autumn campaign. Isobel Lindsay as EVC Publicity favoured one based on a New Deal whereas Jim Sillars as EVC Policy wanted to run on his Conference theme of the Scottish Resistance.[19] After a series of votes, the NEC agreed an integrated campaign with the Scottish Resistance in the autumn and the New Deal in the spring. This was obviously a compromise to keep the various wings quiet. It did not work. The 79 Group faction produced their own suite of publicity promotions to be used by branches they controlled and ignored the official material. There was, however, agreement on demonstrations including assistance to workers at the Lee Jeans factory led by Jim Fairlie, now Senior Vice Chairman and Jim Sillars, opposition to the take-over of the Royal Bank of Scotland by Standard Chartered, a merger between the Royal Bank and Hong Kong and Shanghai Banking Corporation and later, demutualisation of the TSB. For some reason, the SNP had an obsession with banks – one which may now be regarded as prescient!

The issue of Groups arose again. With further reports of bad behaviour by SNG, opinion amongst 79 Group supporters began to swing against it. In August, the 79 Group itself ran into trouble when headlines in the Glasgow Herald bore revelations from the minutes of their August meeting that they were to hold discussions with Provisional Sinn Fein. This led to the Executive, on the initiative of Jim Sillars and Andrew Currie, embarrassed by the militancy of their own Group, prohibiting formal groups from having such contacts[20]. The campaign of civil disobedience had gone off at half-cock with an abortive occupation of the intended Scottish Assembly building on the Calton Hill, Edinburgh. I was fully aware that there was an emerging split in the Group over the republican issue, but for the time being had limited control over the NEC as exemplified when it chose Iain More, the Party's Research Officer to be HQ Director by 12 votes to 11 over my preferred candidate, Alan McKinney.[21]

As the year turned into 1982, there was a by-election in Glasgow Hillhead. This was not good territory for us. The party chose George Leslie who was widely experienced. Members responded and our initially low polling of 12% increased to 14%, a good start when we were desperately seeking to boost our credibility within the constituency from a very low base. Progress was made in the two Labour held wards, but canvassing results in

Anniesland and Hillhead Wards were dire. The SNP had rather contemptuously discounted the chances of the SDP/Liberal Alliance candidate, Roy Jenkins, on the basis that the SDP was an English phenomenon. The Party could not have been more wrong. With huge media support, Roy Jenkins romped home in a late charge that squeezed our vote and pushed us into fourth place. The constituency did not supply a suitable platform to enable the SNP to win. Nevertheless, the result was proof, if any were needed, as to how low the Party had sunk.

Glasgow Hillhead By-election Result (March 1982)

Social Democratic/Liberal Alliance	33.4%
Conservative/Unionist Party	26.6%
Labour	25.9%
SNP	11.3%
Others	2.8%

On the eve of the by-election, the President, Billy Wolfe wrote a letter to the Church of Scotland journal 'Life and Work' objecting to the appointment of the Papal legate as an ambassador from the Vatican and referring to Pope Pius XII as 'the Nazi Pope'. With a papal visit to Scotland due later in the year, this had incendiary implications for the West of Scotland, where sectarianism was a continuing blemish. The letter came too late to affect the outcome of the Hillhead by-election. It did, however, threaten the gravest consequences for the Party's vote amongst Catholics. As result of firm responses by Donald Stewart and me, Billy Wolfe agreed not to publish a further anti-catholic memorandum. This was not enough. Given the growing reaction, I was prepared to initiate disciplinary action which could have led to his suspension or expulsion.

Tom McAlpine and Isobel Lindsay intervened and agreed to procure Billy Wolfe's withdrawal from re-election at the forthcoming Conference. He did so, and I took steps to ensure that the media knew this action was enforced so that there could be no doubt that the Party was seen to have disassociated itself from his views. Action was also taken to re-assure the Catholic Church that the SNP welcomed the visit of his Holiness the Pope and in due course, an invitation was extended, and accepted, for my wife and me to attend the Papal Mass at Bellahouston Park, Glasgow. We were not naïve enough to think that there had been no political damage done to the Party's prospects amongst Catholic voters. The Labour Party would make sure that Billy Wolfe's misguided views were attributed to the SNP as a whole and the affair would take a long time to live down.

Without a boost from Hillhead, the SNP put up 268 candidates in the 1982 Regional Elections. Its vote was squeezed by the SDP/Liberal Alliance from 20.9% in 1978 to 13.4%. The pain was softened with the SNP gaining 23 seats to 20 for the Alliance, and in the medium term, blocking the advance of the Alliance – a strategic necessity if we were to restore our position as Scotland's leading minority party.

In the run up to the Ayr Conference, I knew from sources that the 79 Group was in steep decline with splits arising on the republican issue and was confident enough to brief Bill Clark, political correspondent of the Herald, that the SNP was turning the corner. I had failed to realise that others were following a political agenda that would upset my calculations. The Conference took place in early June 1982 in unusually hot, stifling conditions. The first day's outcome confirmed my view that the Party had seen through the challenge from the 79 Group when Andrew Welsh succeeded in overturning the policy on civil disobedience adopted the previous year by 192 votes to 162.[22] Yet others were not so sensitive and a new Group, the Campaign for Nationalism in Scotland, principally composed of Robert McIntyre, Winifred Ewing and Jimmy Halliday was launched at an evening fringe meeting with the aim of thwarting the 79 Group.

So far as I was concerned my strategy of causing the gradual atrophying of the 79 Group and recruiting their members to a more creative role within the Party had been destroyed. Robert McIntyre wrote to me soon after in justification[23]:

> 'I did not agree with your strictures on the Campaign for Nationalism in Scotland. It was formed to promote the Party's philosophy and policies which were being traduced. I do not agree the '79 group would have faded away as you said to me you thought. Branches were being subjected to concerted attempts at take-over. Before the Conference I attended a meeting in Inverness and the venom that non-members of the '79 Group were subject to was deplorable. I do not think I have ever attended a more objectionable meeting. When the '79ers did not get their way they walked out. The press publicity over the CNS meeting in Ayr would not have occurred had the '79 group not sent along a large contingent to break up the meeting. They claim the right to run a party within a party with its own policies and aims contrary to the SNP but show total intolerance to those promoting the aims of the SNP. I have always regarded that group as outwith the constitution of the Party as another political party.

They do not think they can survive on their own (cf. the SSP and the two SLPs). Therefore they have to find a host organisation on which to prey as a parasite which cannot live without a host which any parasite destroys.'

Regardless of the arguments, the consequences were catastrophic. On the following morning, the newspaper headlines screamed about the civil war breaking out within the SNP. Any hope I had of curing the Party's malaise by patient reconciliation and political self-interest had gone. Angus Lyon, the SNP parliamentary assistant, observed over breakfast, 'This can't go on'. I agreed and made hasty changes to the speech I was due to deliver to the Party later that morning. In it, I highlighted the political damage and gave notice of my intention to propose a resolution the following day that would ban all groups. The impact was immediate. Members of the 79 Group did a public walk-out from the Conference hall to a hail of cat-calls and whistles of derision.

It was by no means sure that I would be able to implement my promise. As Chairman, I had no control over the Conference Agenda. This was in the hands of the separately elected Standing Orders and Agenda Committee and before the commencement of the Conference session, I had to present my resolution to it. To fit the rules, it had to be 'topical'. Whether 'topical' or not, it needed the agreement of the Committee without which I would have to ask Conference to suspend Standing Orders – something that required a two thirds majority and would be even more risky. It was a hard fight, but eventually I received permission by a knife-edge majority to present the following resolution:

> 'This Conference demands the immediate disbandment of all organised political groups within the Party; and declares that membership of the Party is incompatible with membership of any group which has not fulfilled the direction of this Conference within 3 months; and instructs the Chairman and the National Secretary to then immediately take the necessary action under Rules 3, 4, 7 and 66 of the Party Constitution.'

After an impassioned debate, my resolution, seconded by Alan Clayton who was on the left of the party spectrum, defeated by 413 votes to 189 a counter-motion by Alex Salmond seeking to remit the decision to a Special National Council. The resolution then carried by 308 votes to 188. The election results showed a marked swing away from the 79 Group, and at Council on 19 June 1982, the trend was repeated with Alex Salmond and others replaced by mainstream and nationalist representatives.

The resolution gave three months for the groups to make up their minds. This was a mistake since it protracted the appeal processes. Two months would have been a better timescale for early determination of the issue. On the face of it, this should have been the end of the matter. Conference, the highest court of the Party, had laid down the law. Its word was final. In practice, the opposite occurred. The 79 Group had being dying on its feet and its more ambitious members appeared ready to discard it as a platform. The banning resolution was regarded as an affront and the Group suddenly revived and reunited, full of righteous indignation that their 'human right' to form a political grouping in the Party (a notion imported from the Labour Party) had been subverted. Their initial reaction was to hold a meeting, notionally disband and form a 79 Group Socialist Society' that would be open to non-members. Their claim to be a new organisation was not helped by there being no non-SNP members at the time of its reformation! It was a transparent attempt to get round the Conference decision and easy for the SNP National Secretary, Neil MacCallum to discredit. A more intelligent course would have been for them to disband and several months later launch a Scottish Socialist Society with an independent membership. This ill-judgement likely stemmed from arrogance and pique. If they had been patient, there is no way the Party could have extended the ban to a genuine multilateral body, clearly independent of the SNP.

There was a truce with the holding of the Airdrie & Coatbridge By-election on 24 June 1982. This was a very short campaign and SNP activists did not turn out in strength. Given the background of publicised strife and the seat already being poor for the SNP, the result was not encouraging despite the best efforts of the candidate, Ron Wyllie.

Airdrie & Coatbridge By-election Result (June 1982)

Labour Party	55.1%
Conservative & Unionist Party	26.2%
SNP	10.5%
Liberal/SDP Alliance	8.2%

With the effective decision of the 79 Group to continue under another guise, the scene was set for open hostilities where every blow leaked to the media. The National Secretary advised Council on 4 September 1982 that he had written to the Campaign for Nationalism in Scotland, the 79 Group and Siol nan Gaidheal to ascertain their response to the Ayr Resolution. Of these, only the first had responded and agreed to disband. This led to a flurry of questions and a failed attempt was made by Stephen Maxwell to delete this section of the report to allow discussion in December.

On 11 September, the NEC resolved by 15 votes to 2 that Siol nan Gaidheal was an organised political group and that membership of the Party was incompatible with its membership.[24] There was a more complex consideration of the position of the 79 Group, but eventually having had a series of votes on alternatives, the NEC found that the 79 Group Socialist Society was a device intended to remain an organised faction and as it too had not disbanded, its membership and that of its interim committee were likewise incompatible with membership of the Party. SNG office-bearers accepted the position and as no satisfactory response had been received from the 7 of the 9 members of the Interim Committee, letters of expulsion were issued by the National Secretary and confirmed by the NEC on 9 October 1982.[25]

National Council in Glasgow on 4 December was the most fractious I have encountered. The bile poured out! It began with a motion of no confidence in the NEC which I successfully opposed by 183 votes to 42.[26] Later in the day, a motion from Jim Sillars to suspend standing orders to allow direct hearing of the appeals of those expelled (while receiving 126 votes to 124) failed to gain a two thirds majority, and in terms of customary procedure, the appeals were remitted to the Appeals Committee for consideration[27].

While all this was absorbing the energies of the Party, normal work went on. Alan McKinney was appointed HQ Director and Duncan MacLaren resigned as Press Officer. Not helped by the leaking of the National Council papers to the Press, there was yet another by-election in 1982, this time in Glasgow Queens Park where the candidate was Peter Mallan. The Party's Research Officer, Chris MacLean's assessment was of particular interest[28]:

> 'On the three issues on which the SNP has adopted a very high profile over the years, viz independence, nuclear weapons and the EEC, the voters expressed the following opinions: in favour of independence – 40%, in favour of a devolved assembly – 27%,, and for no change – 29%,: not in favour of nuclear weapons in Scotland – 77%, in favour - 19%; in favour of leaving the EEC – 60%, remain in the EEC – 33%. When asked why they were not voting SNP, 32% said it was because of lack of credibility and a further 21% said that they did not know enough about the party; 8% were against independence, 7% because of poor leadership, 4% because the SNP were 'Tartan Tories' and only 1% because the SNP had brought down the Labour government.

Glasgow Queen's Park By-election Result (December 1982)

Labour Party	56%
SNP	20%
Conservative & Unionist Party	12%
Liberal/ SDP Alliance	9.4%
Others	2.6%

Despite an indifferent campaign and poor media coverage, this result was a real achievement. In the prior survey, only 8% of the sample indicated they would vote for us and our vote in the 1979 General Election was 9.7%.

Of course, the 79 Group issue did not go away. By this time the Socialist Society was being established on an ostensibly non-party basis. This did not affect the appeals since the expulsions were legally based on the status of the 79 Group in September. Nevertheless, I sensed that the membership of the Party was taking the view that the NEC was going too far and as my antennae were usually sensitive, made clear to the Press my view that no further action should be taken on the issue of membership of the new Socialist Society meantime. This gained wide coverage and angered mainstream members of the NEC, including the Senior Vice Chairman, Jim Fairlie, Margaret Bain and Colin Bell who succeeded in postponing consideration of the question to February.[29] Internally, there was little progress. The report of the Appeals Committee was not available for National Council in March and my ruling that the matter was *sub-judice* and could not be discussed was challenged, with the vote of confidence being defeated comfortably by 136 votes to 40.[30] In the afternoon session, yet another attempt to suspend standing orders to allow the hearing of the appeals directly failed to get a two thirds majority.[31]

At last, the long drawn out saga reached a conclusion at a special meeting of National Council on 30 April 1983, almost eleven months from the date of the Conference decision. The Appeals Committee had spent around forty hours in considering the case, some of it with the appellants represented by counsel. It found for the National Executive. Prof. Neil MacCormick had come up with an amendment that sought to mitigate the sentence. My first thought was to disallow it, but, after consideration, it seemed to be a possible solution, especially since the NEC majority had fractured. To me, there were three issues. Was the NEC's decision approved in principle? Had the democratic authority of the Party been maintained? What should be the sentence – expulsion or suspension?

On the main issue, Council voted to uphold the expulsions and the procedures by 157 to 138.[32] The debate was reasonably restrained, but tense and Alex Salmond, speaking for the appellants with a complete absence of nerves, made a notable contribution. On the question of sentence, it agreed to Neil MacCormick's motion to commute the expulsions to suspension, but only provided that each suspended member wrote to the Secretary accepting the position and requested the lifting of the suspension.[33] Any appellant not fulfilling this essential condition would remain expelled.

This formula was accepted by an overwhelming majority and the sense of relief amongst the delegates allowed me to turn the feeling to positive advantage by calling forcefully for unity in contesting the General Election. I do not believe the Council believed the Election was imminent but it took place within 6 weeks. In an effort to bandage the wounds, I had to argue forcefully against entrenched opposition in the NEC to approve ex-79 Group member Kenny MacAskill as a candidate. The Party's credibility was still in tatters and the election was a 'no-hoper'. Donald Stewart and I were re-elected comfortably with increased majorities. Other than close outcomes in the constituencies of Banff/Buchan and Moray, there were no gains. This was not a customary General Election. It was held after the Falklands War when the Tories benefited. There is obviously nothing better for a government than a short, sharp, victorious war! The SNP also had to contend with the powerful presence of the SDP/Liberal Alliance, supported by the media. Labour were in disarray in England though not in Scotland. In the outcome, Labour won 41 seats with 35% of the vote, the Conservatives 21 seats with 28.4%, the Alliance 8 seats with 24.5% and the SNP 2 seats, with its support squeezed to 11.8%. There was also a hint for the first time of a committed SNP vote capable of withstanding the cyclical downturns of the past, some of it coming from the second generation of families of those who had first voted for the Party in the sixties.

While the membership rejoiced at the end to the war over the Groups, the four years of internecine warfare – especially in the last year - had weakened the SNP considerably – in prestige, credibility and good will. It was no excuse for the finger to be pointed at the Labour Party which had to fight similar battles over entryism by Militant until Neil Kinnock turned the tide. SNP members have a higher responsibility to their country than internal Party ambition.

Despite the ending of the surface conflict, I was under no illusions. There was a deep seated animosity in the higher levels of the party leadership and a running debate over the future direction of the Party. Jim Fairlie, representing the nationalist wing of the Party put it thus.[34]

> 'It is academic what might have happened if we had gone into that debate (the Council appeal hearing) united as an Executive, even if we had lost the vote. The '79 Group were not in a forgiving mood and spent

> the rest of the 1980s doing what they had been doing as an organised group. They continued to pick off those they wanted to get rid of and the fact the expelled members had been re-admitted before the election of 1983 made no difference to our performance'.

The most difficult part I had to play over the next few years was to cajole and coerce all the leaders of the Party to work together, despite their deeply rooted antipathies. The 1983 general election also administered a shock to the SNP as a whole and in the new mood of realism, my hope was that a new series of policy and publicity initiatives would help bring the SNP back into the mainstream of Scottish politics, and so away from its self-imposed exile in extremism and isolationism.

Chapter 16

New Alliances

Unlike the seventies, Westminster was no longer centre stage, either for the SNP or Scotland. With the defeat of the SNP and the election of a Conservative government, all prospect of progress in delivering devolution vanished. Despite the Tories' promises during the referendum that it was the Labour Government's scheme with which they disagreed and the question of devolution was still open, the reality was otherwise. The Tories were out-and-out unionists and resented the high parliamentary profile enjoyed by Scotland over the previous five years. They had also done well in Scotland in the 1979 election. As for the large majority of Scottish Labour MPs, they had no importance, being merely a branch of the humiliated British Labour Party – and scorned. Scotland was effectively off stage.

Within three weeks of the election, the Government tabled its draft Order repealing the Scotland Act. When Donald Stewart raised the promise from Lord Home that a better Bill would be forthcoming, his intervention was brushed aside by Secretary of State, George Younger who proffered only all-party talks. In my own remarks, I accepted that the issue was exhausted, but they should remember that an ebb tide turns and floods. The Act was summarily disposed of much to the relief of the Labour Party for which devolution had been a running sore.

If the previous Parliament had been a parliament of drama, Westminster was now tamed by an autocratic leader with a large majority and a ruthless disposition. Donald Stewart and I now lacked any parliamentary 'clout'. Bereavement was my first reaction to the loss of my colleagues, heightened by a feeling of political impotence as I realised just how low we had fallen. The only blessing was that my remaining colleague was Donald Stewart. This is not a slight on former colleagues as I am sure my view would have been shared by most of them, if they had been thrust into a group of two. We were completely different in approach and outlook, yet formed an alliance that not even policy difficulties over Europe, devolution and social democracy could shake. We trusted each other completely and our friendship, along with that of our respective wives, Chrissie and Edith deepened as we worked together. We were also well served by our parliamentary staff, Irene Taylor, Angus Lyon and Rona Campbell.

Yet weak as we were, we resolved to keep the SNP flag flying at Westminster until the Party was resurrected as a viable political force. There was no problem over precedence. At Westminster, Donald was the Group Leader and in Scotland, I was Party Chairman. Both of us were still MPs and particularly in my case with activity in Scotland, this gave credibility to my statements.

There was a lot of parliamentary work to do. Over the next eight years, there were many industrial crises with factories closing. In October 1979, I led the fight by seeking an emergency debate on problems with the Scottish economy. Earlier I had spoken on shipbuilding at 1.46 am, a sure indication of the lack of governmental interest. Over the next two years, Donald presented a Gaelic Bill that was defeated. My own Development of Tourism Bill was talked out. This Bill, that sought to give the Scottish Tourist Board power to promote Scotland abroad (then exclusively reserved to the British Tourist Authority), met with a hail of abuse from Scottish Tory MPs. Three years later, the Government produced a similar Bill with not a blush of embarrassment.

Later, Donald Stewart was successful in the ballot for private members' bills and chose the Disablement (Prohibition of Unjustifiable Discrimination) Bill. This Bill had all-party support and none from the Government, so it was duly killed off. Further on, set against the significant number of winter deaths amongst the elderly from hypothermia, I made repeated efforts to progress Cold Climate Bills to give additional benefits to those who lived in the colder areas – a campaign that was not exclusive to Scotland. It attracted support from UK MPs and this led to the Minister, Rhodes Boyson to commission research from York University and for his successor, John Major also to take a profile. In Scotland, there was substantial indignation when the primitive system in force produced a pay-out in the south of England and not in Scotland. Over 30 local authorities registered support for the campaign. There was also a Bill to deal with mergers of Scottish companies.

One issue that could have caused a disagreement with Donald was the Falklands war in 1982. I was always an opponent of British imperialism and approval of the expeditionary force was a large pill to swallow. As international law supported the UK in this case, I rather reluctantly gave Donald support for intervention. Involvement in international matters of this kind was unusual. For the time being, apart from the 'bread and butter' issues, we just had to play for time and be prepared to foment Scottish irritation and outrage, as and when the Scottish people reacted to the Thatcher Government.

With the 1983 election, things began to change. Immediately after the election, I wrote to Bruce Millan Shadow Scottish Secretary with copies to Russell Johnston of the Liberals and Roy Jenkins of the SDP inviting them to discuss Scottish parliamentary opposition to the government. In my letter, I said:

> 'It seems to me a matter of urgency, that all those Scottish parties who can lay genuine claim to the people's mandate, should show their willingness to co-operate in the defence of Scotland's interests. We may

> have campaigned against each other, but we did so in
> the shared knowledge that the Government chosen for
> us by the electors of England, threatened Scotland's
> interests, identity, livelihood and democratic rights.
> Now confronted by that English Tory landslide, we
> should surely recognise that the people of Scotland
> deserve more of us than empty promises to be
> redeemed in five years' time.'

The call was well received within the SNP as a sign that the Party was moving out of its defensive posture. Without the Party securing more MPs in the General Election, its influence over the British opposition parties was muted. There was no positive response from Labour. The Conservative Government's solution to the devolution question had been to hold some meetings of the Scottish Grand Committee in the debating chamber of the former Royal High School, which had been fitted out for the abandoned Scottish Assembly. The meetings ended with a stampede of MPs to catch planes to London! At least it allowed the Scottish Press corps to join their Westminster counterparts in enjoying the tedium of these most provincial of debates.

A few Scottish Labour MPs were irked by the outcome of the election. Labour MPs formed a majority of the Scottish representatives, yet the British Labour Party had lost heavily in England. They expected their Scottish success to give them special consideration, yet they counted for nothing in the unitary United Kingdom parliament. Right from the publication of the Queen's Speech, John Home Robertson MP and John Maxton MP complained that Scotland had rated only twenty words – less than for Hong Kong, and called for a Speaker's Conference on devolution. John Maxton pointed out to the Speaker:

> 'There is a separate Scottish entity, there is separate
> Scottish legislation and there is a separate Scottish
> administration, yet the Labour Party which clearly won
> in Scotland, is not forming the Government in
> Scotland.'

John Home Robertson declared there was a constitutional crisis and pledged that he and his colleagues would battle hard to obtain home rule. Of course, they also recognised that they were UK MPs and this was their weakness. The Tories, drunk with power, were not having any 'snash' from this Scottish element which had no support from the Labour Opposition. On 7 July 1983 Mrs Thatcher bluntly informed Mr Maxton that she would not introduce legislation to establish a Scottish Assembly and on 14 December 1983, Government MPs voted down a Liberal Scottish Parliament Bill. Significantly, fourteen Scottish Labour MPs were missing from the vote so Scottish Labour parliamentarians were mostly lukewarm!

Very occasionally some fighting spirit was displayed. The week before, Scottish MPs were told by the Scottish Secretary at Question Time that the UK Education Minister would shortly make a statement on student grants; yet in the statement by the Secretary of State for Education that followed immediately, there was no mention of the position in Scotland. As Rector of the University of Dundee, I was particularly concerned and raised single-handedly a prolonged series of points of order that brought me close to expulsion until gradually other Scottish MPs, including the shadow Scottish Secretary, woke to the issue. They piled in and filibustered at length until the Speaker conceded and suggested action. At the end of this hour long exchange, when asked whether it had crossed his mind that there was merit in establishing a Scottish Assembly, Speaker Thomas dryly responded that it did frequently.

In Europe, Winnie Ewing had annoyed some members of the NEC in linking up with the Gaullists and Fianna Fail. There was not much choice, since to be an independent was to keep company with some rather strange people and also have limited speaking rights. She made a significant impact on the European Parliament. Compared with her experience of Westminster hostility, she appreciated the sympathetic hearing she received from other European MPs who had no 'hang-ups' about the SNP. It was no surprise when she was re-elected MEP for the Highlands and Islands in June 1984 with her majority increased to 16,277. The SNP's policy on Europe led to an increased vote overall of 17.8%. Winnie's lobbying paid off in the spring of 1985 when, against stiff competition from Athens, she was instrumental in bringing the international Lomé Convention to Inverness.

Effectively, all the action was in Scotland. And with the ending of overt feuding in the Party after the 1983 election, I saw an opportunity to begin the process of altering the SNP's dreadful image and making the Party more acceptable to the electorate. During the summer, I strengthened the political theme that Scotland had been disenfranchised by two successive General Elections in which English voters had chosen Scotland's government. Despite this democratic deficit, I pointed out that since the election in June, the Scottish people had been let down by the British parties which refused to assert a Scottish mandate as a weapon to defend Scottish interests. Blame for this was laid on the Labour MPs who formed the majority of Scotland's representation at Westminster.

Within the Party, I initiated a programme for reform that included the setting up of a Commission to examine the structure and work of the Party and appointed John Swinney, Alex Salmond and Alasdair Morgan, all of whom were rising within the Party, to the team. At the same time, I canvassed for support for my cause to bring the SNP back into the mainstream of Scottish politics and rebuild our popular support. The National Conference at the end of September, 1983 provided the opportunity. Although I had little prospect of changing the Party's mind on non-membership of NATO and armed neutrality, I advocated a softening in our line.[1] This was risky and in due course, when this was rejected overwhelmingly, the Press, who had been well advised of my strategy, recorded it as a personal defeat. The Daily Record report bore the legend, 'The Crown Slips'.

The other issues – Devolution and Europe - were also too close to call. This time, I had the benefit of making the case in my Chairman's speech to Conference, where I chided the Party over its isolationist approach, declaring that:

> 'If we were really serious about obtaining our freedom as a nation, we must be prepared to work within the international scene. For strategic reasons, if none other we must convince other nations that their interests will not be adversely affected by the creation of the Scottish state. Otherwise, they will side with England and refuse to give us the recognition, or influential support we may need.'

And later:

> 'Scotland cannot afford conditional nationalists who put individual policy issues before the national goal. The plain truth is that Scotland has no influence over international events and, for that matter, very little over domestic management so long as we do not have an independent parliament.
>
> Let us take one issue – the EEC. This Party has always – and rightly – opposed British entry. No voice, no entry was one of the slogans used. The terms of entry negotiated by Westminster were diabolically bad. They ruined our fishing industry and failed to provide the industrial jobs needed. These mistakes would not have been made by any Scottish Government.
>
> Of course, it will be for our Government after independence to reach decisions on these matters but

during the election I noted how many industrial workers in export industries have modified their anti-EEC views. Nevertheless if, again we are serious about independence, the EEC offers a first class way of pushing the advantages of political independence without any threat of economic dislocation, however imaginary, which the enemies of Scotland might desperately wish to advance. Within the common trading umbrella, the move to independence can take place smoothly and easily.'

After asking the Party to learn from the results of the General Election, I shifted to the issue of devolution.

'The SNP emerged to prominence in the 1960s and 1970s because our message was credible and relevant. It did not happen by accident. It came because the attitudes and policies of the Party matched the expectations of the electorate. There is a myth which is still being peddled that the SNP stands only for independence – nothing less. That was not true in the sixties or seventies.

Nor is it now true. At the most that tag was accurate for the one and a half years between the 1979 and 1981 Conferences. Nevertheless it has stuck and in my opinion has done us political harm. It gives us a negative image which is all the more galling because it does not reflect Party policy. Instead of being an advantage to the achievement of independence as its supporters wish, it has become a barricade to political progress. It erects a division between us and the electorate. Since independence is dependent on an electorally strong SNP, then automatically, anything which does not assist support of the Party undermines the cause of independence itself.

This Conference has the opportunity to re-assert the policy of the Party and to put the record right. But let me make it absolutely clear so that our members, our people and the media are under no illusions. This Party stands for the independence of the Scottish people, has stood for independence and will continue to strive for that independence until our battle is won.

What we are discussing at this Conference are not our
undisputed fundamental aims but the methods by
which we can bind to our cause the public support
through the ballot box which is essential if we are to
achieve victory. If then our goal is to win the hearts and
minds of the Scottish people, we need to use our
political intelligence as well our fervour. Blind
conviction in a wilderness will lead us and Scotland
absolutely nowhere. Our political intelligence tells us
that we have to make changes. The onus is on those
who want no change to explain why their policies will
be more successful this time than last. Of course,
something may turn up. But this kind of misplaced
political micawberism will serve the SNP no advantage.
We are at the stage where we can either rebuild our
political base or decline to oblivion.
But I also wish to warn those who are too enthusiastic
about the Scottish Assembly. There is no way the SNP
is going to give automatic support to just any form of
devolution. Just as it would be politically impossible to
dismiss any material measure of self-government
which returned industrial or economic power to
Scotland, so, too, it would be a misjudgement on the
part of the SNP to accept any scheme which involves a
'tarted-up' Scottish Grand Committee, a repeat version
of the Labour Party's Scottish Assembly or any other
dubious offer tantamount to electoral fraud. There
must be a bottom line below which we will not go. To
do so would be to repeat the errors of the seventies.
That bottom line can be decided only by this Party at
National Council or National Conference. What is
essential is that we listen to our people and take them
with us. It may be satisfying to berate the electorate
but it is rarely productive. We must add to the politics
of conviction which we have in abundance, the politics
of persuasion at which we were once exceptionally
adept.'

I was taking an extraordinary political risk and gambling that the schisms
and the General Election had altered the mind-set of the delegates. Many of
my main supporters were hand-fasted to opposition to devolution and on
this occasion, I had to pray in aid the moderate mainstream and some of

those who had former affiliations to the '79 Group. I was under no doubt. If I failed to carry the day – and over NATO, I was already one issue down - my credibility would be so blown that resignation would follow.

It was a close run outcome. The debate on devolution took place after my speech. I had had my say in the morning and to avoid overkill was condemned to be a spectator. The resolution sponsored by National Council had the key phrase 'while in no way seeking to obstruct' devolution and was faced with amendments, seeking to strengthen the independence aspect with others softening our attitudes.[2] After a passionate two hour debate in which I faced opposition from Donald Stewart, the Party President, the amendments were defeated and the resolution was passed overwhelmingly. Just to keep my feet on the ground, Conference went on to defeat a proposal for an elected Scottish Convention known to have my support. Happily, a quick briefing of the press allowed me to claim victory and soften the Party's hard line image.

The following day a resolution easing the opposition to Europe, moved by Alex Salmond and supported by Winifred Ewing, passed overwhelmingly giving the Party a platform on which to build a new coalition.[3] The debates had been marked by outstanding speeches by Jim Fairlie and Jim Sillars, and these and other excellent contributions impressed the media who were unaccustomed to such a high level of open debate. On reflection, the 1983 Conference was one that altered the course of the Party radically and in my view for the better. The gamble had paid off. The separatist, isolationist image had been shattered.

From now on, the SNP entered into a more peaceful and constructive phase that made the office-bearers' job easier. Previous tensions had not completely disappeared as individuals and those of likeminded views competed for posts and the press carried leaks of business of the National Executive Committee. Every year, there was a struggle for control over the Standing Orders and Agenda Committee that selected the agenda for the Conference and thus the direction of the Party. With hard work and political skills, the Assistant National Secretary and then the National Secretary, John Swinney ensured that he and Neil MacCallum were in control of Conference business and saw that it was not hi-jacked. Naturally, there were still disputes over strategy, such as involvement in all-party discussions organised by the Campaign for the Scottish Assembly where we agreed to send representatives to a 'working party'. To begin with, my proposal for an elected Scottish Convention to prepare a constitution for Scotland was knocked back by the NEC. It finally passed when an Executive Committee report was approved by National Council on 2 March 1985.[4]

Financially, over the period, the SNP limped along with a small staff and relied on the Neill Trust from income on the capital and contributions towards parliamentary elections. The membership base had taken a knock and the run down of branches in the late seventies had not been repaired, with some constituency associations moving from a multiple branch structure to a single constituency branch. By December 1983, Alan McKinney as HQ Director had made savings of £25,000 without miraculously impinging on HQ services and in his other role of National Organiser believed the key factor was to get the Constituency Associations working, for if they did, the increased membership would solve our short-term financial problems.[5]

And then, there were major changes in the composition of the National Office-Bearers. Alasdair Morgan became National Treasurer in 1983 (the first in that post for a long time to play a political role). Margaret Ewing was elected Senior Vice Chairman (1984) in succession to Jim Fairlie. Alex Salmond was elected Vice Chairman for Publicity (after the resignation of Colin Bell in 1985) and John Swinney was appointed Acting National Secretary on the resignation of Neil MacCallum. Neil had been a very efficient administrator and had carried valiantly the burden of the Party's troubles with an adverse impact on his health. John Swinney had great political ability. He had come though the ranks of the youth movement and helped in the General Election. Alex Salmond was already an experienced and skilful politician. Allan Macartney, later to be a distinguished MEP, also appeared in the team as EVC Organisation (1986) Experienced hands such as Andrew Welsh, George Leslie, Tom McAlpine and Isobel Lindsay gave continuity to the leadership. Irene White was a tower of strength at Headquarters.

Despite the advance to office of some former members of the '79 Group, in 1985 there was a resurgence of effort by the 'hard left' within the Party to win it to their ideology. A pamphlet was published in early 1985 by Kenny MacAskill, Ron Halliday and Charles Reid. It was called 'A New Image For a New Age'. Among other things, it urged 'militant opposition', the 'escalation of civil disobedience', the realisation that 'constitutional change is not enough' and a claim that 'it is incumbent upon the SNP … to become the political vanguard of the Scottish Labour Movement'.

Angus Lyon states[6]:

> 'Some of us were becoming worried about the way we were becoming too identified with the militant left – even to the extent that we might be making SNP candidates unelectable in the future.
> At the 1985 Conference a small grouping was formed to publish a quarterly bulletin called 'Activist' because we wanted to demonstrate that when it came to

matters of Party ideology, strategy and tactics there
were those other than the hard left who could
stimulate debate and develop new ideas. The Co-
ordinating Committee was myself, John Swinney and
Morag Lennie. Issue 1 of 'Activist' was published in
Autumn '85 and the editorial stated that 'Activist'
would reflect two fundamental principles:

1. a belief that the attainment of full independence
   for Scotland is the one and only key to the
   improvement – social, economic and cultural – of
   our nation.
2. a belief in the importance of the SNP conveying to
   the Scottish people a clear vision of what post-
   independence Scotland could – and should –
   be like.

In that first issue, both John and I outlined our own
thoughts on building a strategy for electoral success
and took the militant left to task on some of their
thinking. Morag took them to task on the subject of
mass civil disobedience, arguing that although it could
be a powerful weapon in certain circumstances, it
must be carefully thought through and planned.'

Because of the exertions of John Swinney, the manoeuvrings for control
of the Standing Orders and Agenda Committee were unsuccessful and there
were few shocks at the 1984, 1985 and 1986 Conferences with worthy
policies on exports, women's rights, a workers' charter, land (the most
controversial and carried by 129 votes to 106), steel (more of a campaigning
resolution and setting out the need for Scottish control), transport and a
youth charter. The 1984 Conference, perhaps enhanced by the modern
setting of the Eden Court Theatre, Inverness had a more professional and
attractive feel to it. The credit belonged to Colin Bell, who as Executive Vice
Chairman for Publicity had brought to the post modernising ideas that led to
the improved presentation.

The local elections and European elections helped by marking some
improvements in the fortunes of the Party with us getting into the position
of holding the Highlands and Islands Constituency and winning control of
Angus District Council. They were indicators that we were making progress
after 1979 and the wasted years. The policy debates of 1983 helped shape
a more positive impression of the Party with the public and this in turn

raised the morale of members – and improved their behaviour and contribution. Added to which was the approaching General Election where Margaret Ewing, Alex Salmond and Andrew Welsh were candidates respectively for Moray, Banff/Buchan and East Angus, all very winnable. I took the opportunity to widen the horizons of Conference delegates by introducing a Chairman's Lecture over a Saturday lunchtime where someone who was not a member of the SNP would be asked to address the meeting on a topic of his choosing. The speaker in 1986 was the journalist Neal Ascherson who under the title of 'Don't be Afraid – and Don't Steal' - a quote from Thomas Masaryk, the father of Czechoslovak independence, contrasted the nationalism of that country and Poland. This was followed in 1987 by a thoughtful address by author William McIlvanney under the heading of 'Stand Scotland Where it Did'. And under the name of the Donaldson Lecture, my successors have continued the practice ever since.

The Party held a Special Conference in February 1985, to discuss the Commission of Enquiry Report. It produced streamlining changes to speed up decision making and make the structure more fit for the challenges. Controversial sections, introducing a new post of Leader, amongst other changes to the powers of the Executive, were rejected to the chagrin of some members of the Commission.

On the wider political scene, the SNP was engaged in discussions with the STUC on the closure of Gartcosh finishing mill and devolution. There was singularly little agreement on the constitutional issue. While the STUC was on the whole more sympathetic to a Scottish Assembly (certainly not to independence), it was tied by umbilical links to Labour and was limited in its scope. The SNP had now emerged from isolation and was once more a member (if a radical one) of civic Scotland. Despite there being little sign of Scotland being in rebellion politically against the Thatcher government, there were indications of a moderate increase in support for the SNP in opinion polls. Local election results were on the up in 1985. In the Regional Elections in 1986 under the slogan, 'Turning the Tide for Scotland', there was an improved performance. The Party had got round the road block of the declining Liberal/SDP Alliance and moved into second place with 18.2% (13.4% in 1982). In some of the central belt areas, the vote by district, had improved dramatically.[7]

Percentage Votes 1986 (1982)

Falkirk	41% (12%)	Clackmannan	40% (19%)
Cumbernauld	37% (17%)	Linlithgow	35% (18%)
Clydebank	26% (9%)	Clydesdale	25% (11%)
Livingston	25% (13%)	Kilmarnock	24% (9%)
Stirling	20% (8%)		

In the run up to the 1987 General Election, there was a dispute over the closeness of our relationships with Plaid Cymru. The Plaid had never blown hot over independence as there was very little support for it in Wales. Discussion had taken place on the possibility of cementing an alliance for the next parliament in the hope that we would hold the balance of power. We desperately needed leverage for greater UK relevance during the election campaign, if we were not to be ignored by the UK media whose coverage in Scotland and Wales customarily drowned out Scottish and Welsh issues!

There were meetings between the MPs at Westminster and with the Executives of the two Parties in Edinburgh and London. The pact set out a number of goals for mutual support, and should have been non-controversial. It was heavily fenced with provisions for delivery of the constitutional objectives of each party – and in the case of the SNP, this was a directly elected Scottish Constitutional Convention. Objection was taken within the SNP to our preparedness to offer conditional parliamentary support to one or more of the London parties to achieve constitutional change, something that had brought the SNP to blows in the late seventies. The Conservatives were not to be aided in this way 'in view of their record in Scotland and Wales and their hostility to any form of self-government'. Effectively, this would mean the SNP possibly putting the UK Labour Party in power. When the proposal, jointly presented by both Alex Salmond and me succeeded, there were intimations of dissent.

The idea, however unlikely, that the SNP should uphold a London Government in a minority parliament was too much for delegates and some leading office-bearers.[8] From the point of view of a purist, they were correct. Very few nationalists will make common cause with the state blocking their way to freedom; they would find it easier to make common cause elsewhere, as medieval Scotland did by founding the Auld Alliance with France. But the principal weakness of the SNP ever since 1979 was its lack of political credibility, a factor vitally needed to persuade wavering members of the public to vote for us. So the ploy had two aims – one, to make us electable and two, to lay the foundations for an onslaught on Labour after the election if Mrs Thatcher won again (a gambit rather extravagantly known as the Doomsday Scenario).

The SNP was too weak to enjoy the luxury of purism. Apart from the brutal truth that the Party had the potential to win only a handful of seats, the Conservative Government was well ahead in the polls in England and the likelihood of a hung parliament was minimal. Instead, the main enemy of the SNP was unionist Labour, afraid to use its strength – and arguably its purported mandate - as Scotland's largest party to protect the economic needs of the nation. As early as 1984, I wrote in the parliamentary report to Conference:

'There has been no campaign of parliamentary disruption by the 41 strong group of Scottish Labour MPs. Their 'Scottish mandate' claims now ring hollow.'

The clamant need was to show that only the SNP had the capability of protecting Scotland and in my parliamentary report to Conference 1986, I was able to give a specific example of Scotland's political weakness:

'The crucial parliamentary Debate (on Gartcosh) was postponed by Labour in favour of a debate on the English helicopter company, Westland. By the time we eventually had the debate, the closure notice for Gartcosh had been issued. Once again the contempt in which the Westminster parties hold Scotland and the Scottish people has been clearly demonstrated.'

And then it was the General Election. This time the Party was well prepared. Priorities for contesting constituencies had been worked out and agreed. As Party Chairman, I was given substantial back-up support for the campaign and was deployed fully throughout the country. I enjoyed it hugely – except for the outcome. As the Political Director, Isobel Lindsay reported to the NEC[9].

'She stated that the Party had started the campaign from a low level of credibility in the opinion polls and this had proved difficult to overcome. Press coverage during the campaign particularly in the early weeks had been good and the party had received fair coverage. Toward the end of the campaign, in the final 10 days, the media had started to ignore us.'

Other than during the 1974 elections when the SNP had enjoyed an exceptionally high profile, backed by encouraging polling numbers, the customary fate was for the Party to be ignored by the UK press and the London broadcasters. With this starvation of publicity, so far as the average voter was concerned, we were invisible and not worth voting for. British General Elections are normally fought on British (mainly English) issues and the Scottish dimension was rarely apparent. In an attempt to force the BBC (and thus the IBA) to review their coverage, we raised an action in the Court of Session. It failed at a preliminary stage and this did not help the Party's impact at the outset of what was going to be a difficult exercise.

The 'doomsday scenario' had no impact on raising our profile. It was patent at the outset that the Conservatives were heading for another term, based on their support in England. In Scotland, it was Labour which benefited from anti-Thatcher feeling – not the SNP. In Conservative held seats such as Moray, Banff/Buchan and East Angus, the SNP coalesced the anti-Tory vote and ousted the Conservative MPs. The opposite effect occurred in Dundee East and the Western Isles, where the anti-conservative tide went the way of Labour so the SNP thus lost the two seats it had originally won from Labour. In numerical terms, we were one up in terms of seats won and had an increase in the vote, and this allowed the Party to claim overall success. It was, however, a hollow advance since the central belt strategy had collapsed; and with the loss of Dundee East, in particular, we no longer had parliamentary representation in any industrial area. It was also significant that Angus, Banff/Buchan and Moray were seats previously won by the SNP in 1974 and narrowly lost in 1979.

Summary of Voting 1987 (1983)

Labour	42.4%	(35.1%)	50 seats	(41)
Conservative	24%	(28.4%)	10 seats	(21)
Alliance	9.2%	(24.5%)	9 seats	(8)
SNP	14%	(11.8%)	3 seats	(2)
Others	0.3%	(0.3%)	0 seats	(0)

With Donald Stewart having retired from the Western Isles, I was the one principally affected. Defeat was always on the cards. Dundee East was a tight marginal between Labour and SNP. When I had been selected as a candidate, the Constituency had been exceptionally well organised. With deindustrialisation, Dundee suffered high emigration. There had been no infusion of new talent and gradually, while my attention was focussed on my leadership work, the organisation had run down. It was also politically divided and even the Constituency Chairman, Jimmy Halliday, a former National Chairman, had found it difficult to get people working together to the extent that he gave in his resignation.

Even so, I should have been able to hold on if Tayside Regional Councillors from Angus and Perth had not been manipulated by Dundee Labour Councillors into having the Labour candidate for Dundee East appointed to the high profile role of Council Convener. The Dundee Courier had no doubt this was the reason for the defeat. To be fair to Labour, their campaign was well organised and presented. Their time had come again, and for many Labour activists throughout Scotland, regaining both Dundee East and the Western Isles was more satisfactory than the defeats of many Conservative MPs.

With her substantial network of local contacts, Edith was sure as early as fourteen days from polling day that I would lose. She did not tell me as she did not want me to lose confidence when presenting the national case! On reflection, in the last phase of the election, the anti-Thatcher tide was unstoppable.   It was not only Dundee East that fell that day. Glasgow Hillhead, held by Roy Jenkins of the SDP also went to Labour, I suspect for the same reason and the so-called 'doomsday scenario' had arrived; another hollow Labour victory in Scotland, but the Thatcher Government, on the strength of English votes, was returned for a third term.

It seemed the end. To lose is never pleasant. I had gone into the count aware it was my last. The votes stacked up and although the Labour majority of 1015 was slight, there was never any doubt as to the result. To paraphrase the old saying, those who live by the ballot, die by the ballot. Some things just have to be accepted.

Chapter 17

Poll Taxes, Govan and Conventions

Defeat in Dundee East should have spelled the end of my career as Chairman of the Scottish National Party. Change had been forced upon me and the decision was simple. I needed to find a job. At the age of 49, this would not be easy. There was no safety net for former SNP MPs, and especially for the leader of a political party which had outraged the establishment.

The first task was to sever my leadership role within Dundee East SNP. This was an emotional divorce since I had been a candidate and MP for almost 15 years. But the relationship with some incoming office-bearers had soured. So, shortly after the defeat, I attended my last meeting of the Constituency Association. I thanked sincerely those who had given me support, and politely, those who had not! I told them I hoped to live in Dundee and would give what limited help was possible. They should select another candidate as I would no longer be available. Some Dundee East SNP delegates did not take seriously my announcement that they should find another candidate. The idea that an experienced politician would not wish to regain the seat was outlandish. They did not know that I had come to a further decision – that I would no longer be a candidate anywhere. I had enjoyed the challenges of being an MP – especially when the SNP had held the balance of power. But, eight years of Thatcher Government after the excitements of the seventies was enough and although this experience had been shared with the Labour Party and the Liberal Democrats, it was no consolation. I was bored and did not wish to end my working life marooned on the green benches of the Commons.

I was also feeling the strain of holding down a marginal industrial city constituency. The very real poverty – equal in intensity if not in scale with the east end of Glasgow – had also led to a heavy workload. My fortnightly surgeries lasted between four and seven hours, and on one occasion, after the 1983 General Election, for a mammoth ten and a half hours. For almost all of the time, my office support was provided by Grace Graham, Joan Black and Margaret Taylor as part-time volunteers. It was only in 1986 that improved House of Commons allowances made it possible for me to hire a constituency assistant, Andy Scott, to help with the work. I took the welfare role seriously and indeed it was the most rewarding feature of the job. My home telephone number was in the directory and, although the service was rarely abused, my wife and I did get calls throughout the day and occasionally in the middle of the night. And on one occasion when one of my daughters was alone in the house, Special Branch had put my home under observation because of death threats made from Northern Ireland sources. Being a public figure has many disadvantages. So, although on a competitive level, I was annoyed at losing the contest, after a long holiday, I was grateful to the people of Dundee, who had been extraordinarily loyal over many years, for releasing me from the parliamentary treadmill.

Having served as Party Chairman for eight stressful years, I also had no qualms about abandoning this role and passing the burden to others. Indeed, I had toyed with exchanging this job for that of parliamentary leader if I had been re-elected and the group of SNP MPs was large enough to make an impact. The Conference was due to take place in Dundee in the autumn and this was a suitable occasion to relinquish office. To my dismay, the Party was not going to let me go easily. Not unnaturally, my staunchest supporters such as Margaret Ewing, Winnie Ewing and John Swinney had pitched in and asked me to reconsider. The range of persuasion was wider. Alex Salmond, who would soon put his cap in the ring for Senior Vice Chairman, invited me to lunch and offered his support. This was strange. Alex and I had not been close and although he was not the main irritant during the 79 Group affair, his involvement with others had almost caused the Party to self-destruct. Nevertheless, since he had just been elected MP for Banff/Buchan, he had the platform to be a future leader. If it came to the crunch, his mentor, Jim Sillars was ahead of him in the queue on the Left. Of course, either would have been up against Margaret Ewing who would almost certainly have been elected at that time.

To all, I gave only the answer that I would think things over while I was on holiday. The holiday was long and relaxing, spent touring in Germany, Switzerland – where I met my former colleague George Reid, now working with the Red Cross – and France. Free of care and responsibility, I enjoyed the thought of the new SNP MPs slaving in hot, humid London. The question of continuing in the Chair was not uppermost in my thoughts. If anything, it was the question of getting a job before the meagre redundancy benefit ran out.

On my return, this took priority. I had had several job offers in the law and a three year post of Senior Lecturer at Dundee University that would have tided me over a good way to the next election if I had been minded to stand again. But I had come to a decision. I would retrain as a solicitor – after thirteen years away this was desirable both for me and my clients! My intention was to set up my own law practice in Dundee and I was fortunate to be offered an assistantship with solicitors in Kirkcaldy where I could relearn the trade. This, then, brought me to the question of whether I should continue as Chairman. I was under no illusion. My political standing had been damaged by the loss of Dundee East. I also had no intention of returning to Westminster which would be essential if I wished to retain my political status. If I were to stay in office as Chairman of the SNP, then the job would have to change. I would need to perform a function that would benefit the Party as the role of figurehead did not appeal.

Prior to my election in 1979, the Party Chairman had not been an MP. I resolved to take up the task as chief executive and orchestrate the rebuilding of the organisation. In the eyes of the Party I was still the political leader, but in practice as a 'part-timer' outwith the Commons, I could not have the same public profile. I would leave the public side to the MPs.

The first test was the Conference held in Dundee at the end of September. Unopposed and having 40 nominations, I entered it in strength and was amused when an ungracious speech of welcome by the Labour Lord Provost taunted the SNP over its Dundee loss. Nothing had changed in my absence. Dundee politics was its usual petty, vituperative best! In my address to Conference, I set out fresh targets for achieving Scottish independence, calling on activists to establish a new Scottish dimension. I appealed to delegates that we should build trust from the Scottish people by helping them as individuals, as families and as communities – by making sure that we were always active on the ground and did not just appear at election time. The speech went down well and I had pleasure later when the Party endorsed my views on the need for an international approach to defence. The debate was led by John Swinney who said that Scotland must recognise its strategic geographical position and its international responsibilities. It should seek co-operation with other non-aligned nations such as Finland, Sweden and the Republic of Ireland. A pro-NATO amendment was defeated.[1]

Earlier, the Conference had debated a resolution on how to tackle the issue of the Poll Tax which was accelerating in public concern.[2] Four months before, opposition to the Poll Tax was only one of a number of campaigning issues including the closure of steel works, the political issue of projecting independence as the antidote to Thatcherism, nuclear dumping and designating the Labour MPs as the 'feeble fifty'. The resolution reflected the Party's opposition to the Poll Tax and its support for a local income tax as a replacement.

The problem for the Party was both political and legal. The SNP was not alone in its opposition; dislike of the Poll Tax was shared by the Labour Party, the Liberal Democrats and the STUC. There were two strategies under question – non-registration and non-payment. The Party's lawyers led by Kenny MacAskill had sounded the dangers of non-registration since this could lead to court proceedings with fixed penalties. A non-payment campaign would work only with mass support. And was the Party in danger of being sued by those who followed its advice and were fined or had their bank accounts frozen by the courts? And once started, what was the exit strategy? Then there could be loss of support from the conventionally minded who believed in the sanctity of the law, however unjust that law might be. So although there was pressure on the Party for action, the NEC had to walk on egg-shells. The natural preference was to have a multi-party campaign behind which the SNP could shelter, increase the rhetoric and watch Labour's 'feeble fifty' MPs, squirm and split.

Conference produced a new team of office-bearers – Alex Salmond (the Senior Vice Chairman), Tom McAlpine (Administration), Gil Paterson (Local Government), Allan Macartney (Organisation), Kenny MacAskill (Policy) and Michael Russell (Publicity), a narrow victory over Isobel Lindsay by 210 votes to 209. The team was completed by the re-election of John Swinney and Alasdair Morgan as Secretary and Treasurer respectively. I assumed the convenership of the Senior Office-bearers Committee (SOBS) that co-ordinated the activities of the Party and agreed the duties of the various office-bearers. Mine were to be chief executive, co-ordination of office-bearers and party strategy. Alex Salmond was to be liaison on parliamentary strategy and special responsibility for economic policy. Of crucial importance, Tom McAlpine was to look for new fundraising ideas based on use of the newly computerised membership through mass mailings, all to be part of a more professional approach. National Organiser, Alan McKinney had also been asked to be an observer at the US Presidential election so that the SNP could benefit from American electioneering techniques although this was eventually called off because of a clash with the Glasgow Govan by-election.

Financially, the SNP was on a knife edge. Party finances were stretched although it was hoped there would be no end of year loss as the SNP had no worthwhile reserves. Even when fighting the General Election, it had relied on money from the depleting Neill Trust. It was imperative that other fundraising sources be found. In a new spirit of experimentation, the December National Council divided into workshops whose reports went to the NEC for consideration.

By February 1988, the Poll Tax had become the primary issue. The people of Scotland became outraged, not only over the tax, but having the London Government use Scotland as a guinea pig before deciding to introduce legislation to cover England. Increasingly the all-party deliberations ran into problems and on 13 February, the NEC resolved that we should withdraw from any all-party campaign that did not involve non-payment, and although still willing to be involved in joint ventures, to stand alone in seeking a mandate from the people in the District Elections to lead a mass campaign for non-payment as the most effective opposition to it.[3] Kenny MacAskill was to be at the helm Significantly, this gave us a major campaigning issue for the local elections and kept options open if no mandate was achieved. Even so, there was a minority of NEC members who had reservations.

Nevertheless, by April the NEC decided to bring pressure on the STUC working party by bringing the non-payment issue to a head and by an increased margin of 10 votes to 3 opted to suspend membership of the working party and Joint Campaign to allow the people in the May elections to give a mandate or to wait until the STUC came round to non-payment.[4]

The gamble paid off. The Party doubled the number of District Council seats won and gained 21.3% of the vote, more than the target I had set at Conference. In the previous election, the vote for the SNP was only 11.7%. This put us in second place in terms of votes. Significantly we also achieved a huge number of second places. The impact on Party morale was electric. In my own Report to Council, I commented[5]:

> 'I had the privilege of being in the count in the Kelvin Hall and sharing the joy and exhilaration as the electoral tide turned in our favour even if it was tinged with disappointment at not winning any seats (in Glasgow). This was the best result for 10 years. For those of us who live in areas where the Party is strong, it is educative to remember that a sizable proportion of our members has never known electoral success.'

Although much of the activity of the Party was directed towards improving the quality of the organisation and membership, both of which gave cause for concern, the same Council meeting considered an Executive resolution on the Single European Act. The resolution had sections narrating that the Single European Act did not threaten national sovereignty, posed no problems for existing SNP policy on the EEC and offered opportunities for the Party to avoid association with political or economic separatism.[6] The resolution was gutted with their removal, leaving the policy response in the air – not the best position to occupy in the run up to the European elections scheduled for June 1989. No such hesitation was shown in a further resolution on the non-payment of the poll tax which asked the SNP to lead a popular campaign and called for individuals and other organisations to join with the Party.[7]

The people of Scotland at last were showing some spirit and the Party was genuinely in touch with public opinion. The poll tax was the great issue of the day and at Conference in September, I brought the house to its feet when I threw my weight behind the campaign and declared that I would not pay. It was also at this Conference that the post of Chairman was renamed as 'National Convener'.

Things now moved quickly. There was to be a by-election in Glasgow Govan, which we had last won in 1973 and lost in 1974. Would lightning strike twice, this time in favour of our candidate, Jim Sillars, husband of the original victor Margo MacDonald? Jim adapted the usual identification of the Party on the ballot papers to include the slogan 'No Poll Tax'. The membership rallied round and in a magnificent campaign, Govan was won for a second time with a 38% swing (27.8% from Labour).

Glasgow Govan By-election Result (November 1988)

SNP	48.8%
Labour	36.9%
Conservative & Unionist	7.3%
Social & Liberal Democrat	4.1%
Others	2.9%

As Winnie Ewing had done after Hamilton twenty years before, Jim Sillars embarked on a series of rallies, with the SNP seeking to build its credibility and organisation on the back of this superb victory. The response of the Labour Party was to re-adopt devolution as their counter to the nationalists on non-payment of the Poll Tax. The perfect vehicle for this was to hand. The Campaign for a Scottish Assembly was undergoing a fresh lease of life and had published a document, 'A Claim of Right for Scotland'. A deputation from the National Executive consisting of John Swinney, Alasdair Morgan and Gerry McLaughlan (Assistant Secretary) had met office-bearers of the Campaign in August. They reported to the NEC that the Campaign's objectives were to have a Scottish Assembly created. The Campaign saw their role as articulating and representing demand for an Assembly, drafting the provisions for an Assembly scheme and securing implementation, if necessary, through a referendum.

The SNP delegation had made it clear that participation in a Constitutional Convention would be dependent on there being an open agenda in which all options, including independence within the European Community would be discussed. The SNP delegation took the view that a Constitutional Convention with an agenda restricted purely and simply to debating the creation of a Scottish Assembly was an improper application of the principle of a Constitutional Convention. The true role of the Convention was to consider a number of options representing the diversity of views in Scotland. The recommendations to the NEC were that the National Secretary should write to the Campaign to the effect that our participation would be dependent on independence being discussed, the alteration of references to 'Assembly' to 'Assembly or Parliament' and the requirement that the Convention be a directly elected body, rather than one appointed from historical election results. The NEC considered the report in November and approved the recommendations on participation provided independence, direct election (by a narrow vote of 11 votes to 8) and the raising of the issue of sovereignty of the Scottish people were agreed.[8]

The CSA conceded an open agenda on options, but not the principle of direct election. They proposed a cross-party meeting for 27 January 1989. The NEC agreed to send a delegation composed of Jim Sillars, Margaret Ewing and me and varied the negotiating terms on the recommendation of John Swinney to link Convention membership to the outcome of the forthcoming European Elections on a proportionate basis.

At the January meeting, a gulf opened between the SNP and the Labour Party. From the outset, the Labour Party pushed to expand the membership of the Convention to 150 to include MPs, councillors, the Co-operative Party (a Labour affiliate) and the Trades Unions, most of whom would safely vote the Labour 'ticket'. The SNP and its message of independence would be swamped. Labour flatly refused calls for a referendum, direct election or the European elections being used to determine membership. It was a stitch up. The tactics of the Labour Party were to seize control of the Convention to deliver devolution and nothing more. In hostile and aggressive terms, Donald Dewar MP representing the Labour Party went further. He insisted that the Convention should produce one proposal and not a list of options such as independence, federalism, devolution and current rule from Westminster (the status quo) on which a multi-option referendum could follow. In the knowledge that a loaded Convention would come out in favour of a devolved Scottish Assembly, he made it clear that if the SNP took part, it would be expected to drop its policy on independence and campaign for devolution at the next General Election.

As the meeting developed, Margaret, Jim and I exchanged glances and at the coffee break agreed that the whole affair was a set-up, intended to trap us into abandoning independence in favour of devolution as the sole constitutional option for the Scottish people. As it was clear that we had to report back to the NEC, we, therefore, had the following caveat minuted[9]:

> 'The representatives of the Scottish National Party noted that since the establishment of a non-elected Convention was contrary to established Party policy it was necessary to reserve the position of the Scottish National Party in relation to the membership proposals'.

At the Press Conference afterwards, the other parties spoke warmly of the progress made. The Press noticed our reticence and pallid goodwill. They soon prised out of us the reservation about the composition of the

Convention and our insistence that the Party would need to be consulted. The breaking of ranks by the SNP was the story. The end result was that the SNP received a very bad press. As the next meeting of the NEC was fourteen days away, it was impossible to hold a neutral line and I authorised the consultation of members of the Senior Office-bearers Committee to firm up our position. All those available confirmed that we should make a recommendation to the NEC that the SNP should not take part in the Convention.

All hell broke loose within the Party and media. In the make-up of the SNP, there has always been a significant minority that would be satisfied with a Scottish Assembly, and added to that on this occasion, was a hunger by other SNP activists for progress towards a Scottish parliament. SNP members were well aware that the SNP had given its support to a Constitutional Convention and unaware of the need for the Convention to be representative. They could not understand the perceived *volte face* made by the SNP delegates. So Headquarters began to receive a spate of letters of protest, anger and resignation. A fair number came my way. The divisions broke into the press. Such was the scale of the reaction that John Swinney, the National Secretary and Michael Russell, EVC Publicity felt it was necessary to send a letter to our constituency associations, explaining the reasons for the decision to withdraw. At the same time, we issued a full statement to the press that recorded we had been offered only 8% of delegate entitlement, well below the SNP's fair share and confirmed we would take part in a Convention which genuinely reflected the wishes of the Scottish people as the version on offer would have no constitutional legitimacy and would be rejected by Mrs Thatcher's government. The letter to the Party emphasised that the membership of the Convention was rigged and that the composition took no account of our standing in the opinion polls or support for 'Independence in Europe'. It was made clear that the SNP delegation had been willing to compromise on the demand for a referendum by proposing that Convention elections be held at the same time as the Euro-elections or alternatively to accept the outcome of those elections for appointment of delegates.

Almost immediately, the mood within the SNP changed as members realised we were being forced into a trap. The flow of letters continued, but this time those from the Party were supportive. This did not mean that the issue was settled. There was irritation amongst some NEC members that the decision had been pre-empted by the delegation and Senior Office-bearers. There were also others like Alex Salmond who believed that immediate withdrawal was tactically unwise and Isobel Lindsay who argued passionately that the decision was wrong and should be recalled. There was lengthy discussion. Isobel Lindsay's motion that we take part in the

Convention and review the position in July failed to find a seconder. While the debate took place, a small sub-committee withdrew and prepared this resolution for National Council[10]:

'a)   This Executive endorses the decision of the negotiating team that the Scottish National Party should not take part in the Convention as currently proposed.

b)   The NEC notes with regret the failure of the cross-party meeting on 27 January to agree to a Convention format which would allow the Scottish people a genuine choice on their constitutional future. The present proposed structure will inevitably lead to a devolutionary proposal which the Tory government has already indicated it will veto.

c)   The NEC reaffirms its support for a directly elected Constitutional Convention which would reflect and could deliver the demands of the Scottish people.

d)   If a directly elected Convention is not available, The NEC would recommend to National Council a Convention format which seriously attempts to reflect the wishes of the Scottish people. This could be achieved by:
i   using the European Elections to legitimise the Convention and to seek the Scottish people's mandate for the options that each party is putting within the Convention:
ii   ensuring the approval of the Scottish people through a referendum which will ask them to choose between any scheme for an Assembly, the status quo and an independent Scotland within the European Community:
iii   asserting the sovereign right of the Scottish people to secure national self-determination regardless of any contrary decision taken by the Westminster Parliament.

e)   The NEC will continue to articulate the positive case for a genuine Convention which enables the Scottish people to exercise their right to decide their future.

f)   The NEC instructs the National Secretary to
communicate to the Convention's Business
Committee this resolution and detail of our view
on how the Convention can be improved and
gain legitimacy drawn from the people. Any
response from the Business Committee will be
relayed to delegates at National Council along
with a statement of the NEC position.'

Sub-para. d) (i) was agreed by 17 votes to 5 and Para. f) was accepted
by 16 votes to 6 against a proposal to attend the Business Committee to
express the SNP's position. The resolution as a whole was carried by 22
votes to 1, with Isobel Lindsay being the sole dissentient.

Three weeks later National Council met to vote for or against
participation in the Convention. The hall was packed: the atmosphere
expectant. The large number of delegates looked forward to an exciting
debate. I did not expect an anxious outcome. Too many of the Party's 'big-
guns' supported the NEC. Yet those of a different mind, such as Neil
MacCormick, Mungo Bovey and Paul Scott spoke in favour of a counter-
motion from Isobel Lindsay that the SNP play a constructive role in the
Convention, subject to a summer review. Isobel had a rough reception with
cat-calling. I had to call the meeting to order so that she could be heard and
she bravely carried on in what was her last major speech. In the end, her
motion was defeated by 191 votes to 41. The resolution was carried by 260
votes to 24.[11]

The Convention affair had started as reaction by Labour to the SNP
victory in Govan. For the past nine years, the Labour leadership had let the
issue of devolution languish. In London, Neil Kinnock, the Labour leader had
been a hard- line anti-devolutionist in the seventies. He had not changed his
views. Scots within the Labour leadership such as John Smith and Donald
Dewar who had been favourable, found it politic not to press devolution.
Individual Labour MPs who wanted action were treated as eccentrics and
given no support. But when the SNP began to win once more, Labour had
to respond if it was not to lose its commanding position. The Convention
project was safe since their influence over civic Scotland meant that it was
fully controllable and it would not be permitted to go further than a Scottish
Assembly whose very limited powers would pose no threat to the Union.
The gambit was a good one. It restored Labour's image amongst those who
wanted a devolved Assembly and pushed the SNP cuckoo out of the political
nest. It also acted as a check to the SNP's growing support, but since that
growth stemmed from the anti-poll tax campaign, it did not do as much
harm as it might have done. Indeed, an out-manoeuvring of SNP Councillors

on Tayside Regional Council over the dismissal of cleaners was a far greater political embarassment.

A leading SNP figure did not share this view and pungently stated privately to me:

> 'The Constitutional Convention was a total strategic and tactical failure by us. We had created the momentum of further action on the constitutional question for the first time since 1979 as a consequence of the Govan by-election. We then succeeded in alienating many of those who had been attracted to us by the way we handled our departure from the convention.'

Thanks to the early resolution of the 'stramash' at National Council, the momentum of SNP campaigning was resumed in the run-up to the European elections in June. Here the Party was campaigning in a major election for the first time on the slogan, 'Independence in Europe', trying to give a positive projection of the Party's international outlook and to counter future cries of 'separatism'. I had set a target of 25% of the vote and again the Party hit target with 25.5% and came in at second place in votes. Winnie Ewing won in a landslide with a majority of 44,695. We had a very narrow miss in North East Scotland where Allan Macartney (who suffered most from the Tayside cleaners affair) narrowly lost to Labour which won with a small majority of 3,612.

Because of the Euro-elections, very little time was left for concentrating the SNP's membership firepower in the by-election in Glasgow Central that took place a fortnight later. The Labour organisation was stronger and they went in for canvassing and a poster campaign that took the initiative. They were also helped by a 'general election' effect where rising Labour support in the UK hardened their local vote in Glasgow Central. Not for the first or last time, the SNP encountered negative street-fighting tactics while it campaigned too positively. Despite this, the SNP candidate, Alex Neil did well although the strengthening of the Labour vote was not an encouraging harbinger for the next General Election as it reflected a growing view in the public and media that the Tories could at last be defeated. This would eclipse the SNP strategy of rescuing Scotland from Mrs Thatcher's stranglehold.

Glasgow Central By- election Result (June 1989)

Labour	54.6%
SNP	30.2%
Conservative & Unionist	7.6%
Green	3.8%
Democrat	1.5%
SDP	1.0%
Others	1.3%

The 1989 Conference in Dunoon allowed me to develop a fresh theme by associating us with the new states that were being welcomed into the body of nations following the collapse of the Soviet Union. I contrasted this with Scotland, still without national representation and made a call for a New Scotland to be part of a New Europe. The Agenda itself had few matters of controversy and Conference dealt with 'bread and butter' issues such as a national food strategy, the Scottish Budget, homelessness and broadcasting.

I had pledged to lead the SNP in the next election campaign. Part of my authority came from internal party expectation that I would fight to regain Dundee East. Their delegates came to me during the Conference with an invitation to be their candidate. I put them off till later in the proceedings and news of this leaked into the press. There was no way I could dodge announcing my decision so, when summing up the proceedings at the close of the Conference, I confirmed that I was no longer to be a candidate. I assured the Party that without constituency obligations I would be better able to direct the campaign, I sensed disappointment amongst the delegates that I was no longer willing to lead from the front.

The year was a quiet one by SNP standards, with effort going into fund raising and organisation. With the resignation of Alan McKinney in the spring of 1990, Allison Hunter who had been EVC Organisation took over as Director of Organisation and Kevin Pringle was appointed Research Officer. Iain Lawson, EVC Administration made steady progress towards introducing the Challenge of the Nineties that would in course transform the Party's capability to raise money. Later, Bruce McFee became the SNP's first professional fund-raiser. Indeed, in the whole year the only untoward event was the remitting back at National Council of a detailed Education Policy by 62 votes to 54.[12] Teachers are notoriously difficult to please and many of the morning delegates had also not stayed for the afternoon policy debates: nevertheless, it was dispiriting to see the policy parked after all the work that had been dedicated to it.

The end game approached. In early May, Jim Sillars requested a meeting that took place in my office in Dundee. He told me Alex Salmond was likely to make a bid for the leadership and proposed that we stand together on a joint ticket. During the previous two years, he and Alex had drifted apart and relationships between them and their respective teams were, to put it mildly, not cordial. I was non-committal and promised to think things over and let him know. The news was half expected and there would have been no surprise if I had received a courtesy call from Alex to tell me of his intentions. This was exactly what had happened eleven years before. A leader should know when to stand, what to do when he is in power and when to call it a day. After eleven years, I had reached the last stage. I saw no merit in being involved in what would be a bitter election. The Party needed fresh leadership. I also faced an explosion of work in my legal practice and had less time for politics. My time had run out in both senses. After consultation with Edith, I announced I was standing down and sat back to enjoy the contest. This was between Margaret Ewing and Alex Salmond. Typically, Alex had set up a network of contacts and Margaret had no chance of winning. It would have been better for her to have stood in 1987. Her opportunity had come and gone.

Meantime, running the Party continued. In the Regional Elections in May, the SNP did well with an increased vote of 21.8% (up from 18.2%) and the election of 43 Councillors. The Party went into Conference in Perth with poll ratings in the upper twenties. There were few fireworks, the nearest being a debate on whether the Scottish Steel industry should be nationalised after the closure of the strip steel mill at Ravenscraig with the pro-nationalisation lobby winning by 177 votes to 157.[13] And then the baton was passed to Alex Salmond. The days of my pioneering leadership were over. It would take a further ten years before the SNP would make the great break-through by winning a large number of list seats for the Scottish Parliament with the benefit of proportional representation. As the principal opposition, the character of the SNP would change. It would no longer be a voice in the wilderness. The days of power had begun.

Reflections

It is worthwhile taking an overview of the three decades between 1960 and 1990. When the period began, the SNP was already thirty years old. In 1928, with formation of the National Party of Scotland, the nationalist movement had made a quantum leap from being a lobbyist of the unionist parties to a stand-alone organisation using elections to secure a Scottish Parliament. It did so because that lobbying had got nowhere. True, there were home rule voices in all of those parties. The Independent Labour Party was always more interested in a Scottish parliament than the more London-oriented British Labour Party It is also worth being reminded that the Scottish Party with which the National Party of Scotland had united in 1932 to form the SNP, had its roots in the Cathcart Unionist Party and Liberal elements. Yet the strategy of fighting elections had led nowhere and a large section of the SNP defected in the forties to form the Scottish Covenant Association, another lobbying organisation which, after a bright start, also faded away.

So by 1960, the SNP was suddenly rejuvenated. It was breaking into new territory with the fighting of elections in an organised and professional manner. It had clocked up good results, won Hamilton and had a landslide of support in local elections. Yet there had been deep lows and many disappointments, especially amongst the thousands of new members who came in with the flood. The Party had gained from their enthusiasm and suffered from their inexperience. While it may not have been appreciated by the new members, they were being toughened up, mentally and psychologically.

Again after a dramatic collapse of the SNP in the 1970 General Election, on the back of its iconic 'It's Scotland's Oil' campaign, the seventies permitted the SNP to introduce with greater credibility the concept of independence to a more confident Scottish public and, by election victories in 1974, to induce the unionist parties into making concessions on devolution. These promises were made by coercion, not out of agreement, so that when SNP support slackened, Westminster made sure they were not honoured. It took fifteen years of rule by the Conservative Party to persuade a reluctant Scottish Labour Party that if they were to stave off an SNP revival, a stronger devolution commitment was necessary. And by then, a number of them had been converted genuinely to that cause.

Scotland had also changed. The old male dominated heavy industries had vanished. More females had entered the jobs market. While the service industries rose in importance, unemployment increased and the pool of poverty deepened. Oil was discovered, although little of the benefits of taxation were ploughed into the Scottish economy. At the same time, the British Empire that had once given prospects of employment and opportunity collapsed, taking with it the prestige and power on which the British state had relied. Gradually Scotland moved away from being a deeply unionist nation to one where the benefits of self-rule became more attractive. And it was this slowly developing consensus that led to the Scottish parliament and allied taxation powers being approved in a referendum in 1998.

If there is a lesson to be learned from this second phase of the SNP – the turbulent years when the SNP diced with triumph and disaster – it is that change in a nation occurs slowly. Thirty years is a long time for a person; a short one in the extended life of a nation. Since 1990, the SNP has formed a minority government in the devolved Scottish Parliament. As a minority, it has still to persuade the Scottish Parliament to pass an independence referendum bill. And if it does, will the Parliament agree the wording of the referendum questions the way the SNP proposes? In a referendum, the wording of the questions is critical. And then, the big one, can the SNP persuade the Scottish people to opt for independence? The jump to independence is a large one. And as this history shows, the British State will be the elephant in the room. What role will it play? Will it use the resources of the State to prevent Scotland voting for independence? The way the Government and opposition parties colluded with the civil service to cheat Scotland of the country's oil resources should be salutary. Then, will the UK Government accept the result or will it play for time as it did so successfully over devolution in the seventies? There are lessons to be learned from the SNP's history – and be sure that the British establishment will adapt the template that worked so successfully in the past. Separatism and smears will re-appear; industry and commerce will be encouraged to sow despondency about Scotland's economic future; and attempts will be made to sabotage the confidence that has come from having a devolved Parliament.

So what's new in all that! What is novel is that the SNP is ahead of the gain line. The creation of a Scottish Parliament has taken Scotland part of the way and forming a government has enhanced the credibility of the Party. It is in a far stronger position to withstand the attacks. Yet to win the referendum, the Party will have to penetrate Scottish consciousness as never before and harness the atavistic loyalty to their country that exists within most Scots. There must be a re-emphasis of the sovereignty of the Scottish people and Scottish identity in face of expected external attacks. When the people of Scotland feel wholly Scottish, rather than British, the SNP shall have won.

Despite the bruises of the turbulent years, I have confidence that independence will come, although its shape may change in an ever closer inter-locking world. And who can tell what event will force the issue. In the sixties, it was the anger of the people against industrial decline that drove many to vote SNP. In the seventies, the black gold of oil established faith that Scotland could be a rich and prosperous nation. In the eighties, the hammering of Scotland by Mrs Thatcher and the imposition of the Poll Tax provoked an outcry from which the SNP benefited. Who can tell what the twenty tens will bring. Will the age of austerity brought about by Government debt, leading as it will, to deep cuts in public expenditure and high taxation be the factor that breaks the Scottish people's belief in the long term viability of an increasingly bankrupt Britain?

The key attributes of the SNP, regardless of the odds, are optimism and faith in the Scottish people. When independence comes, the real battle for Scotland's future will begin: when as an independent country, relying on its own endeavours, Scotland will live again and the SNP's vision of the New Scotland fulfilled.

NOTES

Chapter 1
1. Independent & Free – Scottish Politics and the Origins of the Scottish National Party 1918-1945, Richard J. Finlay at p.230
2. SNP/The History of the Scottish National Party, Peter Lynch at p.85
3. Letter from Ian Macdonald 12 January 2007
4. Ibid
5. NEC Minute E63/145 (16 November 1963)
6. Memorandum to NEC circulated by William Wolfe (16 November 1963)
7. NC Minute NC63/47 (7 December 1963)
8. NEC Minute E64/24 (14 February 1964)
9. NC Minute ENC64/16 (7 March 1964)
10. NEC Minute E63/152 (16 November 1963)
11. William Wolfe: Notes for NEC (16 November 1964)
12. NEC Minute –E64 – Special Meetings (6 January 1964) and E64/14 (31 January 1964)
13. NC Minute NC64/6 (31 January 1964)
14. NC Minute NC64/5 (8 February 1964)
15. NEC Minute E64/35 (14 February 1964)

Chapter 2
1. NEC Minute E64/55 (8 April 1964)
2. NC Minute NC 64/24 (6 June 1964)
3. NEC Minute E64/66 (19 June 1964)
4. NEC Minute E64/104 (10 July 1964)
5. NEC Minute E64/144 (11 September 1964)
6. NEC Minute E64/134 (14 August 1964)
7. NEC Minute E64/194 (11 December 1964)
8. NEC Minute E65/3 (8 January 1965)
9. NEC Minute E65/38 (9 April 1965)
10. NEC Minute E65/58 (11 June 1965)
11. NEC Minute E65/90 (13 August 1965)
12. NC Minute NC65/29 (4 September 1965)
13. NEC Minute E65/115 (8 October 1965)
14. NC Minute NC65/30 and NO Report (4 September 1965)
15. NEC Minutes E65/ 115(8 October 1965)
16. NC Minute NC65/41 (4 December 1965)
17. Cmnd. 3550 Report on Speaker's Conference on Electoral Law
18. NEC Minute E68/112 (11 October 1968)
19. Report by National Secretary on BBC Meeting of 18 November 1968

Chapter 3
1. NEC Minute E64/41 (13 March 1964)
2. Internal Conference Resolution 6
3. Report by Convener, Election Committee dated 28 November 1964
4. NC Report by EVC Policy and Development dated 28 November 1964
5. NEC MinuteE65/9 (12 February 1965)
6. NC report by EVC Policy and Development (5 June 1965)
7. NEC Minute E65/50 (14 May 1965)
8. NEC Minute E65/65 (11 June 1965)
9. NEC Minute E66/7 (7 January 1966)
10. NEC Report by Convener, Organisation Committee (14 April 1966)
11. Report by EVC Policy and Development (13 May 1966)

Chapter 4
1. NC Minute NC64/26 (6 June 1964)
2. Letter from Ian Macdonald – ibid
3. NC65/40 Report from Chairman, Arthur Donaldson (4 December 1965)
4. Letter from George Leslie (February 2007
5. NEC Minute E66/22 (16 January 1966)
6. NC Report from Chairman (5 March 1966)
7. Income & Expenditure Statement to 31.12.64
8. NEC Minute E65/74 (9 July 1965)
9. NEC Minute E65/90 (13 August 1965)
10. NC Minute NC65/7 (6 March 1965)
11. Alba Convener's Report (18 August 1966)
12. NEC Minute E66/62 (13 May 1966)
13. NEC Minute E66/79 (8 July 1966)
14. NEC Minute E66/141 (9 December 1966)
15. NEC Minute E66/106 (9 September 1966)
16. NEC Minute E66/80 (8 July 1966)
17. NEC Minute E67/11 (22 January 1967)
18. NC Minute NC67/7 (11 March 1967)
19. NEC Report dated 24 December 1967
20. NEC Minute E68/17 (9 February 1968)
21. NC Minute NC68/9 (2 March 1968)
22. NEC Minute E66/78 (8 July 1966)
23. NC Report by Chairman NC66/22 (3 September 1966)
24. NC Minute NC66/39 (3 December 1966)
25. Letter from George Leslie – ibid
26. NC Minute 67/29 (17 June 1967)
27. Letter from Rosemary V Hall (2007
28. Letter from Ian Macdonald – ibid

29. NEC Minute E67/145 (10 November 1967)
30. NC Report from Chairman NC68/6 (2 March 1968)
31. NC Minute NC68/12 (2 March 1968)

Chapter 5
1. Annual Conference, Bridge of Allan, 16 & 17 May 1964
2. SNP and You – Election Manifesto and 1974 edition.
3. Annual Conference, Perth, 22 & 23 May 1965
4. Conference Resolution 6
5. NC Minute NC65/18 (5 June 1965)
6. NC Minute NC65/42 (4 December 1965)
7. Annual Conference, Edinburgh, 4 & 5 June 1966
8. NC Minute NC67/9 (11 March 1967)
9. Annual Conference, Edinburgh, 2,3 & 4 June 1967
10. Conference Resolution 9
11. NEC Minute E67/155 (8 December 1967)
12. NC Minute NC67/57 (2 December 1967)
13. Annual Conference, Aberdeen, 31 May, 1 & 2 June 1968
14. NC Minute NC68/34 (15 June 1968)
15. NC Minute NC68/74 (30 November 1968)
16. Annual Conference, Oban, 30, 31 May & 1 June 1969
17. NC Minute NC69/40 (6 September 1969)
18. NC Minute NC70/10 (11 April 1970)
19. NC Minute NC69/51 (6 December 1969)
20. Annual Conference, Edinburgh, 29, 30 & 31 May 1970
21. Conference Resolution 9
22. The New Scotland – Your Scotland, Election Manifesto, 1970
23. NC Minute NC70/26 (5 September 1970)
24. NC Minute NC70/38 (5 December 1970)
25. NC Minute NC71/12 and 13 (30 January 1971)
26. NC Minute NC71/10 (30 January 1971)

Chapter 6
1. Letter from George Leslie – ibid
2. Finance Committee Minute 4 (18 July 1968)
3. NEC Minute E69/76 (11 July 1969)
4. NOC Minute (17 May 1969)
5. NC Internal Training Report (6 September 1969)
6. NC Report from Chairman (Billy Wolfe) (6 December 1969)
7. NEC Minute E69/86 (11 July 1969)
8. Scottish Constitutional Sub-Committee Minute SCS5
9. NEC Minute E69/124 (10 October 1969)

10. NEC Minute E70/70 (4 July 1970)
11. National Organiser's Report (6 July 1970)
12. NC Minute NC70/26 (5 September 1970)
13. Director of Communications Report (30 June 1970)
14. NEC Minute E70/78 (8 August 1970)
15. NC Report of Chairman (5 September 1970)
16. NEC Minute E71/49 (8 May 1971)

Chapter 7
1. SNP Research Bulletin, 1970/71, No.5
2. Annual Conference, Rothesay, May 1972 Resolution 2
3. Daily Record, 27 May 1972
4. Thesis: Robert Crawford
5. SNP Research Bulletins, 1970/71, Nos. 6 & 9
6. Campaign Schedule, 15 June 1972
7. Memorandum on Finance, 16 June 1972
8. NEC Minute E72/54 (30 June 1972)
9. NEC Minute E72/58 (30 June 1972)
10. NEC Minute E73/5 (12 January 1973)
11. Herald Report, 28 October 2005
12. McCrone Report 23 April 1973 and Herald Report, 12 September 2005)

Chapter 8
1. Annual Conference, Oban, 30, 31 May & 1 June 1969, Resolution 17
2. NEC Minute E73/109 (14 December 1973)
3. Annual Conference, Elgin 30 and 31 May & 1 June 1974
4. NEC Minute E74/71 (28 June 1974)
5. NEC Minute E74/66 (9 August 1974)
6. NEC Minute E74/76 (7 September 1974)
7. NEC Minute E74/76 (7 September 1974)
8. NEC Minute E74/106 (13 December 1974)
9. NEC Minute E75/31 (11 April 1975)
10. NEC Minute E75/14 (7 February 1975)
11. NC Minute NC75/9 (1 March 1975)
12. NC Minute NC 75/28 (14 June 1975)
13. Annual Conference, Dundee, 26 to 28 May 1977
14. Statement from Isobel Lindsay dated 19 August 2007

Chapter 9
None

Chapter 10
1. SNP Manifesto 1974, P.3
2. Ibid, P.3
3. Ibid, P.11
4. Ibid, Pp. 12-15
5. NEC Minute E74/87 (18 October 1974)
6. NEC Minute E74/106 (13 December 1974), letter from EVC Administration dated 20 December 1974 and E75/4 (10 January 1975)
7. Ibid: E74/106
8. PG Minute Item 1 (11 December 1974)
9. Research Officer's Report to NEC
10. PG Minute Item 1(ii) and Items 3 (i) and (ii) (15 January 1975)
11. PG Minute, Item 5 (19 February 1975)
12. Source: Contact, PG newsletter, 12-18 March 1976
13. Source: Contact, 11/18 November 1976

Chapter 11
1. Conference 29-31 May 1975, Resolution 17
2. Contact, 21-28 May 1976
3. Memorandum from Margo MacDonald to author dated 8 January 1976
4. GBC Minute GBC77/117 (15 November 1977)
5. Joint Meeting of MPs and NEC (4 September 1976)
6. NC Minute NC77/21 (11 June 1977)
7. PG Minutes (23 and 29 June 1977), Items 5 & 1
8. NEC Minute E77/68 (12 August 1977)
9. Research Officer's Report dated 8 May 1978
10. PG Minute (19 April 1978), Item 7
11. Statement from Isobel Lindsay – ibid
12. Ibid

Chapter 12
1. NC Minute NC78/39   (2 September 1978)
2. NC Minute NC78/37 – ibid
3. NC Minute NC78/38 – ibid
4. NC Minute NC78/48 – ibid
5. Memo. of Outcome of Meeting (5 July 1978)
6. NEC Minute E78/63 (30 June 1978)
7. NEC Minute E78/95 (13 October 1978)
8. NEC Minute E78/105 (10 November 1978)

Chapter 13
1. Kilbrandon Commission Report, Cmnd. 5460 and 5460-1
2. Kilbrandon – ibid
3. NC Minute NC74/46 (7 December 1974)
4. NEC Minute E76/38 (14 May 1976)
5. NC Minute NC76/50 (4 September 1976)
6. NEC Minute E76/80 (8 October 1976) and National Organiser's Report dated 21 September 1976
7. NC Minute NC76/58 (4 September 1976)
8. Strategy Committee Minute SC77/10 (5 May 1977)
9. NEC Minute E77/68 (12 August 1977)
10. Statement from Isobel Lindsay – ibid
11. NEC Minutes E78/16 (10 February 1978) and E78/24 (10 March 1978)

Chapter 14
1. NEC Minute E78/4 (13 January 1978)
2. NC Minute NC78/13 (4 March 1978)
3. NC Minute NC79/1 (3 March 1979)
4. Statement from Isobel Lindsay – ibid
5. NEC Memorandum dated 11 January 1979 and E79/5 (12 January 979)

Chapter 15
1. NEC Minute E79/50 (15 June 1979)
2. ICDP (79 Group) Sub-committee Minute (4 July 1979)
3. NEC Minute E79/67 (7 September 1979)
4. Conference 13-15 September 1979 Resolution 30
5. Conference Resolution 41 – ibid
6. Conference Resolution 42 – ibid
7. Chairman's Report to National Council (1 March 1980)
8. National Organiser's Report to NEC (8 February 1980)
9. NEC Minute E80/96 (12 September 1980)
10. NEC Minute E80/105 (10 October 1980)
11. NC Minute E80/80 (6 December 1980)
12. NEC Minute E81/32 (14 February 1981)
13. Conference 28-30 May 1981 Resolution 3
14. Conference Resolution 14 – ibid
15. Conference Resolution 36 – ibid
16. Conference Resolution 57 – ibid
17. Statement by Isobel Lindsay – ibid
18. Letter by Jim Fairlie dated 12 October 2008
19. NEC Minute E81/66 (21 June 1981)

20. NEC Minute E81/111 (9 October 1981)
21. NEC Minute E81/118 (13 November 1981)
22. Conference 3-5 June 1982 Resolution 2, Amendment (a)
23. Letter from Robert McIntyre dated 1 July 1982
24. NEC Minute E82/82 (11 September 1982)
25. NEC Minute E82/91 (9 October 1982)
26. NC Minute NC82/48 (4 December 1982)
27. NC Minute NC82/50 – ibid
28. Report by Research Officer dated 14 January 1983
29. NEC Minute E82/119 (11 December 1982)
30. NC Minute NC83/4 (5 March 1983)
31. NC Minute NC83/8 ibid
32. NC Minute NC83/24 (30 April 1983)
33. NC Minute NC83/26 – ibid
34. Letter from Jim Fairlie – ibid

Chapter 16
1. Conference 29, 30 September & 10 October 1983 Resolution 10
2. Resolution 22 – ibid
3. Resolution 35 – ibid
4. NC Minute NC85/3 (2 March 1985)
5. Memorandum to author by Alan McKinney dated 13 December 1983
6. Memorandum by Angus Lyon, 2008
7. NC Report by EVC Publicity dated 7 June 1986
8. NC Minute NC86/10
9. NEC Minute NEC 87/54 (20 June 1987)

Chapter 17
1. Conference 23-26 September 1987 Resolution 28
2. Resolution 15 – ibid
3. NEC Minute NEC88/13 (13 February 1988)
4. NEC Minute NEC88/31 (9 April 1988)
5. NC Report by Chairman (4 June 1988)
6. NC Minute NC88/31 (4 June 1988)
7. NC Minute NC88/36) – ibid
8. NEC Minute NEC 88/92 (12 November 1988)
9. Record of Cross Party Meeting of Scottish Constitutional Convention
10. NEC Minute NEC89/17 (11 February 1989)
11. NC Minute NC89/10 (4 March 1989)
12. NC Minute NC90/13 (3 March 1990)
13. Conference 19-22 September 1990 Resolution 17

ABBREVIATIONS

Annual National Conference	Conference
Business Reply Cards	BRCs
Edinburgh University Nationalist Club	EUNC
General Business Committee	GBC
National Council	Council, NC
National Executive Committee	National Executive, Executive, NEC
National Organisation Committee	NOC
National Organiser	NO
Party Political and Party Election Broadcasts	PPBs/PEBs
Parliamentary Group	PG
Radio Free Scotland	RFS
Scottish Labour Party	SLP
Scottish Socialist Party	SSP
Scottish Trade Union Congress	STUC
Siol nan Gaidhael	SNG
Social Democratic Party	SDP
Senior Officebearers Committee	SOBS
Strategy Committee	SC

Note: Many of the Committee names and designations changed over the years.

BIBLIOGRAPHY

Douglas, Dick (1995), *At the Helm: The Life and Times of Dr Robert McIntyre*, NP Publications.
Ewing, Winnie (2004), *Stop the World* ed. Michael Russell, Birlinn Ltd.
Finlay, Richard J. (1995, *Independent and Free Scottish Politics and the Progress of The Scottish National Party, 1918-1945* John Donald Publications Ltd.
Jones, Bill (1979), *British Politics today*, ed. Bill Jones & Dennis Kavanagh, Manchester University Press.
Kemp, Arnold, (1993), *The Hollow Drum*, Mainstream Publishing Company (Edinburgh) Ltd
Pittock, Murray (2008), *The Road to Independence? Scotland since the Sixties* Reaktion Books Ltd.
Lynch, Peter (2002), *SNP The History of the Scottish National Party*, Welsh Academic Press.
Stewart, Donald (1994) *A Scot at Westminster* ed. Mary Stewart MacKinnon, The Catalone Press, Canada
Wolfe, Billy (1973) *Scotland Lives* Reprographia

THESIS

Crawford, Robert Mackay (1982), *The Scottish National Party, 1960-1974: an investigation into its organisation and power structure.* Thesis (Ph.D) Glasgow University

MANUSCRIPT AND ORAL SOURCES

Personal Papers
Correspondence
Comments by:
Jim Fairlie
Rosemary Hall
George Leslie
Isobel Lindsay
Angus Lyon
Ian Macdonald
Margo MacDonald
Andrew Welsh

RECORDS

SNP Conference Agendas
SNP National Executive,
Agendas, Minutes, Reports and Memoranda
SNP National Council, Agendas, Minutes and Reports
SNP Sub-Committees, Minutes and Reports
SNP Office-bearers Memoranda
SNP Pamphlets and Leaflets
SNP Collection, ACC.11987, National Library of Scotland
SNP Parliamentary Group, Agendas and Minutes
SNP Parliamentary Group, – Contact Newsletters
Official Reports, House of Commons
House of Commons Library Research Department, Letters & Research Notes

INDEX